Praise for *Stop the Cyber Bleeding*

"Cybersecurity" is the kryptonite of too many healthcare company board meetings. Otherwise intelligent and accomplished people can be intellectually paralyzed by the mere ~~ ~ term. Yet, failure to appreciate cyb riate resource allocation too often perience: the post-breach emergen *leeding*, Bob Chaput clearly and c ~~ ~~ board members with what they need to know and the questions they need to ask to exercise effective oversight in this critical area. Whether your goal is to build a best-in-class Enterprise Cyber Risk Management (ECRM) program or, more modestly, simply to keep your company out of the hacker's crosshairs and off the front pages of the newspaper, *Stop the Cyber Bleeding* is a "must read" now.

—**Ralph W. Davis, serial healthcare board member/
advisor Operating Partner, The Vistria Group**

In his excellent, practical, and timely book, Bob Chaput addresses multiple aspects of ECRM. He first describes the unique challenges of ECRM in today's healthcare environment, given the current cyber risks and regulations. He then offers a well-rounded plan of action on how C-suite executives can provide leadership and oversight for their organization's ECRM efforts. This plan of action is tailored to their specific cyber risks, based on the NIST framework, and includes how to establish an ECRM program and fund it. He finally provides several concrete examples of the benefits of establishing an ECRM program. This book is an extremely valuable guide and should be in the library of every healthcare institution C-suite executive, board member, and IT leader.

—**Dr. Benoit Desjardins, MD, Ph.D., FAHA, FACR, CISSP
Associate Professor, Department of Radiology, Penn Medicine**

Bob Chaput's *Stop the Cyber Bleeding* is a needed call to action. It is a thoughtful explication of the risks inherent in our new digital world. Unlike most such narratives, it also offers a practical approach to manage and mitigate those risks.

—Mark Reynolds, President and CEO, Risk Management Foundation of the Harvard Medical Institutions Incorporated (CRICO)

I know from firsthand experience that the concepts, principles, and actions presented in *Stop the Cyber Bleeding* work to engage and inspire top leaders and board members alike to seriously take up the matter of cyber risk management as an enterprise issue. It's terrific to see Bob codify his practical risk management skills, knowledge, and experience into a book that's easy to read and use. His insightful treatment of the transformation required as a behavior-change matter is incredibly relevant for healthcare organizations. Given the increasing cyber liabilities facing healthcare organizations and their C-suite executives and board members alike, *Stop the Cyber Bleeding* is a must-read today.

—Gregory J. Ehardt, JD, LL.M., Vice President, Compliance and Privacy, CHRISTUS Health

In this book, Bob Chaput provides an excellent summary of the major issues facing healthcare entities with regard to cyber risk management and related security compliance. Bob includes helpful talking points to involve all members of a healthcare organization's workforce in conversations about cybersecurity, including, importantly, the C-suite and board.

—Iliana Peters, JD, LLM, CISSP, Shareholder, Polsinelli PC, Former Acting Deputy Director HHS Office for Civil Rights

While the continuing vulnerability of the healthcare sector to the threat of cyber attacks is well-known, what's less well-understood is how organizations should prepare and implement their strategy to mitigate these threats. *Stop the Cyber Bleeding* offers a smart, practical overview of healthcare cyber risk problems and solutions. Informed by 35-plus years of senior executive experience in information security and risk management, Bob Chaput rejects cookie-cutter solutions, instead explaining why and how risk analysis and threat preparedness should be customized to each organization's setting. This book will be a valuable, actionable guide for healthcare leaders and board members developing cyber risk management plans as essential components of corporate governance today.

—Ann B. Waldo, JD, CIPP, Waldo Law Offices

Chaput hits it out of the park with his book *Stop the Cyber Bleeding*. Bob's decades of risk management experience detailed in this book offer a must-read tutorial for every industry executive. Bob conveys lessons learned from the trenches while delivering street-smart, pragmatic, and tangible strategies toward unraveling the complexities of Enterprise Cyber Risk Management. More importantly, Bob provides evidence for what we cybersecurity professionals have been stating for years: Cyber risk management is not a department within IT—it is an enterprise issue that demands a seat (and a strategy) at the boardroom table!

—James Furstenberg, Ph.D., CISSP, C|EH, GMON, C|ND, C|PTE, CNA, CLFE, ACE, C|SCU, Assistant Professor, Information Security and Intelligence, Ferris State University

The case for ECRM is decisively made; timely and relevant. Successful cyber exploits frequently capitalize on the failure of organizations to focus on, and address, fundamentals. This book is an instruction manual on how to get all of the fundamentals sustainably right. Clear and straight forward guidance for senior executives and board members alike. Ending each section with not only suggested questions to ask, but why and how to ask them is pure genius. Through realistic scenarios and firsthand experiences, Bob takes the reader on a sobering trip across the healthcare landscape. This is a must-read for executives who influence cyber risk and cybersecurity governance.

—Fernando Martinez, Ph.D., CHCIO, CISSP, CISA, CISM, CGEIT, Chief Strategy Officer THA, President and CEO THA Foundation, Texas Hospital Association

At this time of ever-increasing cyber risk, *Stop the Cyber Bleeding* distills, in an easy-to-read, non-technical format, information that every board member and C-suite executive should know to advise and protect their organization. In *Stop the Cyber Bleeding,* Bob Chaput takes his more-than 35 years of experience and lays out the threats faced by healthcare organizations and actions that can be taken to establish a practical Enterprise Cyber Risk Management program to address and mitigate those risks, and how leadership can establish effective oversight of that program.

—Jose Perdomo, RN, MHSA, JD, Senior Vice President, Nicklaus Children's Health System

If you are not yet convinced about investing in enterprise cyber risk management, you will be now. In *Stop the Cyber Bleeding,* Chaput makes a rock-solid, easy-to-read case for 360-degree board-led risk evaluation and mitigation, and provides a detailed road map to accomplish such.

—Michael F. Montijo, MD, MPH, FACP

Bob Chaput does an excellent job in showing, with the proliferation of healthcare data, why cyber risk management has become an enterprise problem that is not optional. He applies the stages of change model to organizations' intentions to develop an enterprise cyber risk management plan. And then he lays out a way to action!

—James O. Prochaska, Ph.D. & Janice M. Prochaska, Ph.D., Authors, Consultants, Speakers, Prochaska Change Consultants

Having performed dozens of successful risk analyses for companies under OCR investigation over the last decade, I can attest to the fact that the principles in this book are absolutely correct. I've known Bob since the very early days of his HIPAA thought leadership, and I was thrilled to see a decade of his hands-on, hard work be put to paper in a way that can be shared with the world. I hope that executives around the country can save themselves the pain and cost of responding to a data breach by applying the sound risk management principles covered in this book. Competent executive leadership will understand that managing cyber risk is just as important as managing any other business risk and that they have to play by the rules of OCR.

—Chris Dansie, Ph.D., CISSP-ISSMP, Associate Professor (lecturer), University of Utah

Bob Chaput's command of healthcare-focused enterprise cyber risk is unmatched in this seminal compilation. *Stop the Cyber Bleeding* should be mandatory reading for organizations and leaders desiring to understand, engage, and execute a program that will reduce enterprise risk and add much-needed maturity to this complex challenge.

—Carter Groome, MBA, CHISL, CFCHE, Chief Executive Officer, First Health Advisory—Cyber Health Solutions

While it is written in an accessible and lively style, this isn't a one-size-fits-all cybersecurity checklist for dummies—it's a smart, well-thought-out discussion of how healthcare organizations need to understand, assess, and mitigate cyber risk. Today, development of a cyber risk management plan at the enterprise level is a governance must-do, and *Stop the Cyber Bleeding* should be on the bookshelves of healthcare CEOs and board members alike.

—Doug Peddicord, Ph.D., President of Washington Health Strategies Group

Bob Chaput continues to elevate the conversation related to cyber risk management. With *Stop the Cyber Bleeding*, Bob clearly and effectively demonstrates why we cannot continue to look at cyber threat as an IT issue . . . This is a leadership issue. This is a trust issue and one that challenges the very foundation of who we are as a health system. As cyber threats continue to become more sophisticated and the stakes climb higher than ever, it is time for bold leaders to stand up and take aggressive action to protect one of the most important aspects of healthcare . . . patient trust and confidence. This book provides the critical information and proven methods for leaders to take control and protect their information, their organizations, and their patients and communities.

—**Tony Burke, CEO, Pivot Health Advisors,**
Former SVP, American Hospital Association

STOP
THE
CYBER
BLEEDING

STOP
THE
CYBER
BLEEDING

What Healthcare Executives
and Board Members Must Know About
Enterprise Cyber Risk Management (ECRM)

HOW TO SAVE YOUR PATIENTS,
PRESERVE YOUR REPUTATION, AND
PROTECT YOUR BALANCE SHEET

BOB CHAPUT

STOP THE CYBER BLEEDING | What Healthcare Executives and Board Members Must Know About Enterprise Cyber Risk Management (ECRM) | How to Save Your Patients, Preserve Your Reputation, and Protect Your Balance Sheet

For information about this title or to order other books and/or electronic media, contact the publisher:

HEALTHCARE CYBER RISK MANAGEMENT

Clearwater Compliance LLC
40 Burton Hills Blvd., Suite 200
Nashville, TN 37215
1–800–704–3394
https://clearwatercompliance.com
cyberbleeding@clearwatercompliance.com

ISBNs:
978-1-7351222-0-5 (print)
978-1-7351222-1-2 (eBook)

Printed in the United States of America

Book design (cover and interior layout) by 1106 Design.

LEGAL DISCLAIMER
Although the information provided in this book may be helpful in informing you and others who have an interest in data privacy and security issues, it does not constitute legal advice. This information may be based in part on current international, federal, state, and local laws and is subject to change based on changes in these laws or subsequent interpretative guidance. Where this information is based on federal law, it must be modified to reflect state law where that state law is more stringent than the federal law or where other state-law exceptions apply. Information and informed recommendations provided in this book are intended to be a general information resource and should not be relied upon as a substitute for competent legal advice specific to your circumstances. Furthermore, the existence of a link or organization reference in any of the following materials should not be assumed as an endorsement by the author or by Clearwater. YOU SHOULD EVALUATE ALL INFORMATION, OPINIONS AND RECOMMENDATIONS PROVIDED IN THIS BOOK IN CONSULTATION WITH YOUR LEGAL OR OTHER ADVISORS, AS APPROPRIATE.

First print edition 2020.

This book is dedicated to my family and especially my wife, Mary, my children, Nicole, Rob, and Joanna, and our beautiful granddaughters, Azza Catherine, Leila Mary, Sofia Hasna, and Reece Belmont.

If I had an hour to solve a problem
and my life depended on the solution,
I would spend the first 55 minutes determining
the proper question to ask.

~ ALBERT EINSTEIN (1879–1955)
 PHYSICIST AND NOBEL LAUREATE

Table of Contents

Foreword

I will always remember the first time I met Bob Chaput. I had just been installed as director of the Department of Health and Human Services Office for Civil Rights ("HHS/OCR") and was now speaking at my first conference on the Health Insurance Portability and Accountability Act of 1996 (HIPAA), an event known as the HIPAA Summit.

I began service at HHS/OCR after the passage of the HITECH Act, a law that was born out of a political consensus to push toward aggressive adoption of electronic health records (EHRs). HITECH's drafters understood that the success of HITECH depended not just on investments in new technologies but also on patient trust that those technologies would keep their charts safe from bad actors. Among the many changes to HIPAA in the HITECH Act was the establishment of a stiff penalty schedule to sanction violations and send the message that compliance needed to be a top priority.

For better or worse, I was the new sheriff in town.

The 2012 HIPAA Summit was a critical opportunity to deliver the message that healthcare organizations disregarded information security at their peril. I asked my public-affairs officer to find me a roll of crime-scene tape, an item not ordinarily available in a building whose mission leaned toward healthcare financing and disease control, rather than surveying murder scenes. Just in time, the night before, the building's security office let us know they had a roll they could share.

In a room of 200 lawyers, CISOs, e-health evangelists, and others, I wrapped the tape around the seats of one quarter of the attendees. The message was delivered and heard: HHS/OCR would thereafter be an enforcement agency in every sense of the word.

As my presentation ended, a man and woman distinguished both by their height and their warm, courtly smiles stood up and introduced themselves as Bob Chaput and his wife and professional colleague, Mary Chaput. They wanted to talk about how they could support our mission. After a few conversations, I understood that among the many vendors in the field, their company, Clearwater Compliance, had actually cracked the HHS/OCR code. They carefully studied our regulations, what we said in public, and, most importantly, the many resolution agreements we were reaching with covered entities that had gone astray.

Their compliance model was based on the recognition that the crown jewel of the HITECH regulations and related HHS/OCR guidance were risk assessment and risk mitigation requirements. These requirements amounted to an expectation that covered entities identify everywhere in the enterprise where electronic protected health information (ePHI) was located and the threats and vulnerabilities to that information and then—on a regular, ongoing basis—to take reasonable risk mitigation measures to minimize or eliminate those risks.

If the healthcare industry learned from me that HHS/OCR was serious about enforcement, I learned from Bob a sensible, real-world way to manage health information risk in a way that my agency would find also amounted to compliance.

As a former senior healthcare executive in publicly traded companies himself, Bob also cracked another code—for organizations to be successful at managing these information and compliance risks, senior executives and the board must set the right tone. I made this point throughout my HHS/OCR tenure, and my successors affirmed it in numerous cases.

The importance of the kinds of executive and board-led risk management strategies that Bob recommends in this book has only grown over time. In the years since Bob and I met, the threats to electronic health information have grown rather than shrunk. While a large portion of breach reports in those early years involved physical loss or theft of devices containing protected health information, more recent years included ransomware attacks and electronic intrusions with the intent to steal PHI and sell it on the dark web. Anyone who pays attention recognizes that these are threats that fundamentally affect patients' access to safe and competent care.

I was fortunate after I left federal service to work again with Bob and Mary as they worked to bring their expertise to a wider audience. I myself was now a private lawyer, assisting the very types of organizations we once pursued as enforcers, and Bob's lessons rang truer still as we navigated preventable breaches and the HHS/OCR investigations that inevitably followed.

And it matters. Our transition to a modern healthcare information environment depends critically on patient trust. Patients need to trust in the safety of their data in order for healthcare delivery to be the type of partnership that assures that patients achieve the best outcomes, to which senior executives and the board have a fiduciary responsibility.

At the end of the day, it all really is about the patients—and that is the most fundamental thing that Bob and his team recognize.

~ LEON RODRIGUEZ, FORMER HHS/OCR DIRECTOR (2011–2014),
PARTNER, SEYFARTH SHAW LLP

Preface

I wrote this book to help C-suite executives and board members provide the leadership and oversight needed to stop what I call "cyber bleeding," that is, the pain, loss, and harm our patients are experiencing as an unintended consequence of the digitization of our healthcare industry. In addition to the electronic health record (EHR) stampede, with biomedical devices now connected to our networks *and* implanted in or attached to our patients, the compromise of these data, systems, and devices can cause grave loss or harm—up to and including death or disability.

Contemporaneous with the explosion of healthcare data, systems, and devices, the reality we're facing today is that cyber attacks on healthcare organizations are increasing specifically because of the value of this health information and the relative ease with which it can be compromised. The compromise of health information, including not only clinical data (e.g., sexually transmitted disease diagnoses) but also administrative data (e.g., insurance ID cards), can cause loss or harm to our patients. It can be used for ransom money, medical identity theft, adverse employment decisions, fraudulent use of medical services and/or illegal acquisition of prescription medications—all of which may result in additional loss or harm to our patients.

The reputational, financial, and strategic consequences of cyber attacks and other exploits can be far-reaching for your healthcare organization as well. These consequences extend even to personal liability for C-suite executives and board members because of your duty of care and fiduciary responsibilities.

This book is based on what I've learned throughout my career. My 35-plus years of experience includes serving as an executive in global healthcare organizations such as GE, Johnson & Johnson, and Healthways. During this time, I have always had responsibility for privacy, security, regulatory compliance, or cyber risk management. About 10 years ago, I started Clearwater Compliance, a firm dedicated to helping organizations with HIPAA compliance risk management and cyber risk management for healthcare organizations. Over time, I have discovered significant deficiencies in how healthcare organizations are approaching compliance and cyber risk management.

The single biggest deficiency I have observed is the failure of organizations to invest in cybersecurity based on their unique risks. You must start with *your* unique vision, mission, strategy, values, and services, examine all *your* unique data, systems, and devices that support *your* unique business, and then identify all *your* unique cyber exposures across *your* entire enterprise. This failure to identify *your* unique risks usually leads to a one-size-fits-all, checklist-based approach to cybersecurity. The upshot is overspending to treat perceived risks and underspending on *your* real risks.

This book, therefore, is a business book about ECRM, because ECRM is a business matter. Creating an ECRM program requires the leadership of the C-suite executives and the oversight of the board. ECRM is not an "IT problem"; furthermore, handled properly, it can become a business enabler. To be successful at leveraging ECRM to be a business enabler, the C-suite and board must engage. Yet, many are uncertain how to do so. This book shares what I've learned and provides tangible, actionable guidance, and recommendations on how to establish, implement, and mature a formal ECRM program.

This book is specifically designed to be used by healthcare C-suite executives and board members who want to fully execute their duty of care and fiduciary responsibilities to their patients. For ECRM to be effective, the entire organization must be engaged in the program. Although this book is written especially for C-suite executives and board members, I am confident that the ECRM information I have shared will also be useful to other managers and professionals in organizations throughout our healthcare ecosystem. For it requires all of us, working together, to safeguard the critical healthcare information assets on which our healthcare system—and your organization—are so critically reliant.

As I am finalizing this book, we are experiencing the rapid spread of novel coronavirus, a threat emanating from one of the four general threat source categories discussed further in the book. That threat, in turn, has caused other new cyber attacks to spike as adversaries look to take advantage of weaknesses in healthcare organizations due to fear, uncertainty, and disruption, all further underscoring the importance of Enterprise Cyber Risk Management (ECRM). Historically strong governance of the risk management function is now helping many organizations mitigate novel coronavirus risks, a black swan for many. Cyber risks ought not be your organization's next black swan, given all we know today. It is, arguably, the single biggest emerging risk your organization faces. There's a great deal to learn from this ECRM book that will also assist you with our current public-health crisis.

~ BOB CHAPUT, FOUNDER AND EXECUTIVE CHAIRMAN
CLEARWATER

Abbreviations

- ACHE: American College of Healthcare Executives
- AEHIS: Association of Executives in Healthcare Information Security
- AHA: American Hospital Association
- AHIA: Association of Healthcare Internal Auditors
- ANSI: American National Standards Institute
- ARRA: American Recovery and Reinvestment Act of 2009
- ASHRM: American Society of Health Care Risk Management
- BAA: Business Associate Agreement
- CAH: Critical Access Hospital
- CAP: Corrective Action Plan
- CapEx: Capital Expenditures
- CCPA: California Consumer Privacy Act
- CFR: Code of Federal Regulation
- CGEIT: Certified in Governance of Enterprise IT
- CHCIO: CHIME Certified Healthcare CIO
- CHIME: College of Health Information Management Executives
- CIA: Confidentiality, Integrity, and Availability
- CIO: Chief Information Officer
- CISA: Certified Information Systems Auditor

- CISA: Cybersecurity & Infrastructure Security Agency, U.S. Department of Homeland Security
- CISM: Certified Information Security Manager
- CISO: Chief Information Security Officer
- CISSP: Certified Information Systems Security Professional
- CMS: Centers for Medicare and Medicaid Services
- COBIT: Control Objectives for Information and Related Technologies
- CPA: Certified Public Accountant
- CRICO: Consolidated Risk Insurance Company; insures all of the Harvard medical institutions and their affiliates
- CRISC: Certified in Risk and Information Systems Control
- CT scan: Computerized Tomography (CT) scan
- CT: Computerized Tomography
- ECRM: Enterprise Cyber Risk Management
- ECRMS: Enterprise Cyber Risk Management Software
- EH: Eligible Hospital
- EHR: Electronic Health Record
- ePHI: electronic Protected Health Information
- ERM: Enterprise Risk Management
- EU: European Union
- FBI: Federal Bureau of Investigation
- FDA: Food and Drug Administration
- FERPA: Family Educational Rights and Privacy Act
- FTC: Federal Trade Commission
- GDPR: General Data Protection Regulation
- GISS: Global Information Security Survey

- GLBA: Gramm-Leach-Bliley Act
- GRC: Governance, Risk Management, and Compliance
- HCCA: Health Care Compliance Association
- HIMSS: Healthcare Information Management and Systems Society
- HHS: Department of Health and Human Services
- HIPAA: Health Insurance Portability and Accountability Act
- HITECH Act: Health Information Technology for Economic and Clinical Health Act
- HVAC: Heating, Ventilation, and Air Conditioning
- IDN: Integrated Delivery Network
- IRM|Pro®: Information Risk Management | Professional, Clearwater's ECRMS solution
- ISA: Internet Security Alliance
- ISO/IEC: International Organization for Standardization (ISO) and the International Electrotechnical Commission (IEC)
- IT: Information Technology
- IV: Intravenous
- KLAS: KLAS Research
- M&A: Mergers and Acquisitions
- MPL: Medical Professional Liability
- MU: Meaningful Use
- NACD: National Association of Corporate Directors
- NEMT: Non-Emergency Medical Transportation
- NIST SP: NIST Special Publication
- NIST: National Institute of Standards and Technology

- OCR: Office for Civil Rights
- OpEx: Operating expenses
- PACS: Picture Archiving and Communication System
- PB: Petabytes
- PCI DSS: Payment Card Industry Data Security Standard
- PHI: Protected Health Information
- PI Program: CMS's Promoting Interoperability (PI) Program
- PII: Personally Identifiable Information
- PIN: Personal Identification Number
- PMO: Project Management Office
- ROI: Return on Investment
- SaaS: Software-as-a-Service
- SIEM: Security Information and Event Management
- SOC: Security Operations Center
- TCO: Total Cost of Ownership

Challenges

CHAPTER 1

When Something "Cyber" Happens

First, do no harm.

~ HIPPOCRATES

The Attack

Mrs. Smith, a polarizing politician, has a cough. Her voice is hoarse, and she has also been feeling tired and weak. She's been a little bit "off" in her recent public appearances, so much so, that the media have been speculating about what health issues she might be dealing with.

She visits an internist in your organization. The internist orders a regular (non-stat) CT (Computerized Tomography) scan. However, unbeknownst to the hospital, a hacker has already infiltrated the radiology department network. The evening before Mrs. Smith's CT scan, when janitorial staff entered the building to clean, a man slipped into the radiology department and placed a "man-in-the-middle" device on the network near the CT scanner. It took only seconds for him to position the simple device, which enabled a wireless access point to the network.

With the device in place, the hacker is able to intercept and modify the CT scan images. It's a fairly easy task for the hacker, since transmission of the images between the CT scanner and the picture archiving and communication system (PACS) is not encrypted. The hacker uses his access to erase the evidence of cancerous nodules from Mrs. Smith's CT scan.

When the radiologist reviews the modified scan, he sees no evidence of tumors. He forwards his analysis to Mrs. Smith's internist. Her physician calls her with the good news: the CT scan shows no evidence of cancer.

Because of the misdiagnoses, Mrs. Smith's lung cancer goes untreated. She dies within the year. Her family files a medical malpractice lawsuit against your organization.

Far-fetched?

Not at all.

Researchers in Israel have demonstrated the feasibility of just such an attack.[1] The device they used to infiltrate a hospital network is simple, inexpensive, and available on Amazon.com. The researchers also demonstrated that experienced radiologists were unable to identify modified CT scans—and therefore made incorrect diagnoses based on the modified images.[2]

But, you say, that scenario could never happen at my organization! Unfortunately, it is all too possible. Cyberattackers have hundreds, if not thousands, of ways to gain access to and compromise your organization's devices, networks, and protected health information (PHI). The attacker could use spear phishing (a targeted, fraudulent email) to trick the radiology department administrative associate into revealing her username and password or for inadvertently downloading malware onto the network. Even if the administrative associate had limited network privileges, a hacker could "privilege-escalate" from her account and then execute malware. An outside attacker could hack into your PACS because of an unpatched Microsoft Windows operating system vulnerability. An unhappy employee with excessive system permissions and access could have downloaded CT scan images from your PACS server.

The fact is, the healthcare industry continues to be the single most targeted industry for cyber attacks,[3] and your organization might be next (if you haven't been attacked already).

As the CT scan hack illustrates, the consequences of cyber attacks on healthcare organizations can be far-reaching. Patient lives can be at risk, for example, when a ransomware attack disrupts a provider's ability to deliver services. Your organization's finances and reputation can be put at risk as well. Violations of the privacy and security requirements spelled out in the Health Insurance Portability and Accountability Act of 1996 (HIPAA) can result in fines, penalties, and corrective actions being levied against your organization. More recently, litigation related to data breach incidents has demonstrated an increased risk of personal liability for an organization's directors and officers.

The bottom line?

Cyber risk management (CRM) is not "just an IT problem." Cyber risk management is an *enterprise* risk management issue with consequences that can impact every stakeholder in your organization, from individual patients to C-suite executives and members of the board. It is not possible to separate "cyber risk management" from your enterprise's overall risk management program. That is why I always refer to cyber risk management as *enterprise* cyber risk management (ECRM).

The First Cyber-Driven Medical Malpractice Lawsuit?

Could inadequate cybersecurity lead to a medical malpractice lawsuit? A recent article in the *National Law Review* stated, "Negligent security practices are considered an ethical liability. Poor cybersecurity can lead to malpractice suits, even if a security breach does not occur."[4] You certainly do not want your organization to be the first healthcare organization to have a headline like the one in figure 1.1 to appear in your local newspaper.

Figure 1.1 *A Future Medical Malpractice Headline*

I am not a lawyer, and nothing in this book should be construed as offering legal advice. It is helpful, however, to note how "medical malpractice" and "negligence" are defined in the law and how these definitions might apply in the case of a cybersecurity incident. Three elements characterize medical malpractice under the law. The first element is:

> *(1) A violation of the standard of care.* The law acknowledges that there are certain medical standards that are recognized by the profession as being acceptable medical treatment by reasonably prudent healthcare professionals

under like or similar circumstances. This is known as the *standard of care*. A patient has the right to expect that healthcare professionals will deliver care that is consistent with these standards. If it is determined that the standard of care has not been met, then negligence may be established.[5]

On this point, note that healthcare organizations tend to think of medical malpractice and negligence in terms of *clinical* standards of care. But as healthcare has become dependent upon digital information, systems, and devices, standards of care have developed around how that digital information is handled. I will have more to say about this in a later chapter, but suffice it to say that, between HIPAA regulations, Office for Civil Rights (OCR) guidance, and National Institute of Standards and Technology (NIST) guidance, *de facto* standards of care related to cybersecurity and ECRM have emerged. (Please note that I reference NIST standards related to CRM throughout this book, and I discuss various NIST standards and approaches. In Chapter 10, I discuss why I recommend using them to establish, implement, and mature your ECRM program). These standards provide a benchmark by which organizations may be judged when determining "reasonable" behavior with respect to cybersecurity.

The second two elements that characterize a case of medical malpractice are:

(2) *An injury was caused by the negligence.* For a medical malpractice claim to be valid, it is not sufficient that a healthcare professional simply violated the standard of

care. The patient must also prove that he or she sustained an injury that would not have occurred in the absence of negligence. An unfavorable outcome by itself is not malpractice. The patient must prove that the negligence caused the injury. If there is an injury without negligence or negligence that did not cause an injury, there is no case.

Establishing a case of negligence, then, requires four elements:

1. the existence of a legal duty that the defendant owed to the plaintiff;

2. defendant's breach of that duty;

3. plaintiff's sufferance of an injury;

4. proof that defendant's breach caused the injury.[6]

(3) The injury resulted in significant damages. Medical malpractice lawsuits are extremely expensive to litigate, frequently requiring testimony of numerous medical experts and countless hours of deposition testimony. For a case to be viable, the patient must show that significant damages resulted from an injury received due to the medical negligence. If the damages are small, the cost of pursuing the case might be greater than the eventual recovery. To pursue a medical malpractice claim, the patient must show that the injury resulted in disability, loss of income, unusual pain, suffering and hardship, or significant past and future medical bills.[7]

Have I numbed you with legalese? I admit that is a lot of technical language. But understanding these concepts is important because they have implications for your organization's approach to ECRM. Among those implications is an increasing acceptance on the part of the courts regarding the role executives and directors play in ensuring your organization's cybersecurity.

The Increasing Liability of Directors and Officers

In addition to potential medical malpractice liability, another means by which executives and directors can be held liable for ECRM failures is through the concept of *duty of care*. To understand this connection, you need to understand terms and definitions related to the responsibilities of your executives and board members.

A *fiduciary* is a person or business with "the power and obligation to act for another (often called "the beneficiary") under circumstances which require total trust, good faith, and honesty."[8] By this definition, healthcare organization board members and C-suite executives act as fiduciaries for the people their organization serves. Fiduciaries, by definition, have legal responsibilities and obligations. One of those responsibilities is the *duty of care*.[9] In layman's terms, a board member's duty of care means, "When engaging in hospital business, trustees must use the same level of judgment they would use in their own, personal business activities."[10]

In negligence cases, *duty of care* is a requirement that a person "act toward others and the public with the watchfulness, attention, caution, and prudence that a reasonable person in the circumstances would use. If a person's actions do not meet this *standard of care*, then the acts are considered negligent, and any damages resulting may be claimed in a lawsuit for negligence."[11]

In other words, *duty of care* refers to the legal responsibility of the organization or individual (for example, a healthcare organization, executive leaders, or board of directors members) to act in a reasonable manner toward the people they are responsible for (for example, patients). The measure used to determine whether the defendant's actions were, in fact, reasonable is the *standard of care*.

Recent data breach litigation shows how corporate executives and board members can be at risk of personal liability when a cybersecurity incident occurs. For example, in 2013, cyber-attackers hit retailer Target and gained access to the company's computer network via credentials stolen from a third-party vendor. The attackers installed malware and were able to gain access to 41 million customer payment card accounts.[12] As a result of this breach:

> . . . litigation was filed, regulatory and congressional investigations commenced, and heads rolled. Banks, shareholders, and customers all filed lawsuits against the company. Target's CEO was shown the door. And Target's directors and officers were caught in the crossfire. In a series of derivative lawsuits, shareholders claimed that the retailer's board and C-suite violated their fiduciary duties by not providing proper oversight for the company's information security program, not making prompt and accurate public disclosures about the breach, and ignoring red flags that Target's IT systems were vulnerable to attack.[13]

In Target's case, the shareholder derivative lawsuits filed against the company's officers and directors were dismissed. But the case underscores "the critical oversight function played by corporate directors when it comes to keeping an organization's cyber defenses up to par."[14]

Derivative litigation was also brought against Yahoo, Inc., for data breaches that occurred in 2014 and 2016. The $29 million settlement, which was approved in January 2019, "represents the first significant recovery in a data-breach related derivative lawsuit targeting directors and officers for breach of fiduciary duty."[15] In an article reviewing the implications of the Yahoo case, Attorney Freya K. Bowen, of law firm Perkins Coie, said:

> . . . a series of prominent and widely publicized data breaches, combined with the growth of a cybersecurity industry designed to assist corporations in protecting against cyber attacks, may have created a corporate cybersecurity standard of care . . . In other words, the very development of stronger cybersecurity protections and controls may have created a known duty to act. The Yahoo data breach derivative litigation could be a harbinger of this trend. Many of the suit's allegations assert a bad-faith failure by the directors to adequately monitor the corporation's cybersecurity system, including through their failure to adequately fund the corporation's data-security infrastructure and through their refusal to approve necessary security updates.[16]

The 2017 Equifax Inc., data breach, which impacted 147 million consumers, was settled in July 2019, at a cost of at least

$575 million and potentially up to $700 million.[17] The litigation that followed the Equifax data breach also named certain officers and directors of the organization.[18]

> Although the court granted the motion to dismiss with respect to most of the officers and directors, it denied it as to the Equifax's former CEO, who was alleged to have personal knowledge of the inadequacies in Equifax's cybersecurity system. This ruling makes Equifax the first major data-breach related claim against a corporate officer to survive a motion to dismiss. These cases, along with the increase in cybersecurity-related derivative and securities actions, indicate that directors and officers of major corporations may face an increased risk of personal liability in connection with data breaches.[19]

Class-action lawsuits continue to be filed against healthcare organizations on behalf of victims of data breaches. Among many others, these suits have been filed against UCLA Health, Community Health Systems, Quest Diagnostics, and Virginia Mason. It would not be surprising to see derivative lawsuits filed against these healthcare C-suite executives and board members for violation of their duty-of-care responsibilities.

HIPAA's Perspective: Reasonable Diligence

When it comes to measuring the adequacy of your organization's approach to ECRM, legal definitions related to fiduciary responsibilities and duty of care are not the only standards that apply. HIPAA is the foundational legislation for the data security and privacy requirements that apply to any entity that "creates, receives, maintains, or transmits protected health information."[20]

HIPAA's language related to the enforcement of data security and privacy requirements includes these three terms and definitions:

- *Reasonable cause* means an act or omission in which a covered entity or business associate knew, or by exercising reasonable diligence would have known, that the act or omission violated an administrative simplification provision but in which the covered entity or business associate did not act with willful neglect.

- *Reasonable diligence* means the business care and prudence expected from a person seeking to satisfy a legal requirement under similar circumstances.

- *Willful neglect* means conscious, intentional failure or reckless indifference to the obligation to comply with the administrative simplification provision violated.[21]

OCR uses these definitions to evaluate the scope of responsibility an organization holds for lack of compliance with regulatory requirements. It also uses these definitions to determine the scope of civil money penalties in cases of noncompliance.

The point is, whether you consider the legal definitions and standards related to negligence and malpractice or the legislative terms related to HIPAA compliance, they both boil down to the same question. In the event of a cybersecurity incident or data breach, the courts and OCR want to know the same thing: did your organization do everything, within reason, that it could to prevent the incident from happening? Or did your organization demonstrate "negligence" or "willful neglect" with respect to your ECRM responsibilities?

It's important to remember that, even though up to this point I've been focusing on data breaches, they are only one part of the bigger ECRM picture. The HIPAA Privacy and Security Rules are meant to ensure the confidentiality, integrity, and availability (CIA) of PHI. Data breaches typically involve violating confidentiality—but that is only one leg of the CIA triad. A comprehensive ECRM program will help protect your organization's data, systems, and devices from compromises of confidentiality, integrity, *and* availability, not just from data breaches. For example, in the scenario that opened this chapter, both the confidentiality *and* the integrity of patient information was compromised by the cyber attack. In other cases, such as a ransomware attack, the availability of the information is compromised. I will have more to say about CIA in subsequent chapters.

Best-Case Scenario

The CEO of a large, national ambulatory surgery center (ASC) organization once told me, "Taking care of our patients' information is just as important as taking care of our patients." His commitment to information security served as a touchstone for his organization as they built their ECRM program.

A robust, proactive ECRM program is your organization's best defense. In the first place, if executed properly, an ECRM program will minimize the risk of an incident occurring. But if/when a cybersecurity incident or data breach does occur, an effective ECRM program can help shield you and your organization from claims of negligence or willful neglect. Imagine if the CT scan hack I described at the beginning of this chapter happened to your organization or if another kind of cybersecurity incident or data breach occurred. Your phone would be ringing. The media would be pressing your organization for a statement. They might even ambush you on your way to or from your office, shouting out questions about your organization's culpability.

In a best-case scenario, you would be able to defend yourself and your organization by honestly and unequivocally communicating the following points:

- Our board has been and is proactively engaged in ECRM.

- Our board has adopted and communicated strong governance principles which require a risk-based (not checklist-based) approach to ECRM.

- Our executive team is responsible and accountable for ECRM, and we have formed a cross-functional team of leaders across our organization to execute our ECRM strategy.

- We have adopted the NIST Cybersecurity Framework and use it as the basis for our ECRM program.

- We have implemented the internationally recognized NIST process for ECRM (NIST Special Publication 800–39 and NIST Special Publication 800–37).

- We engage with our liability insurance brokers on a regular basis to inform our risk transfer and risk retention decisions.

- To ensure progress and continuous process improvement of our ECRM program, we monitor all changes in our program, measure our program maturity annually, and execute continuous improvement plans.

- In recognition of the dynamic nature of cyber risks, we conduct ongoing risk analyses and execute risk management plans to ensure that any risks we accept are below our risk appetite.

Some of these statements might not be meaningful to you at this point. That's OK. My goal in writing this book is to give you the understanding and actionable information you need to be able to establish or improve your organization's ECRM program. When you have implemented the steps I outline in this book, you will be able to make the statements above, with the confidence and knowledge that you have put into action a program that meets accepted standards of care for managing cybersecurity risk, protecting your patients and your organization from cyber threats.

The Bottom Line

Information is literally the "lifeblood" of your healthcare organization. Especially today, with the mass digitization of healthcare and the explosion of electronic healthcare data, systems, and devices, your ability to ensure the CIA of your patient information is critical to your organization's success.

In addition to information, another essential currency in healthcare organizations is trust. There is perhaps no other industry more based on trust than healthcare. Patients entrust their healthcare providers with detailed, sensitive information about themselves, and they trust that that information will be protected. It's important for all of your stakeholders, but especially for your patients, that you maintain their trust by establishing, implementing, and maturing an ECRM program.

Talking about ECRM may seem technical and complex, and, yes, it can be both. But it is important to remember that the role of executive leadership and the board is to provide informed direction and oversight for your organization's ECRM approach, activities, and strategy. It is not the board's role to micromanage cybersecurity efforts in the field, but to provide leadership, guidance, and oversight that optimizes your organization's cybersecurity efforts.

An oft-used phrase that describes the board's role is, "eyes open, nose in, fingers out." This way of thinking can be applied to a board member's approach to ECRM, as well. "Eyes open" means be informed: understand what it means to have an effective ECRM program in place. "Nose in" means understand where your organization is in relationship to legal requirements, best practices and standards related to ECRM, and provide leadership with respect to closing any gaps between established ECRM practices and your organization's approach. Finally, "fingers out" means leave the details of execution to your organization's appropriate team members.

Many executives and board members struggle with where and how to focus their organization's ECRM efforts. I suggest beginning with the following three steps—keeping in mind that the board's role is to provide oversight for these activities, not to personally implement them. Note that I will explain each of these steps in greater detail in subsequent chapters:

1. Identify, and then prioritize, all of your organization's unique cyber risks.

2. Discuss, debate, and settle on your appetite for cyber risk, i.e., determine what level of risk your organization is prepared to accept.

3. Manage each risk, making informed decisions about which risks you will accept and which you will treat (avoid, mitigate, or transfer), and then execute on that plan.

Discussion Questions for Your C-suite and Board

As this chapter has made clear, the risk of a catastrophic cyber attack on your healthcare organization is real. The first step in addressing this risk is engaging C-suite executives and board members in a conversation about what cyber risk is, what the potential adverse impacts could be on your organization, and what steps can be taken to establish or improve your ECRM program.

I have included discussion questions at the end of each of the chapters in this book to help you begin that conversation. As you think about your organization's preparedness to deal with cybersecurity incidents, here are some questions to get you started:

1. Have your C-suite executives and board members discussed their *fiduciary responsibility* with respect to managing cyber risk?

2. What is your C-suite and board members' understanding of their *duty of care* with respect to managing cyber risk?

3. How would your organization's existing cybersecurity program measure up against HIPAA's definition of *reasonable diligence*?

4. Have your C-suite executives and board members been updated on the privacy, security, and breach notification regulatory enforcement environment in the last 12 months?

5. In the event of a successful cyber attack on your organization, how prepared is your CEO to address patients, internal stakeholders, regulatory agencies, business partners, external stakeholders, the community, and the media, with strong, unequivocal messaging about your ECRM program?

6. What steps can your organization take to ensure that ECRM is included in your organization's overall enterprise risk management program?

CHAPTER 2

Your Organization's Top Challenges

(And How ECRM Can Help)

*Cyber crime is the greatest threat
to every company in the world.*

~ GINNI ROMETTY, CEO, IBM[1]

Hospital and healthcare organizations are facing especially challenging times. Profit margins are shrinking as costs rise. Legislation, policies, and regulations are changing so fast—sometimes even reversing course depending on who is in charge—that healthcare organizations have a hard time keeping up. Nontraditional organizations, like Apple Inc. and Google, are positioning themselves as healthcare industry disruptors, eager to claim a share of the $6.0 trillion in annual healthcare spending projected to take place in the U.S. by 2027.[2]

With so many challenges to deal with, how does your organization justify allocating time and resources to ECRM? The truth is, ECRM has an important role to play in meeting many of the challenges the healthcare industry is facing. ECRM's role includes playing both offense and defense, to ensure and advance your organization's strong, competitive positioning.

Protecting the Balance Sheet

The cost of delivering healthcare continues to rise, squeezing profit margins across the industry. A recent survey of hospital CEOs found that financial challenges were hospitals' top concern.[3] No single driver is responsible for these financial challenges, but a perfect storm of multiple drivers has converged to make protecting the balance sheet more challenging than ever:

- *Labor costs* are increasing. Healthcare is a labor-intensive business. *The Atlantic* reported that healthcare surpassed retail and manufacturing to become the U.S.'s largest employer in 2018.[4] At the same time as the demand for healthcare workers is rising, the national unemployment rate dropped from 9.8 percent (January 2010) to 3.6 percent (January of 2020).[5] Because of the skills, certifications, and licensing required of healthcare professionals, the mismatch between job openings and job seekers is even wider in healthcare than in the tech industry.[6] That puts upward pressure on labor costs.

- *Pharmaceutical costs* are rising. An American Hospital Association (AHA) survey found that "over 90 percent of surveyed hospitals reported that inpatient drug price increases had a moderate or severe effect on their ability to manage costs."[7]

- *Technological advances and investments in new technologies* have been estimated to drive between 40 to 50 percent of healthcare-cost increases.[8]

- The *digitization of healthcare*, through the adoption and maintenance of electronic health records (EHRs), continues to impact healthcare organization budgets. The global spend on EHRs was calculated to be $25 billion in 2017.⁹ Much of those initial expenditures occurred as a result of the Centers for Medicare and Medicaid Services (CMS) EHR Incentive Program. However, as anyone who has ever implemented software realizes, software is not a once-and-done proposition. Ongoing investment is required to keep it updated, functional, and effective.

As rising costs impact the industry, it is more important than ever to protect your organization's balance sheet. One way to do so is to have a mature ECRM program in place to minimize the risk of compromising healthcare data, systems, and devices. Ironically, as increased digitization has increased efficiencies in healthcare administration and clinical delivery, it has also increased opportunities for cyber attacks. After all, a hacker gaining access to EHRs on a hospital network can do a lot more damage than a thief who breaks into a physician's office and finds a cabinet full of paper charts.

I'll have more to say about the potential costs of a data breach in Chapter 5, but let me give you a sneak peek here: The financial consequences of a data breach include penalties, fines, legal and other fees, settlements, and reputational damage, in addition to operational repercussions. A share of those financial consequences are the settlement amounts or civil money penalties associated with enforcement actions levied by OCR for HIPAA violations. In 2018, OCR had a record year, collecting a total of $28.7 million from enforcement actions against 10 different entities.[10] Of that total, $3 million was from a single settlement with Touchstone Medical Imaging for breaches of unsecured electronic protected health information (ePHI), impacting more than 300,000 individuals.[11] HHS reported:

> OCR's investigation further found that Touchstone failed to conduct an accurate and thorough risk analysis of potential risks and vulnerabilities to the confidentiality, integrity, and availability of all of its electronic PHI (ePHI), and failed to have business associate agreements in place with its vendors, including their IT support vendor and a third-party data center provider as required by HIPAA.[12]

Even though OCR collected less in enforcement actions in 2019 ($12,274,000), the number of breaches reported to OCR in 2019 is 33 percent higher than in 2018.[13] The number of individuals involved in those breaches has grown even more substantially, at 195 percent.[14] In addition, in 2019, we saw the first-ever OCR settlements driven by consumer complaints, a trend I expect to continue. OCR enforcement is not going away.

It's been said that "the best defense is a good offense." One certain way that healthcare organizations can protect their balance sheet is by proactively managing cyber risk to minimize the risk of compromised data, systems, and devices, and the downstream costs associated with such an incident.

Conquering Compliance Complexities

Healthcare organizations arguably navigate more layers of regulation than just about any other industry you can think of.

Increasing federal legislation, policies, and regulations; complex state legislation, policies, and regulations; now, even global policies and regulations impact the way healthcare agencies do business. A survey conducted by *Managed Healthcare Executive* identified "complying with policy changes/government requirements" as the No. 1 challenge facing healthcare organizations in 2019.[15] The survey included executives from all types of healthcare organizations, including providers, benefit management organizations, health plans, long-term care organizations, and group purchasing organizations.

An American College of Hospital Executives (ACHE) survey of hospital CEOs identified "governmental mandates" as their No. 2 concern, behind financial challenges.[16] Survey respondents identified their top-five concerns related to governmental mandates as follows:

1. CMS regulations

2. Regulatory/legislative uncertainty affecting strategic planning

3. Cost of demonstrating compliance

4. State and local regulations/mandates

5. CMS audits[17]

Even as healthcare organizations are struggling with federal and state level regulations, new global regulations are coming into play. One example of this is the European Union (EU)

General Data Protection Regulation (GDPR), which became effective May 25, 2018.[18] This regulation was designed to protect the data privacy of all EU citizens, but its application extends beyond the European Union. The GDPR protects EU citizens no matter where they are in the world; as such, compliance with the GDPR's data privacy regulations must be taken into account regardless of whether an organization maintains a physical presence in the EU or not.[19]

That became abundantly clear in early 2019, when France fined Google 50 million euros (about $57 million) for noncompliance with GDPR protections.[20] More recently, the U.K. Information Commissioner's Office (ICO) proposed a fine of $230 million for British Airways and a fine of $123 million for Marriott (for the loss of 339,000,000 guest records).[21] The maximum GDPR fine is four percent of a company's global turnover or 20 million euros, whichever is greater.[22]

In addition to CMS regulations, HIPAA requirements, GDPR requirements, and state and local requirements, some healthcare organizations (such as an academic medical center) may also be subject to the requirements of the Family Educational Rights and Privacy Act (FERPA), the Gramm-Leach-Bliley Act (GLBA), and the Payment Card Industry Data Security Standard (PCI DSS).

How can a comprehensive ECRM program help with regulation complexities? Almost all of the regulations and standards I have mentioned (including HIPAA, CMS, GDPR, GLBA, FERPA, and PCI DSS) include language and requirements about conducting a comprehensive risk analysis as part of your organization's data privacy and security program. In other words, a mature ECRM program can provide the foundation for meeting the data privacy and security requirements of a number of diverse mandates and regulations. It's the equivalent of the proverbial "killing two birds with one stone," only in this case, establishing and implementing an ECRM program has the potential to kill significantly more than two birds. Because a comprehensive ECRM program can meet the requirements of multiple mandates, it can both simplify and enhance the effectiveness and efficiency of your organization's compliance activities.

Facilitating M&A Activity

A survey by Definitive Healthcare identified consolidation as the most important trend impacting the healthcare industry in 2019.[23] In 2018 alone, Definitive Healthcare tracked 803 mergers and acquisitions (M&A), and 858 affiliation and partnership announcements. A separate survey, conducted by Capital One, identified M&A as the preferred growth vehicle for 44 percent of healthcare executives, indicating that M&A activity in the healthcare industry will not be slowing down any time soon.[24]

What role does ECRM play in M&A? A big one, it turns out. One of the drivers of healthcare M&A activity is "using data more effectively to improve quality and outcomes, such as through personalized medicine or interoperable data exchange."[25] And wherever "healthcare" and "data" intersect, data security and privacy considerations are close at hand.

In fact, a global survey of M&A professionals by the Merrill Corporation found that "data privacy" concerns were among the most likely factors to sink a healthcare M&A deal, right after "political uncertainty" and "investor confidence."[26] The same survey found that "data privacy compliance" is the second-hardest part of getting a healthcare deal right, with "talent assessment" being the first consideration.[27]

I've seen this concern play out in real time. One private equity firm contacted me in the early stages as they were planning to sell one of their data analytics portfolio companies. Their goal in reaching out to Clearwater was to ensure that cybersecurity and ECRM were a non-issue in any potential transaction. (Clearwater is the healthcare compliance risk management and cyber risk management firm that I founded in 2010. See "About Clearwater" at the end of the book.) Clearwater helped them identify and remediate cyber risk exposures and also helped them assure their compliance with HIPAA Privacy, Security, and Breach Notification regulations. In the end, when a strategic acquirer performed due diligence, ECRM was a non-issue. The transaction was consummated without a hitch.

Contrast that experience with Verizon's acquisition of Yahoo in 2017. Although not a healthcare industry deal, the dynamics of the transaction are instructive. After Verizon agreed to acquire Yahoo, Yahoo disclosed two massive data breaches that had occurred in 2013 and 2014.[28] As a result of the disclosure, the two companies negotiated a reduction of $350 million in the purchase price.[29]

Due diligence related to cyber risk is critical whether your organization is positioned to acquire another organization or to be acquired. As the Yahoo example shows, inadequate ECRM can drop your organization's enterprise value. On the flip side, if you acquire another organization without conducting due diligence around cyber risk, you could find yourself taking on more risks and liabilities than you can afford to take on. Regardless of whether your organization is primed to acquire another organization or to be acquired, it is important to build M&A considerations into your ECRM program.

Competing with Disruptors

Here we are, well into the 21st century, more than 10 years since the Health Information Technology for Economic and Clinical Health Act (HITECH)—part of the American Recovery and Reinvestment Act of 2009 (ARRA)—was passed, creating incentives to bring healthcare's use of digital tools, including EHRs, into the modern era.

And yet—after an estimated $38 billion in investments from the U.S. government—there is still plenty of room for improvement.[30] Many EHRs function in ways that are neither clinician-friendly nor patient-friendly, and genuine digital interoperability isn't yet a reality.[31] For example, in my own experience, I was personally responsible for downloading, printing, and faxing my lab results from one prestigious academic medical center to another prestigious academic medical center, both of which, by the way, use the same EHR. No wonder the healthcare industry is ripe for disruption.

For this particular scenario, Apple came to my rescue. In January 2018, Apple introduced an update to its Health app to allow patients to view their medical records on their iPhone.[32] At the time of the announcement, Apple stated:

> The updated Health Records section within the Health app brings together hospitals, clinics and the existing Health app to make it easy for consumers to see their available medical data from multiple providers whenever they choose. Johns Hopkins Medicine, Cedars-Sinai, Penn Medicine, and other participating hospitals and clinics are among the first to make this beta feature available to their patients.[33]

The newest version of Apple's Health app is organized around four categories of healthy behaviors: Activity, Sleep, Mindfulness, and Nutrition.[34] In addition, as of August 2020, the number of providers working with Apple to make health records available in the app has increased to more than 1,000 providers, in states ranging from California to Connecticut.[35]

In their 2018 report on healthcare industry disruption, PricewaterhouseCoopers (PwC) identified "Technology Invaders" as one of four types of disruption models shaking up the healthcare industry (the other types are: Vertical Integrators, Employer Activists, and Healthcare Retailers).[36] PwC describes Technology Invaders as "technology companies seeking to grab a greater foothold in healthcare."[37] Apple is only one example of a "Technology Invader." Other examples include Google, Amazon, Uber, and Lyft. PwC notes that, among the capabilities these companies bring to the table, are a "strong knowledge of consumer behavior; knowledgeable employees, and innovative culture; general trust of consumers; and strong analytics and technological capabilities."[38] As global players, these companies bring more mature ECRM experience to the table, as they are required to meet stringent compliance, data privacy, data security, and risk management standards from around the world. These "Technology Invaders" tend to allocate more resources to ECRM, as well.

Amazon is another tech company/disruptor making big moves in the healthcare space. Amazon established Haven Healthcare in 2018 with partners Berkshire Hathaway and JPMorgan Chase.[39] Haven's vision, as posted on its website, says in part:

> We believe it is possible to deliver simplified, high-quality, and transparent health care at a reasonable cost. We are

focused on leveraging the power of data and technology to drive better incentives, a better patient experience, and a better system. Our work may take many forms, and solutions may take time to develop, but Haven is invested in making healthcare much better for all of us.[40]

While it remains to be seen how innovations by companies like Apple and Amazon will ultimately impact traditional healthcare providers, it's clear that these "Technology Invaders" are experts at leveraging data—with the intent to improve the consumer experience as well as improve patient outcomes.

Interestingly, technology companies' strengths—deep experience in leveraging big data—may have a downside with consumers. It turns out, consumers don't necessarily trust big tech to handle their data with the requisite attention to security. Rock Health's 2018 Digital Health Consumer Adoption survey, which

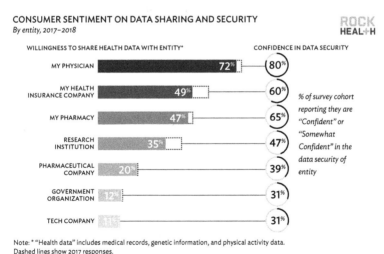

Figure 2.1 *Consumer Sentiment on Data Sharing and Security*

Source: Rock Health Digital Health Consumer Adoption Survey. https://rockhealth.com/reports/beyond-wellness-for-the-healthy-digital-health-consumer-adoption-2018/.

they have been administering for four consecutive years, turned up some interesting data about consumer trust.[41] In general, consumers are more willing to share data with their physicians (72%) than with tech companies (11%) (figure 2.1).[42] Even so, consumers lost confidence in highly trusted entities like physicians and health plans between 2017 and 2018, likely due in part to increased awareness of data security issues.[43]

What this information points out is that all healthcare organizations—whether traditional or disruptive—need to pay attention to data privacy, data security, and ECRM issues. Because consumers are paying attention to data privacy and security, they want to know that their personal data will remain secure and private if they entrust your organization with it.

One example of a disruptor that took a proactive approach to ECRM is Uber Health. Beginning in 2017, Uber began partnering with healthcare organizations to address the need for reliable transportation for patients. Studies have shown that lack of reliable transportation can be a barrier to healthcare access.[44] Uber took a proactive approach to cybersecurity when developing the Uber Health platform. Since 2017, Uber has worked with Clearwater to conduct ongoing risk analyses and ensure the organization satisfies HIPAA requirements, since, in the course of providing transportation services, the company now deals with ePHI.[45] Uber Health makes clear in its marketing that it has developed its platform with attention to HIPAA compliance, including HIPAA's cyber risk management requirements.[46]

By taking a proactive approach to ECRM, Uber has been able to earn the trust of provider partners as well as of patients. As of mid-2019, Uber Health boasted more than 1,000 provider partners.[47] The takeaway is that, in order to compete effectively with these disruptors, healthcare organizations and their business associate partners must pay attention to ECRM, whether that means establishing and implementing an ECRM program or maturing an existing one.

Your Organization's Reputation

Healthcare doesn't work, at any level, without trust. Patients come into the system full of uncertainties: What's wrong with me? Can it be fixed? Can I trust these professionals and this organization to help me? For patients to move forward in the system, they have to trust that their healthcare professionals and organizations are motivated and competent to act in the patient's best interest. Studies have shown that trust impacts a broad scope of patient behaviors, from their willingness to access healthcare in the first place, to their choice of provider, to their compliance with recommended treatments.[48]

Your organization's trustworthiness—as measured by your reputation—can directly impact revenue. One study found a relationship between a hospital's online reputation and its financial performance: hospitals with a high "reputation score" demonstrated 29 percent higher revenue per bed than hospitals with a low "reputation score" (per an analysis of online reviews).[49]

Gallup conducts an annual "Confidence in Institutions" poll to determine how Americans' confidence levels in a variety of institutions have changed over time. Overall, Americans' confidence in most institutions (the church, Congress, big business, public schools) has declined over the 40-plus years Gallup has been collecting data.[50] This decline in confidence shows up in healthcare as well. In 2004, 44 percent of survey respondents said they had either a "great deal" or "quite a lot" of confidence in "the medical system."[51] In the same year, only 17 percent said they had "very little" confidence in the medical system. Contrast that with the 2019 numbers: a little more than one-third (36%) said they had either a "great deal" or "quite a lot" of confidence in "the medical system," while the percentage who said they had "very little" confidence in the medical system increased to nearly one in four (24%).[52]

The digitization of healthcare—and increased consumer awareness about the impacts of data breaches and growing patient-safety risks—has put a new question in the minds of healthcare consumers. In addition to wondering whether their providers are competent at medical treatment, they are also wondering if their providers can be trusted to keep their medical information private and secure. A 2018 survey of businesses across a variety of business types, regarding data protection, found that "damage to customer trust and their business' reputation were greater concerns for firms than lost revenue and fines."[53]

I've seen this play out. One large, urban health system experienced several data breaches in succession. Per the HIPAA Breach Notification Rule, the health system notified the affected individuals, HHS, and the media.[54] A regional competitor immediately rolled out a public relations campaign, based on the theme, "How can you entrust your *healthcare* to an organization that can't even protect your *healthcare data*?"

Warren Buffet has been quoted as saying, "It takes 20 years to build a reputation and five minutes to ruin it. If you think about that, you'll do things differently."[55] I would add only that, in the modern digital era, it takes ten nanoseconds, not five minutes, to ruin a reputation—five nanoseconds for a breach to occur, and five nanoseconds for news of that breach to spread across the globe, once it's been discovered.

PwC's 20th Global CEO Survey found "69 percent of CEOs said it is becoming much more difficult for businesses to earn and keep trust in a digital world."[56] And that is where ECRM comes in. An organization with a comprehensive and mature ECRM program in place is not only proactively managing their cyber risk but also proactively managing their reputation.

Leveraging ECRM to Address Your Organization's Challenges

The healthcare industry is experiencing a time of unprecedented change. Challenges include financial challenges, regulatory challenges, M&A activity, threats from disruptors, and reputational challenges. The digitization of healthcare has contributed a new dimension to these challenges—a dimension that can be addressed, in part, with a comprehensive ECRM program.

An effective ECRM program can protect against financial challenges by reducing the risk of compromises to the CIA of health information, the systems that process this information, and the devices that gather it. Data breaches, ransomware attacks, and other compromises of patient information not only put your patients at risk but also risk the financial well-being of your organization, due to fines, legal and other fees, settlements, and other costs and/or medical malpractice lawsuits related to compromised data, systems, and devices.

A comprehensive ECRM program can help your organization achieve compliance not only with HIPAA regulations but also with many other regulations and standards (including CMS, GDPR, GLBA, FERPA, PCI DSS and others) that apply to organizations that create, receive, maintain, or transmit protected consumer information, including protected health information.

A mature ECRM program can facilitate M&A transactions. Inadequate cyber risk management can sink an M&A deal by decreasing the value of the organization to be acquired. If your organization is in the position of acquiring other organizations, inattention to cyber risk management can negatively impact the acquiring organization's cybersecurity, by introducing weaknesses into the overall system. A mature ECRM program can ensure that whether your organization is looking to acquire or to be acquired, cybersecurity issues will not stand in the way.

A dynamic ECRM program can help traditional organizations compete in a market full of "Technology Invaders." Traditional healthcare organizations will need to address cyber risk fully and completely in order to match the level of overall technology sophistication and ECRM experience these innovators bring to the table. At the same time, innovators in the field (such as Apple) will need to prove to patients and providers that they understand and can manage the specific security and privacy requirements that apply when dealing with patient data.

Finally, a robust ECRM program can be leveraged proactively to establish and maintain consumer trust and protect your organization's reputation. A PwC survey of consumers on attitudes toward cybersecurity found "85% of consumers will not do business with a company if they have concerns about its security practices."[57] In this digital age, it is more important than ever that organizations demonstrate trustworthiness and maturity in their approach to data protection.

Historically, healthcare organizations have approached ECRM only as an "IT problem." ECRM has been relegated to an isolated cost center and considered, at best, a necessary cost of doing business. The truth is that, in the digital age, ECRM is actually a business enabler. Effective ECRM enables organizations to securely deploy consumer-centric, technology-based innovations that engage customer trust and encourage customer confidence. It is time to stop treating investment in ECRM as an afterthought and instead recognize the enterprisewide role ECRM has to play in helping organizations meet all of their business challenges. As senior leaders and board members, you have the opportunity to provide the oversight and leadership needed to leverage ECRM as a competitive advantage.

Discussion Questions for Your C-suite and Board

ECRM might seem like just another challenge for your organization to address. But viewed from a different perspective, establishing or maturing your organization's ECRM program actually presents you with an opportunity to strengthen your organization's competitive position. The following questions will help you start thinking about how ECRM fits into the "big picture" of all of the challenges facing your organization.

1. What are the top challenges your hospital or health system is facing over the next three to five years?

2. Do you view ECRM as a challenge or as an opportunity?

3. How important is it to protect your organization from the fines, fees, settlements, and other costs associated with the compromise of CIA of patient data (e.g., data breach, ransomware attack, etc.)?

4. How important is it to ensure that your organization demonstrates compliance with HIPAA and other relevant regulations and standards (GDPR, GLBA, FERPA, PCI DSS, etc.) regarding data privacy and security?

5. Is your organization likely to be involved in any M&A activity in the next several years? Would your organization's privacy and security posture pass the due diligence process of a potential acquiring organization? Does your organization have the capacity and resources to perform rigorous ECRM due diligence on a potential acquiree?

6. Is your organization prepared to go toe-to-toe with healthcare industry disruptors with respect to your ability to protect your healthcare data, systems, and devices from compromise?

7. What reputational consequences would your organization incur in the event of a compromise of the CIA of protected patient data?

8. What additional organizational challenges might a robust ECRM program help you address?

CHAPTER 3

The Healthcare
Cyber Risk Problem

The health sector is in desperate need
of a cyber hygiene injection.

~ JAMES SCOTT, SENIOR FELLOW, INSTITUTE
FOR CRITICAL INFRASTRUCTURE TECHNOLOGY [1]

The Problem Is Real:
Risky Perfect Storm Ahead

As far back as 2014, the FBI issued a Private Industry Notice (PIN) warning of increased cyber intrusions against healthcare systems.[2] The alert cited a number of reasons for the increase, including the transition from paper records to EHRs, a higher financial payout for medical records on the black market, and "lax cybersecurity standards" in the industry.[3] The alert went on to state that "the healthcare industry is not as resilient to cyber intrusions" as other critical infrastructure sectors (e.g., energy, financial services, transportation systems, etc.) and that healthcare is "poorly protected and ill-equipped to handle new cyber threats exposing patient medical records."

Six years later, the FBI's alert is still relevant. Cyber attacks on healthcare organizations continue to increase. In addition, the healthcare industry's attack surface has increased exponentially. And, unfortunately, most healthcare organizations are still ill-prepared to deal with these increasing threats. Together, these trends combine to create a risky perfect (cyber) storm for healthcare organizations.

Cyber Attacks on Healthcare Organizations Are Increasing

Cyber attacks are a fact of life for anyone connected to the internet. A University of Maryland study found that the typical computer with internet access is attacked by hackers every 39 seconds: that's an average of 2,244 times each day.[4]

Healthcare is no exception. A recent survey of healthcare organizations found that 39 percent experience cyber attacks on a daily or weekly basis, 15 percent experience attacks on a monthly basis, and 21 percent experience attacks once or twice a year.[5] Nearly one in five (18%) *do not know* how often they experience cyber attacks, and 6 percent stated they had never experienced a cyber attack.[6] Considering the facts that cyber-attackers often operate in a stealth mode and that these percentages capture only *known* attempts at intrusion, these numbers likely underrepresent the true scope of attacks. Even without statistics, any number of daily headlines tell the story:

- Erie County Medical Center (ECMC), a 602-bed hospital in Buffalo, New York, was the victim of a ransomware attack on Palm Sunday in April 2017 that, ultimately, infected more than 6,000 of ECMC's computers with a common variant of ransomware called SamSam.[7] ECMC says patient records were never compromised during the incident. ECMC decided not to comply with a nearly $30,000 ransom demand; ECMC officials estimated expenses tied to the incident were around $10 million.[8] "What happened to us was a wake-up call for the entire community," said Thomas Quatroche Jr., the medical center's chief executive officer. "Any major institution that wants to improve cybersecurity will have to make investments just like this."[9]

- In 2018, the American Medical Collection Agency (AMCA), a medical-billing firm, experienced a data breach that exposed the information of nearly 20 million people.[10] AMCA clients Quest Diagnostics and LabCorp suffered patient-data breaches as a result of the AMCA breach. After disclosure of the initial and subsequent data breaches, AMCA lost its clients and incurred millions of dollars in expenses. AMCA filed for bankruptcy in 2019.[11]

- In 2019, insurer Dominion National discovered unauthorized access to servers that potentially compromised the data of 2.96 million patients.[12] Further investigation found that the hack may have been initiated in 2010, nine years before it was eventually discovered.[13]

As of July 1, 2019, more than 216 breaches, representing 9,911,355 records, were under investigation per the HHS/OCR Breach Portal.[14] In just the first six months of 2019, more patient records were impacted by data breaches than during the entire year of 2018.

Healthcare's Attack Surface Is Increasing

Healthcare data, systems, and devices are more voluminous, more visible, more valuable, and more vulnerable than ever. The industry's transition from paper to digital records—prompted by the CMS EHR incentive program—took place over a relatively short period of time. Between 2008 and 2017, the percentage of acute care hospitals using EHRs increased from 9 percent to 96 percent.[15] This means that the number of organizations that create, receive, maintain, and/or transmit ePHI has increased at least tenfold in the last decade.

The scope of these systems has expanded as well. I am not talking only about EHR systems when I talk about where ePHI is located. Besides EHRs, there are clinical information applications, lab and medical specialty applications, medical billing and claims processing applications, payment processing applications, and financial management and reporting applications. In addition, as the achievement of interoperability in the U.S. healthcare system has continued to be a priority, healthcare organizations are sharing data with an increasing number of third-party partners. (Third-party partners are known as *business associates* in HIPAA parlance).

At the same time that the number of organizations leveraging digital patient information has increased, the volume of data has increased as well. Technological advances (e.g., advances in imaging technology) and emerging technologies (e.g., genomics, consumer fitness devices) have contributed to an explosion of healthcare data. A Dell EMC study estimated that the average healthcare organization managed 8.41 petabytes (PB) of data in 2018.[16] (For reference, a single PB of data is the equivalent of 500 billion pages of standard typed text).[17] The same study also found that the healthcare data growth rate was 878 percent between 2016 and 2018, far exceeding the data growth rate of 569 percent across all other industries for the same time period.[18]

Simultaneous with the increase in the number of organizations dealing with digital healthcare data and the increase in the volume of that data has been an increase in the number of systems and devices generating and using that data. Twenty-five years ago, the phrase "Internet of Things (IoT), hadn't yet been coined.[19] Compare that to today: 87 percent of healthcare organizations expect to have Internet of Medical Things (IoMT) technology implemented by the end of 2019.[20] It has been estimated that more than 3.7 million IoMT devices are in use today.[21] Innovations from smart infusion pumps to real-time location-tracking systems are helping healthcare organizations deliver care more effectively. But the flip side of this innovation is an increase in attack surfaces for cyber criminals. Of those healthcare organizations who have already implemented IoT, 89 percent reported having experienced an IoT-related security breach.[22]

Nonclinical technology is also part of the expanding attack surface in healthcare. From facilities security systems to internet-connected HVAC systems—any system with a hospital network or internet connection presents additional potential vulnerabilities that must be assessed and considered.

Healthcare Is Underprepared

The unintended consequences of the digitization of the healthcare industry include operational disruption, greater legal and compliance exposures, new patient-safety concerns, patient-trust issues, potential reputational damage, possible medical malpractice lawsuits and supply-chain or third-party exposure. With so much at stake, why is healthcare so far behind other industries when it comes to cybersecurity?

One reason is that, prior to the CMS EHR incentive program, healthcare lagged behind other industries in the adoption of digital technology in general. The banking industry, for instance, went digital decades before healthcare did. The first automatic teller machine (ATM) that allowed customers direct access to their accounts was unveiled by Lloyds Bank in the United Kingdom in the early 1970s.[23] That's 35 years before CMS launched its EHR incentive program. The consequence is that the banking industry has deeper, broader experience in digital data and transactions—including experience in maintaining the security and privacy of that data—than the healthcare industry does.

A 2017 report by the Health Care Cybersecurity Task Force identified a number of reasons why the healthcare industry is still behind when it comes to cybersecurity (figure 3.1).[24]

The report cited multiple reasons for the healthcare industry's lack of cybersecurity preparedness:

- *Lack of security talent*: The majority of health delivery organizations lack full-time, qualified cybersecurity personnel.

- *Legacy equipment*: Many healthcare organizations are using equipment that is running on old, unsupported, and vulnerable operating systems.

- *Premature connectivity*: In the healthcare industry's rush to go live and demonstrate Meaningful Use, per CMS requirements,

HEALTHCARE CYBERSECURITY IS IN CRITICAL CONDITION

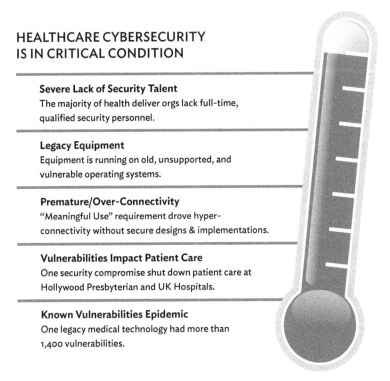

Severe Lack of Security Talent
The majority of health deliver orgs lack full-time, qualified security personnel.

Legacy Equipment
Equipment is running on old, unsupported, and vulnerable operating systems.

Premature/Over-Connectivity
"Meaningful Use" requirement drove hyper-connectivity without secure designs & implementations.

Vulnerabilities Impact Patient Care
One security compromise shut down patient care at Hollywood Presbyterian and UK Hospitals.

Known Vulnerabilities Epidemic
One legacy medical technology had more than 1,400 vulnerabilities.

Figure 3.1 *Healthcare Cybersecurity Is in Critical Condition*
Source: Bob Chaput, Executive Chairman, Clearwater. Adapted from *Report on Improving Cybersecurity in the Health Care Industry.* Health Care Industry Cybersecurity Task Force. June 2017. Accessed August 31, 2019. https://www.phe.gov/Preparedness/planning/CyberTF/Documents/report2017.pdf

cybersecurity concerns sometimes got put on the back burner or treated as an afterthought. Connectivity was put in place before consideration of secure design and implementation.

- *An open, sharing culture*: In order to deliver effective care, data has to be easily accessible to clinicians. There is sometimes tension between the accessibility needed for timely care delivery and the privacy and security practices needed to protect patient data.

- *Viewing cybersecurity as an IT challenge*: The report notes that the tendency to approach cybersecurity reactively (rather than proactively) and as an IT responsibility (rather than an enterprisewide responsibility) is common in the healthcare industry.

- *Lack of understanding of the risks cyber threats pose*: Many in the healthcare industry, from clinicians in the field to organizational leadership, lack an awareness and full understanding of cyber risk.[25]

Defining the Problem: What Is Risk?

Before I proceed further, it's important to define the problem. What is risk, at its most basic level? Risk is about loss or harm; risk management is about minimizing or mitigating the potential for loss or harm.

We All Manage Risks Every Day

Each of us makes decisions related to risk on a regular, if not daily, basis. We may choose to drive our own car to work or to commute with another driver. We may exceed the speed limit when we're driving, accepting a risk in order to make an appointment. We may or may not have set a password or PIN on our personal mobile phone. We may or may not lock our front door when we leave home. We may or may not have a security system set up at our home.

These examples of risk management decisions from our daily lives can be used to illustrate two important concepts about risk:

1. For risk to exist, there must be an *asset*, a *threat*, and a *vulnerability*.

2. Rating the level of risk is a function of the *likelihood* of a bad thing happening and the *impact* were that bad thing to occur, given what controls may be in place.

It's essential to understand these concepts about risk before getting into the specifics of treating cyber risk within healthcare organizations. Let's look at these concepts in light of the everyday examples I used above.

For Risk to Exist, There Must Be an Asset, a Threat, and a Vulnerability

Risk comprises three components: an *asset*, a *threat*, and a *vulnerability* (figure 3.2). If all three of these components aren't present, then you don't have risk. Think about your home. Your home is an *asset*. What are the *threats* to your home? One possible threat could be a burglar. How *vulnerable* is your home to this threat? Well, if you leave your front door unlocked when you leave the house, you may be more vulnerable to a burglary than if you lock it securely behind you when you go. So, the *vulnerability* in this case is an unlocked front door.

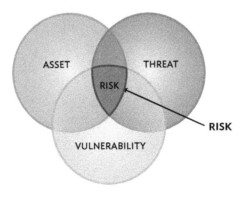

Figure 3.2 *Risk Exists Where an Asset, a Threat, and a Vulnerability Intersect*
Source: Bob Chaput, Executive Chairman, Clearwater.

All three components must be in place for risk to exist: an asset (your home), a threat (a burglar), and a vulnerability (an unlocked door). If there is an asset and a threat, but no vulnerability (e.g., you live in Fort Knox), there is no risk.

The asset-threat-vulnerability combination is known as a "risk scenario." I use the notation {asset-threat-vulnerability} to indicate a risk scenario. In the instance described above, the risk scenario would look like this: {your home-burglar-unlocked door}.

Other variables—beyond the {asset-threat-vulnerability} combination—are at play as well. Which brings us to the second important concept to understand about risk: risk is a function of likelihood, impact, and controls.

Risk Is a Function of Likelihood, Impact, and Controls

The rating of any particular risk is a function of three variables: likelihood, impact, and controls.

- *Likelihood* refers to the probability that a given threat is capable of exploiting a given vulnerability

- *Impact* refers to the extent of the harm that can occur if a vulnerability is exploited

- *Controls* are the measures, safeguards, strategies, methods, and tools used to mitigate risk by lowering the likelihood or impact

Let's revisit the home example for a moment. Your home is an asset. The threat is a burglar. The vulnerability is that your front door is unlocked when you leave. What is the *likelihood* that your home will be burglarized? One source extrapolated from FBI crime data to calculate that 1 in every 36 homes is burglarized each year.[26] Many variables impact the likelihood of your particular home being burglarized. For example, 34 percent of burglars enter through the front door.[27] This directly relates to our vulnerability—leaving the front door unlocked. In fact, burglars will sometimes knock to see if anyone is home and then try the doorknob to see if it is unlocked—an open invitation for the intruder.[28]

What about *impact*? If you just bought the home and haven't moved anything in yet, the impact may be negligible. But if you keep valuables in your home—such as cash or expensive jewelry—the impact could be high. You could experience a high degree of loss if a burglar gains entrance. If you are home when the burglar breaks in, you become another *asset*, and the impact could be even higher, as home invasions can end in violence.

Finally, what *controls* do you have in place to minimize your risk? Do you lock your front door? Do you have a deadbolt on your front door? Do you have a security system? Do you live in a gated community?[29] All of these *controls* can help mitigate your risk.

Risk in a Healthcare Organization

Now let's see how these concepts apply to healthcare cyber risk. In healthcare, your assets include your data, your systems, and your devices, as well as supporting assets such as building management systems and HVAC systems. Loss or harm occurs when there is a compromise of the CIA of these assets. The HIPAA Security Rule specifically states that covered entities and business associates must "ensure the confidentiality, integrity, and availability of all electronic protected health information."[30] But the concept of protecting the CIA of healthcare organization assets is bigger than HIPAA and more than a HIPAA-compliance issue. It is a patient-safety issue. As the Health Care Industry Cybersecurity Task Force concluded in 2017:

> The healthcare system cannot deliver effective and safe care without deeper digital connectivity. If the healthcare system is connected but insecure, this connectivity could betray patient safety, subjecting them to unnecessary risk and forcing them to pay unaffordable personal costs. Our nation must find a way to prevent our patients from being forced to choose between connectivity and security.[31]

What kinds of loss or harm to patients can result from the compromise of the CIA of your organization's data (ePHI), systems, or devices? Figure 3.3 identifies some of the possibilities.

These losses have significant implications not just for patients but for the entire organization. Yet one recent global survey found that only 18 percent of organizations say that information security (cyber risk management) fully influences business strategy plans on a regular basis.[32]

Problem-Solving: Understanding Your Role in Ensuring an Effective Approach

Given that cyber risk is on the rise, and given these fundamental concepts related to risk, how do C-suite executives and board members begin to approach the problem? The following concepts will help you begin to approach ECRM in your organization in a meaningful way.

Confidentiality	Integrity	Availability
(for example, a data breach that results in unauthorized access to ePHI)	*(for example, an undetected modification of patient records)*	*(for example, a ransomware attack that shuts down operations)*
Identity Theft	Incorrect Diagnosis	Delayed Admittance
Reputational Damage	Incorrect Treatment	Delayed Diagnosis
Relationship Damage	Incorrect Prescriptions	Delayed Surgery
Employment Damage	Incorrect Billing Charges	Delayed Prescriptions
Financial Damage	Contaminated Clinical Trial	Delayed Discharge
Anxiety	Identity Theft	Diagnosis Errors
Depression	Reputational Damage	Treatment Errors
Suicide	Theft	Death

Figure 3.3 *Potential Loss/Harm Caused by a Compromise of Data, Systems, or Devices*

Source: Bob Chaput, Executive Chairman, Clearwater.

Risk Management Is About a Holistic Program, Not a Particular Tool

To effectively manage risk, you have to approach it with a programmatic, ECRM perspective. No single tool will solve the problem of cyber risk. Simply installing a deadbolt on your front door doesn't solve the home-burglary problem. It can help, but it doesn't, by itself, eliminate the problem. If you live in a high-risk neighborhood (and healthcare is a high-risk neighborhood in terms of cyber risk), you will want to carefully inventory the valuable assets you want to protect in your home (cash, jewelry) and design a home security program that will protect these assets. For example, not only might you install a deadbolt on the front door, you might also invest in a safe box to store your cash and jewelry. You might also decide to install and subscribe to a home-alarm system that will alert you when an intrusion occurs.

Likewise, managing cyber risk in your healthcare organization is not about investing in the latest, greatest tool. Implementing the latest encryption tool or the latest web vulnerability scanning tool *may be* appropriate and helpful. But without considering the overall context of your organization's risk environment, investments in the cybersecurity tool *du jour* may be a waste of your resources. Furthermore, if you have identified all of your risks upfront, then you will be able to recognize controls that can give you more value by mitigating more than one risk.

Risk-Based Versus Checklist-Based Cybersecurity

An effective risk management program begins with an inventory of your organization's specific assets and an assessment of your organization's specific threats and vulnerabilities. Back to our home security example: Google "home security checklist," and, in an instant, you'll see a number of one-size-fits-all checklists designed to ensure the security of your home. One checklist recommends:

- Install a deadbolt on every exterior door

- Purchase and install a security bar on every sliding glass door

- Install locks on all windows

- Install security bars on your windows

- Install motion-detector outdoor lights on your home's exterior

- Purchase a safe box for valuables such as cash and jewelry, and bolt it to the floor

The problem is that home security isn't one-size-fits-all (and neither is cybersecurity). If you just follow a checklist, you might end up spending money on things you don't need. At the same time, you might neglect to consider a safeguard that's not mentioned in the list.

For example, the checklist above suggests purchasing and installing a security bar on all windows, but if you live on the 20th floor of a condominium building, this suggestion is irrelevant to you. Buying security bars for your 20th floor windows would be a waste of resources and would not improve your home security.

On the other hand, what if your single-family home happens to have a skylight? The list above does not include any recommendations for securing skylights. And yet skylights are one of many vulnerable entry points burglars may use to invade your home.[33]

As you can see, simply using a checklist approach is not the best way to establish your home security program. First you need to inventory your assets. Do you keep cash, jewelry, and/or other valuables, in your home? Or do you keep your valuables in a lockbox at the bank? Does your home have sliding glass doors? Does your home have a skylight? Then, you need to identify and consider threats and vulnerabilities that apply to your assets in order to determine your specific risks.

The same thing is true for your ECRM program. Without knowing your unique exposures, how can you make wise decisions about how to treat them? The foundation for an effective ECRM program is risk assessment. The risk assessment includes an inventory of **all** of your assets (data, systems, and devices as well as supporting systems), identification of the threats and vulnerabilities associated with each asset, and a rating of the likelihood and impact of each threat. Only then will you be able to effectively determine what safeguards or controls to implement. Without an accurate inventory of the assets you are trying to protect, you cannot develop an effective ECRM program. Without an understanding of your unique risks, you can end up underspending or overspending on your ECRM program, because you won't have the information you need to make the wisest possible investment decisions.

In my experience, the single biggest error organizations make is the failure to identify all their unique risks. I have seen this problem in both large and small healthcare organizations. As you can see from the home security example, the necessary first step to risk management is a detailed consideration of your unique assets, threats, and vulnerabilities. You cannot make good decisions about how to deploy scarce resources for controls without the first critical step of identifying your organization's specific risks.

Once you have identified all of your risk scenarios {asset-threat-vulnerability} and prioritized them using their risk rating, it can be helpful to reference a list of controls as you consider how to minimize and/or mitigate your greatest risks. Controls are a critical component of risk management, however, they should not be considered in a one-size-fits-all manner as the basis for your organization's ECRM program.

C-suite Executives and Board Members Do Not Need to Know How to Spell "Ransomware" or "Cryptojacking"

Hopefully, it is clear by now, that as a C-suite executive or board member, you do NOT need to be a cybersecurity expert to lead your organization's ECRM efforts effectively. It's the same as with your home security program: you do not need to know how to install a deadbolt. You do not need to design and manufacture a safe box. You do not need to build and install a home security system from scratch. You *do* need to know how these potential safeguards fit into the bigger picture of protecting your home, but you do not need to be personally responsible for designing or installing them. You also need to understand your level of risk (e.g., do you live in a high-risk community or not?) in order to make smart decisions about investing your risk management dollars. If you live in a low-crime neighborhood, maybe you will be comfortable simply installing the deadbolt and purchasing the safe box but will forgo the home security system. (I will talk more about risk appetite in Chapter 5).

In other words, the board and C-suite do not need to dictate the technical details of your organization's ECRM program. Instead, the board should provide oversight for the ECRM program, and C-suite executives should provide leadership. But this oversight and leadership occur at a strategic, not tactical, level. Too many organizations approach ECRM as an afterthought and end up mired in tactical/technical/spot-welding activities. They respond reactively to the threat *du jour,* whether that be cryptojacking, IoT-device threats, mobile malware, or something on the horizon yet to be named. The tactical/technical/spot-welding approach does not result in an effective ECRM program. For an ECRM program to make a meaningful difference, you need to take a strategic/business/architectural approach. That is why oversight and leadership from the board and C-suite are essential, and that approach is what I will cover in the following chapters.

Only the board and C-suite have the business-wide perspective and authority to ensure that your organization's ECRM efforts align with your overall strategic goals and enterprise risk management program. The board and C-suite have the scope and power to allocate scarce resources strategically, including human resources, capital expenditures (CapEx) and operating expenses (OpEx), to establish, implement, and mature an effective ECRM program.

As I will state several times throughout this book, the single most important decision you will make about ECRM is *how* you're going to conduct ECRM. Your ECRM program must transcend time, your current assets, today's threats and vulnerabilities, and your current safeguards. They will all change, as this is not a once-and-done event. Ultimately, as a C-suite executive or board member, your goal is to invest the right amount in ECRM to treat risks in a way that is acceptable for your organization and its stakeholders as you execute on your vision, mission, strategy, values, and services.

Discussion Questions for Your C-suite and Board
Leadership's awareness of, and engagement in, ECRM is essential to developing an effective program. Leon Rodriguez, former director of the Department of Health and Human Services' Office for Civil Rights, once said, "HIPAA compliance needs to be owned by the entire organization. It needs to be owned by the leadership of the organization."[34] The same is true for your organization's broader ECRM program, of which HIPAA compliance is only one component. The following questions will

help you think about your role in providing leadership for your organization's ECRM program.

1. Healthcare organizations are a big target for cyber-attackers. Has your organization been subject to one or more cyber attacks in the last 12 months? If this is information you do not currently have, who in your organization has this information?

2. Early in this chapter, I made the point that the health-care industry's attack surface is increasing exponentially. Think about whether this is true for your organization: Are you handling increasing volumes of digital data? Is your network expanding with the use of IoT and IoMT devices? In addition to your EHRs (if applicable), how many other systems and applications are part of your network ecosystem?

3. Some of the significant breaches mentioned in this chapter were due to data sharing relationships with business associates/third-party partners. Does your organization interact with third-party partners in a way that should inform your ECRM program?

4. Has your organization conducted a comprehensive, detailed risk assessment, identifying and rating your unique risks (assets/threats/vulnerabilities)?

5. Is your organization using a risk-based approach to ECRM or a checklist-based approach? That is, are you

making risk mitigation decisions (e.g., what controls to implement) based on your unique exposures, or are you implementing someone else's checklist of controls?

6. Does your organization currently approach ECRM from a tactical/technical/spot-welding perspective? Or does your organization approach ECRM from a strategic/ business/architectural perspective? Which approach do you think is more effective?

7. Do considerations about cyber risk inform your business strategy and planning efforts?

8. Does your vision, mission, strategy, values, and services inform your ECRM program? Are they well-aligned?

9. Do you believe you need to be an expert in technical cyber risk topics in order to provide effective, strategic ECRM direction for your organization? Why or why not?

CHAPTER 4

The Unique Challenges of Conducting Enterprise Cyber Risk Management

Many executives are declaring cyber as the risk that will define our generation.

~ DENNIS CHESLEY, GLOBAL RISK
CONSULTING LEADER, PWC, USA[1]

R isk management is certainly not a new concept in the healthcare industry. Healthcare organizations have been managing risks related to patient safety and professional liability for a long time. What's changed in healthcare enterprise risk management is that enterprise *cyber risk* management has moved to the forefront in a very short time. Cyber risk wasn't even on the healthcare industry radar 20 years ago. Now, with the digitization of healthcare, cyber risk has become a risk with the potential to impact every other type of business risk a healthcare organization manages.

ECRM has much in common with traditional risk management. After all, for any type of risk management, you need to start by identifying, rating and prioritizing your organization's unique risks, before determining how your organization will treat those risks. However, ECRM also comes with some unique challenges that don't necessarily apply to other types of enterprise risk management. These challenges relate to your organization's *understanding* of ECRM, *engagement* with ECRM, and *execution* of ECRM. Understanding ECRM's unique challenges will help you lead your organization in establishing and maturing your ECRM program.

Challenges Related to Understanding ECRM

The relatively new—and dynamically evolving—nature of cyber risk means that many organizations are not "up to speed" on the history, nature, breadth, and relevance of cyber risk. After more than 25 years of working with healthcare organizations to identify, rate, prioritize, and treat cyber risk, I've found the following clarifications to be helpful.

Yesterday's Cyber Risk Is Not Today's Cyber Risk

Over the past 10 years, the healthcare industry's understanding of cyber risk has evolved through four distinct phases, emphasizing four different aspects of cyber risk. Understanding these four different phases gives context for where healthcare cyber risk began and where it is now.

HIPAA was enacted in 1996.[2] The HIPAA Privacy Rule went into effect in 2003, and the HIPAA Security Rule went into effect in 2005.[3] In the early 2000s, HIPAA enforcement efforts were complaint-driven and reactive, resulting in minimal compliance efforts. That changed with the passage of the HITECH Act. The HITECH Act changed breach reporting requirements, expanded the types of entities subject to HIPAA's Privacy and Security rules, increased penalties for lack of compliance, and increased enforcement activities. These changes ushered in the first phase of cybersecurity in the healthcare industry: The Compliance phase (figure 4.1).

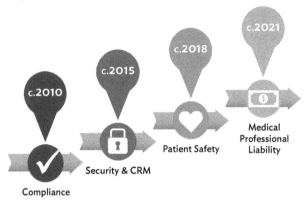

Figure 4.1 *The Evolving Focus of Cyber Risk in the Healthcare Industry*
Source: Bob Chaput, Executive Chairman, Clearwater.

In 2015, data breaches at Anthem, Premera Blue Cross, Excellus BlueCross BlueShield, and others exposed the data of more than 193 million individuals.[4] These breaches reinforced the idea that cybersecurity in healthcare was about more than simply HIPAA compliance. It became clear that cyber risk was a security issue. Healthcare organizations increased their efforts around security and cyber risk management, ushering in a new phase of cyber risk focus: The Security and Cyber Risk Management (CRM) phase.

Around the same time as these data breaches were occurring, connected medical devices were gaining acceptance—and providing new opportunities for cyberattackers. As early as 2011, security researcher Jay Radcliffe demonstrated how he could remotely hack into and disable an insulin pump.[5] In 2013, the Food and Drug Administration (FDA) issued guidance on cybersecurity and medical devices. In 2017, the FDA recalled an implantable pacemaker over concerns that it was vulnerable to hacking.[6] By 2018, incidents like these led to a new cybersecurity focus within the healthcare industry; I call this the Patient Safety phase.

Now, as we enter 2021 and beyond, the healthcare industry has entered a new phase: the Medical Professional Liability phase. As of the writing of this book, there has not yet been a highly publicized, cyber-driven, medical malpractice lawsuit. But progressive organizations know that it is coming, and they are working hard to get ahead of this trend. More and more organizations are connecting the dots between cyber risk, patient safety, and medical professional liability. They are rightly beginning to view ECRM as an *enterprise* risk management issue, not an IT problem, and elevating ECRM's role within their organizations accordingly.

ECRM Interfaces with Many Layers of Regulations

As I previously discussed, healthcare organizations are subject to a number of privacy, security, and breach notification rules that range from local to state to federal to international regulations. This means that your ECRM program is not only an important business requirement but also required by law. The key sources of regulations related to data privacy, security, and breach notification include the following:

- *HIPAA*—HIPAA, as I've previously noted, is the acronym for the Health Insurance Portability and Accountability Act of 1996. HIPAA's Privacy, Security, Enforcement, and Breach Notification Rules, as articulated in the Omnibus Final Rule, which was published in 2013, provide the foundation for the healthcare industry's privacy and security laws.[7] It is the standard against which HIPAA compliance is measured. The privacy, security, and breach notification rules that are part of HIPAA apply to PHI, a broad category that encompasses many different types of clinical and administrative data. PHI is defined as "individually identifiable health information."[8] Every organization that "creates, receives, maintains, or transmits protected health information" is required to comply with HIPAA.[9]

- *State Laws*—As of this writing, the U.S. has not enacted any single, overarching data protection legislation.[10] States, however, are another matter. All 50 states and the District of Columbia require that residents be notified in the case of a data breach of practically any type of personally identifiable information (PII), including PHI.[11] State definitions of protected information and breaches, and regulations around notification, vary widely. One trend that is evident across state-initiated privacy and security regulations is an emphasis on *risk-based* information security. In this respect, state laws are mirroring HIPAA's requirements for risk-based data security measures based on comprehensive risk analysis.

- *The Federal Trade Commission (FTC)*—The FTC is "an independent U.S. law-enforcement agency protecting consumers and enhancing competition across broad sectors of the economy. The FTC's primary legal authority comes from Section 5 of the Federal Trade Commission Act, which prohibits unfair or deceptive practices in the marketplace . . . This broad authority allows the Commission to address a wide array of practices affecting consumers, including those that emerge with the development of new technologies and business models."[12] The FTC has increasingly been leveraging its authority to protect consumer privacy and personal information. The FTC's focus on data privacy and security has the potential to impact your organization. One recent example of the FTC's perspective and influence is the 2019 settlement with Facebook. The final settlement included the following requirements:

✓ The organization must establish an ongoing Independent Privacy Committee

✓ The organization must engage an external firm to conduct an initial Independent Privacy Program Assessment and to continue to conduct such assessments every 2 years for the next 20 years

✓ Each fiscal quarter, the Principal Executive Officer and the Designated Compliance Officer(s) must sign a certification related to the establishment, implementation, and maintenance of a Privacy Program compliant with the requirements of the settlement

✓ Conduct risk assessment and risk management prior to modifying products, services, or practices, or implementing new products, services, or practices[13]

Although this particular example (Facebook) is from outside of the healthcare industry, healthcare is not exempt from

FTC scrutiny. The FTC has cited numerous healthcare organizations (CVS Caremark/CVS Pharmacy, Rite Aid, Accretive Health, and GMR Transcription Services, for example) for violating the FTC Act. FTC enforcement is based on the idea that, by failing to secure consumers' private information, organizations are engaging in unfair and deceptive practices.[14]

- *Europe's General Data Protection Regulation (GDPR)*—As I noted in Chapter 2, the GDPR went into effect in May 2018. The GDPR protects EU citizens no matter where they are in the world; as such, compliance with the GDPR's data privacy regulations must be taken into account regardless of whether an organization maintains a physical presence in the EU or not.[15]

Compliance Does NOT Equal Security

Despite the importance of compliance with applicable laws and regulations, it is important to clarify that regulatory compliance does not equal security. Many organizations operate under the misconception that compliance with the original HIPAA legislation (enacted more than 20 years ago) or the HIPAA Security Rule (effective 15 years ago) is sufficient. I'm using the term "compliance" here in the sense of a checklist approach to regulatory requirements: Simply ticking off boxes on a controls checklist or list of best practices or the HIPAA Security Rule itself and calling it good does not translate into effective security.

That is not sufficient to secure your organization's data, systems, and devices. And multiple OCR enforcement actions demonstrate that this type of "checklist" exercise doesn't meet HIPAA Security Rule requirements for an effective ECRM program, either. An effective ECRM program is more complex, more specific, and more nuanced than marking off a checklist.

For example, the HIPAA Security Rule doesn't require just one type of assessment: it actually requires that organizations conduct three different types of assessments (figure 4.2).

Non-Technical
Compliance Assessment
45 CFR §164.308(a)(8)

Risk Analysis
45 CFR §164.308(a)(1)(ii)(A)

COMPLIANCE

SECURITY

TEST & AUDIT

Technical Testing
& Audits
45 CFR §164.308(a)(8)

Figure 4.2 *The Three Types of Assessments Required by the HIPAA Security Rule*
Source: 45 CFR §164.308; graphic illustration by Bob Chaput, Executive Chairman, Clearwater.

It is important that your organization understands the differences between these three types of assessments in order to implement a program that is compliant with the HIPAA Security Rule. But for our purposes here, what I want to emphasize is that one of the three required assessments is the *risk analysis*. This analysis, which identifies and documents your organization's unique assets, threats, and vulnerabilities, is what provides the foundation for an effective ECRM program. And a comprehensive ECRM program—not compliance, in and of itself—is what ultimately keeps your organization secure.

Cyber Risk Is Inseparable from the Other Risks Your Organization Faces

Cyber risk does not exist in isolation. A successful cyber attack doesn't just threaten your organization's PHI or other sensitive data; cyber risk is inextricably linked to the other risks your organization faces. A successful cyber attack could trigger an enforcement action by a regulatory body, such as OCR or the FTC. A ransomware attack could lead to business interruption and an expensive payoff to resume operations. Other consequences might include damage to your organization's reputation, lost customers and revenues, a medical malpractice lawsuit, or a negligence lawsuit against C-suite executives and board members.

Downstream, the consequences can also turn into talent-acquisition challenges, higher cost of capital, and higher insurance premiums. An adverse cyber event can result in serious negative financial, regulatory, reputational, and clinical consequences.

The story of Accretive Health, a company that provided medical billing and revenue-management services to hospitals around the U.S., is a case in point. Accretive experienced a data breach in 2011, when an employee laptop, containing 20 million pieces of information on 23,000 patients, was stolen from the employee's car.[16] Accretive was accused by the Minnesota Attorney General of repeated privacy breaches.[17] Subsequent regulatory-enforcement actions included a $2.5 million settlement per a federal lawsuit brought by the Minnesota Attorney General as well as a 20-year enforcement action from the FTC.[18] Over the course of these controversies, Accretive's stock dropped from a high of $30 per share to $8.02 per share; in 2014, Accretive was delisted from the New York Stock Exchange.[19] The company lost $79.6 million in 2014 and $84.3 million in 2015.[20] (Note: In 2017, the company was reincarnated as R1 RCM, Inc.)[21]

Challenges Related to Engagement with ECRM

As I've mentioned before in this book, for too long, cyber risk management has been seen as the sole province of your organization's IT department. By now, I hope it is clear to you that cyber risk is NOT an IT problem: it's a business risk problem. For that reason, it is essential to facilitate engagement in ECRM across the enterprise, starting with C-suite executives and the board. As I've worked with organizations to establish, implement, and mature their ECRM programs, I've discovered three common "errors of engagement" that hinder effective ECRM.

Error #1: Believing You Need to Be a Technical Expert to Engage with ECRM

I keep emphasizing this point because it is an important one: as a C-suite executive or a board member, you do not need to be a technical expert to provide effective ECRM leadership and oversight for your organization. There is nothing about cyber risk that makes it more complicated than the other complex risks that hospital and health system C-suite executives and board members already address. Remember, for the board, the mantra is "eyes open, nose in, and fingers out" when it comes to oversight responsibilities.[22] Whether it is the risk of a competitor stealing market share, the risk of your organization's credit rating being lowered, the risk of non-compliance with Stark or Anti-Kickback regulations, the risk of making a False Claim, the risk of medical malpractice or the risk of spills and falls in the hospital, risk is all about loss or harm. To begin, you need to understand what assets are at risk and the frequency and severity of risk events that may cause loss or harm to these assets.

Ultimately, once you understand your risks and rate them, you will work toward treating risks that are above your "risk appetite" to lower their risk rating such that the risks are acceptable. Whether you're addressing risks in your organization or in your home, it's about assets, threats to those assets, and vulnerabilities in protecting those assets—and then, making an assessment of the frequency and severity of your unique risk scenarios.

The same is true of cyber risks. In conventional cyber risk terminology, we typically see the words "likelihood" and "impact" in place of "frequency" and "severity," respectively. Otherwise, it's pretty much the same.

While I've already touched upon many important ECRM terms and concepts, in *Chapter 5, ECRM Essentials for the C-suite and Board Members*, I'll take a deeper dive into all the necessary terminology for which you need a good working definition in order to execute your leadership and oversight responsibilities.

Error #2: Absence of Board/Executive Support

Executive-level support for ECRM is essential. I have worked with many dedicated Chief Information Security Officers (CISOs), Chief Compliance Officers (CCOs), and Chief Information Officers (CIOs) across the country and have seen too many of them struggle to get effective ECRM programs in place without executive support and engagement.

Without appropriate oversight and leadership, decisions about treating cyber risk will default to the wrong level of your organization. No disrespect intended toward your CISO, CCO, or CIO, but these individuals often do not have the full strategic context of your organization. An enterprisewide, strategic perspective—the perspective held by the C-suite and board—is absolutely essential to implementing an effective ECRM program.

In addition, executive-level engagement helps drive engagement at all levels of your organization. Executive-level support helps break down the siloed management (Error #3, below) that often hinders the implementation of an effective ECRM program.

OCR frequently finds that lack of executive engagement is a contributing factor to HIPAA violations. In 2016, an OCR investigation into multiple data breaches found that Oregon Health & Science University (OHSU) had "widespread and diverse problems."[23] OHSU settled with OCR/HHS for $2.7 million.[24] Jocelyn Samuels, OCR Director at the time, said, "This settlement underscores the importance of leadership engagement and why it is so critical for the C-suite to take HIPAA compliance seriously."[25]

I get it: I know that healthcare C-suite executives and boards are busy. You are already dealing with many challenges. But deciding whether to provide executive and board support is, in and of itself, a risk management decision. It's an important decision that should not be taken lightly.

Error #3: Siloed ECRM Management

ECRM is not a departmental issue: ECRM is an enterprise issue. But I repeatedly see ECRM relegated to some siloed section of an organization. Then, when an attack occurs, the response devolves into finger-pointing, blaming, and "not my job" defensiveness. The fact is that ECRM is everybody's responsibility. But without a C-suite-led, collaborative, and coordinated approach, your organization's ECRM program will be inefficient and ineffective.

I've facilitated many ECRM sessions in which it's the first time that key leaders of functional areas or lines of business have been in the same room, discussing cyber risk and ECRM. I've overheard comments like, "I didn't know we had a policy and procedure about acceptable use of company laptops!" and "Since when have we not allowed the use of Starbucks Wi-Fi? I still use it." These comments show how important it is to have enterprisewide engagement in cyber risk management.

This means that everyone—from board members, to human resources leaders, to the Chief Medical Officer (CMO), to the Chief Financial Officer (CFO)—should be involved in your organization's ECRM program. Below are just a few examples of the roles various stakeholders have to play in supporting your organization's ECRM program (Please note that these examples are adapted, with permission, from the original *Cybersecurity Cheat Sheets for the C-suite and Board* developed by the Advisory Board):[26]

- *Chief Audit Executive (CAE)*—Audit executives already play an integral role in enterprise risk management. Given the unique relationship CAEs have with their boards, they have the opportunity to:

  ✓ Ensure that ECRM is formally integrated into the organization's audit plan

  ✓ Insist on making ECRM a "team sport," encompassing all departments

✓ Lobby to make ECRM discussions an agenda item at every board meeting

✓ Provide the C-suite executives and board with assurance that the ECRM program is working, through internal IT and security audits and coordinated external audits

✓ Help the organization estimate the potential cost of a data breach to your organization

- *Chief Human Resources Officer (CHRO)*—Threat sources that healthcare organizations face include malicious insiders, careless insiders, and workforce members who simply make a mistake and open a malicious email. The implementation of an organization's cybersecurity program depends heavily on members of the workforce being well-trained and per-formance-measured on privacy and security policies and procedures. The CHRO can contribute to the success of the organization's ECRM program in multiple ways, including:

✓ Ensuring that the right privacy, security, compliance, and risk management talent is on board to operationalize the organization's ECRM program

✓ Assisting in the development of privacy and security policies and procedures

✓ Assisting with the development and delivery of privacy, security, and breach notification training to all members of the workforce

✓ Enforcing sanction policies to ensure all members of the workforce are held accountable for privacy and security

- *Chief Medical Officer (CMO)*—ECRM has become a patient safety and professional liability matter for hospitals and health systems. With the digitization of healthcare, clinicians across your organization are now dependent on data, systems, and devices that impact patient safety, quality of care, and access to care. The CMO contributes to the success of your ECRM program in many ways and can:

  ✓ Help the organization "connect the dots" between the CIA of these data, systems, and devices, as well as quality care, safe care, and timely access to care

  ✓ Ensure that clinicians have a seat at the table as new security controls are considered and take into account the impact of the implementation of security controls on clinician productivity and morale

  ✓ Advocate for "security-by-design" that ensures risks are considered before new healthcare data, systems, or devices are implemented

  ✓ Make ECRM and cybersecurity a standing and ongoing training program for all clinicians

  ✓ Advocate that your business continuity plans remain current and consider the potential adverse patient impact if critical data, systems, and devices become unavailable

- *Chief Financial Officer (CFO)*—A core theme of this book is to help your organization make more informed decisions about the allocation of scarce human and financial resources to your ECRM program. The CFO, as a core member of the executive team, has a unique view of financial resources across the organization. To fulfill his or her cyber risk responsibilities, he or she should:

  - ✓ Understand and communicate the financial consequences of the compromise of the CIA of critical data, systems, and devices

  - ✓ Work with C-suite colleagues to establish appropriate OpEx, CapEx, and human resource budgets to manage cyber risks to an acceptable level in the organization

  - ✓ Establish the financial analysis methods that your organization will use to judge the value or return on investment (ROI) of cybersecurity investments

  - ✓ Participate in and support making ECRM an executive-led, cross-functional initiative outside the sole purview of the CIO and/or CISO

I could detail how other leadership roles have ECRM responsibilities, but you get the idea. ECRM must be a board- and executive-led initiative, with engagement across and up and down your entire organization.

Challenges Related to Execution of ECRM

Finally, the third set of challenges unique to ECRM are challenges related to *execution*. This may be the area in which the challenges of ECRM are least similar to the other risk management challenges your organization encounters.

Level of Effort

As I stated earlier, ECRM begins with the identification of all of your organization's assets (healthcare data, systems, and devices) and a detailed analysis of all of the potential threats and vulnerabilities that comprise the unique and specific risks to your assets.

What does this mean in practical terms? Let's revisit the personal assets example for a moment: your home is one asset, and your car is another asset. Each asset is subject to numerous *threats*, from classic threat categories such as: accidental (think poor drivers, careless teenager, etc.), adversarial (think vandal, arsonist, burglar, etc.), structural (think defect in home construction, poor recent car repair job, power surge, etc.), or environmental (think lightning strike, earthquake, hurricane, mudslide, tornado, etc.). There are easily dozens, if not hundreds, of potential threats to consider for each asset.

Remember that risk is composed of an asset, plus a threat, plus a vulnerability. In the personal asset scenario, the threat sources may exploit potentially dozens of vulnerabilities you may have. For example, your current vulnerabilities may include depleted smoke-detector batteries, lack of home security system, failure to take defensive-driving course, no lightning arrestors on home, no safe in which to securely store valuables, etc.

If you consider just these two assets (your home and your car) and just, for ease of arithmetic, 10 possible threats and 10 possible vulnerabilities, the set of asset-threat-vulnerability combinations to consider when completing your home risk analysis is 200 (i.e., 2 assets x 10 possible threats x 10 possible vulnerabilities) before even considering what controls you may have available to consider when rating the risk. If there were only 10 controls available to help lessen the possibility of a certain threat exploiting a certain vulnerability, we would now be considering a total of 2000 scenarios (i.e., 2 assets x 10 possible threats x 10 possible vulnerabilities x 10 possible controls).

When we come back to cyber risks and your organization's information assets, the number of scenarios quickly explodes into the millions. Remember, each asset has multiple threat sources, and each threat source exploits multiple vulnerabilities (figure 4.3).

Asset	Threat	Vulnerability
Laptop	Burglar steals laptop	No encryption
Laptop	Burglar steals laptop	Weak passwords
Laptop	Burglar steals laptop	No tracking device
Laptop	Careless user drops laptop	No data backup
Laptop	Shoulder-surfer views screen	No privacy screen
Laptop	Lightning strikes electrical system, causing power surge	No surge protection

Figure 4.3 *Partial, Simplified List of Laptop Risks*
Source: Bob Chaput, Executive Chairman, Clearwater.

What's my point? There is a lot of work to be done, especially at the onset. Risk analysis is not something that can be conducted, documented, or maintained using a simple Excel spreadsheet as your assets, threats, vulnerabilities, and controls evolve. Risk analysis, as a part of ECRM, is a complicated enough task that it is worth considering using specialized software to facilitate and document your ECRM program. Software development is not a core competency of most healthcare organizations. Just as most healthcare organizations would not consider writing their own EHR software, ECRM is an instance where using specialized software can make cyber risk assessment and cyber risk management easier to conduct, easier to document, easier to implement, and easier to maintain (I provide more detail about the value of using specialized software in Appendix B: *Enterprise Cyber Risk Management Software [ECRMS]*).

As I've worked with various organizations on cyber risk management, I've often heard, "That is way too much work" and "OCR cannot possibly require that level of detail!" But the requirement for this level of detail is codified in the HIPAA Security Rule. The HIPAA Security Rule states that organizations must conduct "an accurate and thorough assessment of the potential risks and vulnerabilities to the confidentiality, integrity, and availability of electronic protected health information held by the covered entity or business associate."[27]

Furthermore, countless OCR statements related to HIPAA violation settlements and corrective actions have reiterated the importance of conducting a comprehensive risk analysis. To name just one example, OCR's 2016 Resolution Agreement and Corrective Action Plan (CAP) with the University of Massachusetts, Amherst (UMass), stated:

UMass shall conduct a comprehensive and thorough
Risk Analysis of the potential risks and vulnerabilities to the confidentiality, integrity, and availability
of electronic protected health information (ePHI)
held by UMass. This Risk Analysis shall incorporate
all UMass facilities, whether owned or rented, and
evaluate the risks to the ePHI on all of its electronic
equipment, data systems, and applications controlled,
administered, or owned by UMass or any UMass entity,
that contain, store, transmit, or receive ePHI. Prior to
conducting the Risk Analysis, UMass shall develop
a complete inventory of all of its facilities, electronic
equipment, data systems, and applications that contain
or store ePHI that will then be incorporated into its
Risk Analysis.[28]

So, the bad news is that conducting an OCR-Quality® Risk
Analysis requires a lot of up-front work. (NOTE: The term
"OCR-Quality® Risk Analysis" describes the specific, proprietary
tools and processes Clearwater uses to conduct risk analysis.
Clearwater's approach addresses not only all the requirements
defined in HIPAA regulations but also OCR's expectations as
spelled out in OCR guidance documents and OCR enforcement
action documents (e.g., resolution agreements, corrective action
plans, notices of final determination) describing the failures of
organizations cited for HIPAA violations.) The good news is
that, once you've completed your organization's initial, comprehensive risk assessment—using the appropriate software—then
maintaining the currency of the assessment (also required by
HIPAA) becomes much easier.

Lack of Expertise

Lack of cybersecurity talent is a challenge impacting all industries, not just healthcare. The Center for Cyber Safety and Education has estimated that unfilled cybersecurity jobs will reach 1.8 million by 2022.[29] A recent study by the Information Systems Security Association (ISSA) and Enterprise Strategy Group (ESG) found that 74 percent of organizations have been impacted by the cybersecurity skills shortage and that the cybersecurity skills gap has continued to increase over time.[30] Cybersecurity professionals are in a "sellers' market," with 77 percent of cybersecurity professionals reporting being solicited at least once per month for other opportunities.[31]

Healthcare organizations, in particular, are having trouble staffing Chief Information Security Officer (CISO) roles. As late as 2014, many hospitals and healthcare organizations did not even have a CISO role, so now they are playing catch-up in staffing. This talent gap represents a significant challenge to all healthcare organizations but especially those in rural or remote areas. Outsourcing of certain cybersecurity tasks and contracting with virtual CISOs are two ways that some healthcare organizations are dealing with this talent shortage.[32]

Acknowledging the Challenges and Moving Forward

It's important to acknowledge the challenges associated with ECRM. At the same time, it's clear that conducting ECRM is not optional. There is too much on the line—from patient safety to professional liability to enterprise financial security. How then, can your organization move forward in the face of these challenges?

The answer to challenges of *understanding* is education. By simply picking up this book and reading it, you are helping to broaden your own understanding of cyber risk and ECRM. If you choose to share this book with your C-suite colleagues or board members, you can further expand your organization's understanding of ECRM. You can also take advantage of many free resources, including articles, white papers, and webinars, to enhance your understanding of cyber risk and ECRM. (See the *Stop the Cyber Bleeding* resource page at https://www.clear watercompliance.com/stopthecyberbleeding for a list of online resources to enhance your understanding.)

Of course, these actions will enhance your *own* understanding of ECRM, but what about the understanding of your organization as a whole? The answer to challenges of *enterprisewide understanding, engagement,* and *execution* of ECRM are behavioral and developmental in nature. To explain what I mean, let's use an example from healthcare. I am going to borrow from the transtheoretical model (TTM) of behavior change, developed by James O. Prochaska and Carlo di Clemente. TTM—sometimes also referred to as a "stages of change" model—proposes that health behavior change comprises progress through several predictable stages.[33] In my experience working with organizations to establish, implement, and mature ECRM programs, I have found that most organizations go through very similar stages of inaction/action as they move toward implementing ECRM (figure 4.4).

The first stage is Precontemplation—or more simply, "not ready." (In fact, in ECRM, there may be a stage even before this one, called "complete denial.") At this point in the process, the organization is either blissfully unaware of the cyber risks they face, or they are vaguely aware that cyber risk might be a problem, but they are choosing the "stick your head in the sand" approach.

The next stage is Contemplation, a.k.a., "getting ready." The fact that you picked up this book is a sign that you, as an

Stage	Description	As Applicable to ECRM
Precontemplation (Not Ready)	May be unaware a problem exists or in denial; not planning to take action.	Organization does not view cyber risk as relevant or important.
Contemplation (Getting Ready)	Recognize a problem exists; starting to look at pros/cons of taking action.	Organization is beginning to think about the importance of ECRM and about whether and how it might approach this task.
Preparation (Ready)	Intent to take action within the immediate future or already taking small steps toward change.	ECRM has been identified as an organizational priority; organization makes plans to establish, implement, or mature its ECRM program.
Action (Taking Action)	Taking specific, overt steps to change.	Organization engages a partner to conduct an OCR-Quality® Risk Analysis as a first step toward establishing, implementing, or maturing its ECRM program.
Maintenance (Sustaining Action)	Sustaining positive changes; working to prevent relapse.	Organization actively maintains its ECRM program via the alignment of governance, people, process, technology, and engagement.

Figure 4.4 *Stages of Organizational Change with Respect to ECRM*

Source: Bob Chaput, Executive Chairman, Clearwater. Adapted with permission from Prochaska, J.O. & Prochaska, J.M. (2016). *Changing to Thrive: Overcome the Top Risks to Lasting Health and Happiness.* Center City, MN: Hazelden Publishing. ISBN 13:9781616496296.

individual, or perhaps, your organization, is beginning to consider that cyber risk is a problem you need to address. At this stage, you might be thinking about the pros and cons of engaging in ECRM and even investigating some possible approaches to the problem.

The third stage is Preparation. At this stage, the organization is ready to act and is committed to taking action within the immediate future. Here, the organization may have taken steps such as committing to ECRM as an organizational priority. Also, at this stage, the organization might begin seeking a deeper understanding of cyber risk via readings or participation in webinars or similar opportunities.

The fourth stage is Action, i.e., taking specific, overt steps to address the problem. With respect to ECRM, these steps might include educating the C-suite and/or board by inviting an expert to address the topics of cyber risk and ECRM. The organization might begin allocating resources (time, staff, and resources) to ECRM activities. It's often at this stage, as well, that the organization might address challenges of execution by giving strong consideration to engaging the services of a partner with deep experience and expertise in ECRM within the context of the healthcare industry. Because of the level of effort and expertise required and the shortage of cybersecurity talent, sometimes the most feasible solution for initiating or maturing your ECRM program is to engage the services of a partner with expertise in this area. See Appendix A: *What to Look for in an ECRM Company and Solution* for guidance on selecting a competent ECRM partner. The most helpful, immediate first action your organization can take would be engaging a partner to conduct an OCR-Quality® Risk Analysis, since comprehensive risk assessment is the essential first step toward establishing, implementing, and maturing your organization's ECRM program.

The fifth stage is Maintenance. As I've mentioned before, ECRM is not a once-and-done project. Cyber risk, including cyber threats and types of cyber attacks, are continuously evolving. At the same time, your organization is evolving as well: service offerings change, technology changes, processes change, facilities change, personnel change, assets change. An effective ECRM program continuously monitors and adapts to the changing internal and external environment, ensuring that risk management is a relevant and ongoing process within the organization.

This developmental, multi-stage process, adapted from the TTM model of behavior change, can help your organization transcend the challenges of ECRM and move toward establishing an effective ECRM program. You begin by determining what stage of change your organization is in currently. After all, any major business transformation is about behavior change, which usually begins with C-suite leaders and the board.

Discussion Questions for Your C-suite and Board

In this chapter, I described challenges of understanding, challenges of engagement, and challenges related to execution that can hinder the establishment of an effective ECRM program. The following questions will help you think about these challenges as they relate to your organization and about how you might move your organization toward embracing ECRM as an enterprisewide initiative.

1. Do you feel that, personally, you have a good understanding of the cyber risks your organization faces?

2. Which of the four "phases" of cyber risk understanding best describes your organization's perspective on cyber risk? That is, does your organization view ECRM as a compliance matter? A security matter? A patient-safety matter? A reputation matter? A professional-liability matter? Or all of the above?

3. Do you know whether your organization is compliant with all relevant regulations, including HIPAA, applicable state regulations, FTC standards, and GDPR? If you are not sure whether or not your organization is fully compliant, how would you verify this information?

4. To what extent are you, as C-suite executives and board members, providing executive support, guidance, and governance to your organization's ECRM program?

5. What is the breadth of the cross-functional engagement in ECRM at your organization? Think through all of the C-level executives in your organization. Are all of them engaged in your organization's ECRM program? If not, think about the reciprocal relationship between their respective functions and your organization's risk management program. Can you see a role for each C-suite executive in your organization's ECRM program? If not, why not?

6. What is the depth of your organization's cyber risk and ECRM talent? Would your organization benefit from engaging the services of a partner with ECRM expertise?

7. What stage of change is your organization in with respect to establishing, implementing, and maturing your ECRM program? Are you not even thinking about cyber risk at this point? Or thinking about it but not certain what to do next? What actions might your organization take to move to the next step?

SECTION TWO

Actions

CHAPTER 5

Learn ECRM Essentials for the C-Suite and Board

If you wish to converse with me, define your terms.

~ VOLTAIRE

When you first engage in conversations about your organization's cyber risk and cybersecurity, you may feel as if you are trying to speak in a foreign language. ECRM can seem quite technical and complex, but it is actually quite understandable once you have a good set of working definitions of some of the fundamentals. The goal of this chapter is to provide you with clear definitions of the key terms, phrases, and concepts you need to understand in order to provide appropriate leadership and oversight for your organization's ECRM program.

20 Terms You Need to Be Able to Use in a Sentence

When the executive team and board are discussing this quarter's financial results, it is important that everyone understands terms like "revenue," "operating margin," and "net income." Any ambiguity in the understanding of those terms can lead to miscommunication. Likewise, in order to have a meaningful and productive conversation about cyber risk and cybersecurity, everyone at the table needs to be able to speak with precision and understand the differences between a risk, a vulnerability, and a threat, among other terms. There's no need to memorize these terms; there will not be an exam. Refer back to this chapter as your glossary whenever necessary.

The fact is that cyber risk and cybersecurity encompass so many different terms and concepts, one could write an entire book on terminology alone. (It's been done. One of the best references on the subject—and my main resource in writing this chapter—is the glossary compiled by the Computer Security Resource Center (CSRC) at NIST. This comprehensive glossary can be accessed online at: https://csrc.nist.gov/glossary/).

In your free time, you might find it interesting to browse the NIST Glossary. In the interests of saving you some time, I've summarized the most critical terms, phrases, and concepts in the following pages. Understanding these terms and concepts will enable you to provide meaningful and appropriate cybersecurity guidance and oversight to your organization.

1. Risk

Risk is about the possibility of loss or harm. Risk is a function of the *likelihood* of a given *threat* triggering or exploiting a particular *vulnerability* and the resulting *impact* on the organization. (The terms in *italics* are further defined below). Risk is not, therefore, one single factor or event but the combination of variables (assets, threats, vulnerabilities, controls) that, when considered together, can have an adverse impact on your organization or its stakeholders. Cyber risk, in the context of healthcare, arises through the compromise of the CIA of your healthcare data, systems, or devices. *Usage Example*: "Have we assessed our enterprisewide cyber risk?"

2. Resilience

Resilience is the ability to continue to: (i) operate under adverse conditions or stress, even if in a degraded or debilitated state, while maintaining essential operational capabilities; and (ii) recover to an effective operational posture in a time frame consistent with mission needs.[1] In its April 2014 Private Industry Notification, the FBI wrote "The health care industry is not as resilient to cyber intrusions compared to the financial and retail sectors; therefore, the possibility of increased cyber intrusions is likely."[2] The ultimate goal of your ECRM program is to make your organization more resilient to ensure the continuity of medical services to your patients. *Usage Example*: "Do we have an ECRM program in place to support our organization's resilience requirements in case of a cyber attack?"

3. Risk Problem We're Trying to Solve

This is not the definition of a term but a fundamental concept that is important to understand. Given that your organization's cyber risk arises through the compromise of the CIA of your healthcare data, systems, or devices (see risk definition, above), then you must (1) identify, and then prioritize, all of your organization's unique cyber risks, (2) discuss, debate, and settle on your appetite for cyber risk, i.e., determine what level of risk your organization is prepared to accept, and, (3) manage each risk, making informed decisions about which risks you will accept and which you will treat (avoid, mitigate, or transfer), and then execute on that plan. It's that simple. That's the fundamental problem we're trying to solve.

4. Cybersecurity

Cybersecurity describes the ability to safeguard, protect, and defend the CIA of all of your healthcare data, systems, and devices against all reasonably anticipated threats and vulnerabilities, below your risk appetite (see definition #16, below). *Usage Example*: "Have we integrated cybersecurity into our overall enterprise risk management program?"

5. Assets and Information Assets

Assets may include major applications, general support systems, high impact programs, the physical plant, mission critical systems, personnel, equipment, or another logically related group of systems.[3] System or information assets include any associated software, hardware, data, administrative, physical, communications, or personnel resources. In numerous documented enforcement actions (Resolution Agreements and Corrective Actions Plans) directed at noncompliant healthcare organizations, OCR has variously defined information assets as:

- ". . . all electronic equipment, data systems, programs, and applications controlled, administered, owned, or shared by [organization name] or its affiliates that contain, store, transmit, or receive [organization name] ePHI . . ."[4]

- "all . . . electronic equipment, data systems, and applications controlled, administered or owned by [organization name] or any [organization name] entity, that contain, store, transmit, or receive ePHI."[5]

- "all of its facilities, electronic equipment, data systems, and applications that contain or store ePHI . . ."[6]

As you can see, OCR's definition of an asset is broad and inclusive. The typical healthcare organization has thousands of assets, if not tens of thousands, when you include all of the different categories of assets that exist:

- *Traditional information assets.* Traditional information assets include IT systems and applications. They include EHRs, clinical information applications, lab and/or medical specialty applications, medical billing and claims processing applications, email applications, company intranet websites, human resources management applications, network file sharing applications, electronic data interchange (EDI) applications, fax applications, payment processing applications, financial management and reporting applications, and other applications and systems.

- *Biomedical information assets.* Biomedical assets include items such as patient monitoring devices, so-called "smart" rooms, implantable devices, and remote wellness and chronic disease management applications.

- *Internet of Things (IoT) information assets.* IoT assets include biomedical devices, as well as internet connected assets such as facilities security and building management; real-time location services (RTLS) for assets, employees, patients, and visitors; and networking hardware, software, security, and services.

Usage Example: "When we complete our acquisition of XYZ Health, we will need to inventory all of their information assets in order to incorporate them into our ECRM program."

6. Threats/Threat Sources

A threat is any circumstance or event with the potential to adversely impact organizational operations (including mission, functions, image, or reputation), organizational assets, or individuals through an information system via unauthorized access, destruction, disclosure, modification of information, and/or denial of service.[7] Threats come from a variety of sources. A common way to categorize threat sources is:

- *Accidental.* Accidental threats occur without malice or intent on the part of the user. Examples of accidental threat sources include an employee who sends out a group email containing ePHI to the wrong recipients or an equipment operator at a nearby construction site cutting fiber-optic cable connecting you to your cloud-based EHR.

- *Adversarial.* Adversarial threats are characterized by the malicious intent of the perpetrator. The perpetrator may be an individual, a group, a competing organization, or a hostile nation-state. A common type of adversarial threat is "insider threat," which originates inside the organization (e.g., a disgruntled or untrained employee).

- *Environmental.* Environmental threat sources include natural or man-made disasters (fire, flood, earthquake, tornado, etc.) and unusual natural events (e.g., sunspots/solar flares, pandemic).

- *Structural.* Structural threats include the failure of IT equipment or a utility service, such as a failed hard drive, poorly written code in a software application, or loss of telecommunications infrastructure or electrical power.

An effective ECRM program will consider all reasonably anticipated threat sources and possible threat events. It's important to base your ECRM program on a comprehensive assessment of your organization's unique threats, rather than simply responding to the latest "threat *du jour.*" The specific threats that are making headlines today (malicious URLs, web attacks, formjacking attacks, cryptojacking, and ransomware) will be replaced by new threats tomorrow.[8] Your organization's best defense is to take a proactive approach to assessing risk across the organization, rather than simply react to today's headlines. *Usage Example*: "Does our ECRM program address relevant environmental threats?"

7. Threat Events

A threat event is an event or situation that has the potential to cause undesirable consequences or impact.[9] When your organization conducts a risk analysis (see definition #13, below), it is important to brainstorm and consider all types of reasonably anticipated threat events, even if you believe they are highly improbable or even if you've never experienced them before.

For example, although California has experienced accidental power outages before, 2019 marked the first year that preemptive power outages were used so frequently and on such an expansive scale. Healthcare providers have had to rethink their disaster protocols to deal with this new environmental threat event.[10] *Usage Example*: "As we develop our ECRM program, we need to consider all possible threat events that our organization might encounter."

8. Vulnerability

A vulnerability is a flaw or weakness in system security procedures, design, implementation, or internal controls that could be exercised (accidentally triggered or intentionally exploited) and result in a security breach or a violation of the system's security policy.[11]

Security engineers and operations staff often confuse conducting *vulnerability scans* with completing a *risk analysis* (see definition #13, below). Vulnerability scans are important but do not comprise real risk analysis. Vulnerability scans provide a long list of weaknesses but fail to take into account the rest of the risk factors. To return to our home example for a moment: if you do not have a deadbolt lock on one of your exterior doors, that could be a vulnerability. But you don't just run out and install deadbolt locks. If you live in a gated community (a control) and you have external motion detectors in your home security system (another control), the likelihood of a burglar exploiting the lack of a deadbolt on a single door may be very low.

Vulnerabilities that are related to your information assets might include: dormant user accounts, accounts with inappropriate/excessive user permissions, inadequate device or data encryption, bad software code in custom applications, weak passwords, and insufficient program governance, among others. You can determine your organization's specific vulnerabilities by conducting a comprehensive, enterprisewide risk analysis. *Usage Example*: "I am concerned about the lack of encryption on the laptops and mobile devices that store PHI. Do you think this is a vulnerability that creates risk we ought to treat?"

9. Controls

As a reminder: risk exists only when an asset, a threat, and a vulnerability are present simultaneously (see definition #1, above). The ultimate goal of your ECRM program is to implement reasonable and appropriate controls to ensure your risks are rated below your risk appetite. Controls (also referred to as *safeguards* or *countermeasures*) are the tools your organization uses to mitigate risks to an acceptable level.

Security controls are the management, operational, and technical controls (i.e., safeguards or countermeasures) prescribed for an information system to protect the CIA of the system and its information.[12] The HIPAA Privacy Rule and the HIPAA Security Rule refer to controls as "safeguards."[13] Both rules reference three types of safeguards:

- *Administrative*. Administrative safeguards encompass things like policies and procedures, governance, the security management process, risk analysis, risk management, training, and business continuity plans.

- *Technical*. Technical controls encompass the typical controls you might think of when you think of cybersecurity, including firewalls, encryption, intrusion detection/prevention systems, etc.

- *Physical.* Physical safeguards include things like building-security systems, guards, gates, biometric-access controls, and fire-suppression systems.

Note that technical safeguards are only one of three types of safeguards or controls. Establishing and maturing your organization's ECRM program is, arguably, your most critical administrative control. You can't achieve cybersecurity by engaging in a technical controls arms race. For controls to be effective, your organization needs to take a considered approach, based on an examination of your unique business and your organization's unique assets, threats, and vulnerabilities. *Usage Example*: "I know we've talked about purchasing a new intrusion detection system, but before we discuss that, are we sure we have the appropriate administrative controls in place?"

10. Likelihood

Likelihood is the chance of something happening.[14] The first step in conducting a comprehensive, enterprisewide, risk analysis is to identify all possible risk scenarios {asset-threat-vulnerability}; the next step is to rate them. Likelihood is one of two factors (the other being "impact," defined below) used to rate risks. In the context of insurance, the analogous terms you will likely hear are "frequency" and "severity." Your Chief Risk Officer and professional liability insurance broker usually use these latter two terms.

NIST explains that the likelihood of occurrence is a weighted risk factor based on an analysis of the probability that a given threat is capable of exploiting a given vulnerability (or set of vulnerabilities).[15] An example of a scale on which to assess likelihood is shown in Figure 5.1:

Rating	Description	Percent Likelihood in Next 12 Months	Frequency May Occur
1	Rare	5%	Once every 20 years
2	Unlikely	25%	Once every 4 years
3	Moderate	50%	Once every 2 years
4	Likely	75%	Once every 16 months
5	Almost Certain	100%	Multiple times per year

Figure 5.1 *Risk Likelihood Scale*
Source: Bob Chaput, Executive Chairman, Clearwater.

For example, suppose you are assessing the likelihood of one of your organization's unencrypted laptops being lost by a careless employee in the {laptop-careless employee-no encryption} risk scenario. It's been estimated that a laptop is lost every 53 seconds![16] Given this statistic, it is likely that all healthcare organizations will lose at least one laptop each year. In that case, the likelihood rating would be "Almost Certain," a "5." In assessing likelihood, you should take into account what controls you do have in place. In this risk scenario, while the laptops may not be encrypted, the organization may have a very strong password policy in place that may lower the likelihood of accessing the laptop's data. *Usage Example*: "What is the likelihood that one of our employees will lose a laptop containing ePHI this year?"

11. Impact

Impact from a threat event is the magnitude of loss or harm that can be expected to result from the consequences of unauthorized disclosure of information, unauthorized modification of information, unauthorized destruction of information, or loss of information or information system availability.[17] In other words, the impact assessment is based on the extent of compromise of the CIA of your organization's data, systems, or devices.

Just as with likelihood, a scale be used to assess impact (figure 5.2).

Rating	Description	Example Considerations		
		# Records Breached	Downtime	Organization Cost in $
1	Insignificant	<100	Minutes	$10,000
2	Minor	100–499	2 hours	$20,000
3	Moderate	500	4 hours	$200,000
4	Major	5,000	8 hours	$2,000,000
5	Severe	50,000	24 hours	$20,000,000

Figure 5.2 *Risk Impact Scale*
Source: Bob Chaput, Executive Chairman, Clearwater.

Continuing with the {laptop-careless employee-no encryption} risk scenario from the definition above, if that lost laptop was known to contain about 5,000 ePHI records, a rating of

"Major" or "4" would be assigned. Similarly, when considering impact, you should consider what controls you have in place. In this risk scenario, while the laptops may not be encrypted, the organization may have a mobile device management solution in place that allows for remotely wiping the laptop's data. Such a control may reduce the impact of this risk scenario. *Usage Example*: "What is the impact on our organization from one lost, unencrypted laptop?"

12. Risk Rating

The risk rating for each risk scenario {asset-threat-vulnerability} is determined by considering both the likelihood (definition #10, above) and the impact (definition #11 above) of the threat event occurring. In the {laptop-careless employee-no encryption} risk scenario I described in the last two definitions, the risk rating would be "5" (likelihood scale) multiplied by "4" (impact scale), resulting in a total risk rating of 20 for this particular risk scenario. (Note that, since both the likelihood and impact scales have five levels of ratings, the highest possible risk rating would be 5 x 5, or 25.). Calculating the risk rating for all risk scenarios results in an initial, natural ranking of risks from most serious to least serious (figure 5.3).

This information may inform the C-suite and board members' deliberations when determining a risk appetite for the organization. Or, the C-suite and board members may set a risk appetite in advance of their first risk analysis. The ratings also provide an inherent starting point for the prioritization of risks. *Usage Example*: "What risk rating did we calculate for the risk scenario in which a laptop is lost or stolen?"

Asset	Threat Source/ Event	Vulnerability	Likelihood	Impact	Risk Rating
Laptop	Burglar steals laptop	No encryption	High (5)	High (5)	25
Laptop	Burglar steals laptop	Weak password	High (5)	High (5)	25
Laptop	Burglar steals laptop	No asset tracking	High (5)	High (5)	25
Laptop	Careless user drops laptop	No data backup	Medium (3)	High (5)	15
Laptop	Lightning strikes home	No surge protection	Low (1)	High (5)	5
Laptop	Shoulder-surfer views screen	No privacy screen	Low (1)	Medium (3)	3
Etc.	There are dozens more risk scenarios to consider with each category of laptops.				

Figure 5.3 *Sample Excerpt from a Risk Register*
Source: Bob Chaput, Executive Chairman, Clearwater.

13. Risk Analysis or Risk Assessment

Risk analysis and risk assessment are synonyms used to describe the same process: the process of identifying, estimating, and prioritizing risks to organizational healthcare data, systems, and devices.[18] The single biggest issue facing healthcare organizations today is the failure or inability to identify all of their unique risks, i.e., the failure to complete a comprehensive risk analysis. How are you possibly going to treat your risks if you do not know what all your risks are? *Usage Example*: "In the event of a data breach, the first thing OCR is going to ask us is if we have completed an enterprisewide, comprehensive risk analysis. Have we done that?"

14. Risk Management

Risk management refers to the broader ongoing program and supporting processes deployed to manage risks to organizational operations (including mission, functions, image, and reputation), organizational assets, individuals, and other organizations.[19] *Usage Example*: "Our risk management program encompasses our entire organization and all information assets."

15. (Enterprise) Cyber Risk Management (ECRM)

ECRM is (or should be) incorporated into your organization's overall enterprise risk management program. ECRM deals specifically with the *cyber* risks that can result in loss or harm to your organization. ECRM has multiple components, including the development of a risk register from your risk analysis that serves as the basis of informed decision-making related to cyber risks. The countermeasures or controls that are implemented to treat risks at or above your organization's risk appetite (see definition below) form the basis of your organization's cybersecurity strategy. *Usage Example*: "Our ECRM program enables us to deploy our resources effectively to prevent loss or harm from cyber attacks."

16. Risk Appetite (a.k.a. Risk Threshold, a.k.a. Risk Tolerance)

Once you identify and rate your risks, you must decide which risks you will treat (see definition #17, below) and which will you simply accept. Risk appetite is generally defined as the level of risk an organization is willing to assume in order to achieve a potential desired result. Setting, communicating, and adjusting your organization's risk appetite is one of the most important C-suite and board responsibilities with respect to your organization's ECRM program. For example, in the risk scenario where a careless employee loses an unencrypted laptop, if that risk is assigned a likelihood of 5/5 and an impact of 4/5, then the risk rating for that scenario is 20. If the organization's risk appetite is set at 15, the organization will not accept this risk but treat it in some way (i.e., avoid, mitigate, or transfer the risk). But if the organization's risk appetite was set at 22, the organization would simply accept this risk. *Usage Example*: "What percent of the risks we identified and rated in our most recent risk analysis is above our risk appetite?"

17. Risk Treatment Choices (a.k.a. Risk Response Choices)

Once your organization has identified all of the possible ways in which there can be a compromise to the CIA of your assets, you need to rate each one (see definition #12, above) by taking into account the likelihood and impact of each risk scenario. Risks that are rated below your risk appetite are risks that you will typically simply *accept*. For risks at or above your risk appetite, you will have to determine whether you will *avoid, mitigate,* or *transfer* that risk. These four choices—accept, avoid, mitigate, or transfer—are fairly standard in the treatment of any type of risk. An example of risk mitigation would be to implement encryption on all laptops, so that, even if a careless employee lost a laptop, whoever found it could not access the data on it. An example of risk transfer is to increase an organization's cyber liability insurance limits to help cover any potential damages. *Usage Example*:

"Given that this particular risk is rated right at the risk appetite we defined, what risk treatment choice would you recommend?"

18. ECRM Framework

A framework provides a high-level model that assists organizations in defining their desired cyber risk management outcomes in alignment with their overall organization vision, mission, strategy, values, and services. The framework which I recommend is the Cybersecurity Framework created by NIST.[20] A colleague in the industry once described the NIST Cybersecurity Framework to me this way: "The NIST Cybersecurity Framework provides a template for your organization's cybersecurity framework. The rest is up to you. It's like having a palette of colors to paint a canvas. The colors are what you combine to create your painting; your painting is going to be what cybersecurity looks like for your specific organization. The NIST Cybersecurity Framework gives you that palette to start with."[21]

At the highest level, the NIST Cybersecurity Framework "palette" starts by identifying five key functions that your ECRM program must perform: Identify, Protect, Detect, Respond, and Recover. I will go into greater detail about the advantages of using the NIST Cybersecurity Framework in Chapter 10. *Usage Example*: "I recommend we consider adopting the NIST Cybersecurity Framework to help align and articulate our desired ECRM program outcomes with our organization's vision, mission, strategy, values, and services."

19. ECRM Process

The ECRM framework defines the "what" of your ECRM program: what outcomes are you setting out to achieve? The

ECRM process, on the other hand, describes the "how" of your ECRM program. What specific, repeatable actions are your organization going to take to achieve the cybersecurity outcomes you described in your framework?

The cyber risk management process I recommend is based on guidance provided in "Managing Information Security Risk" (NIST Special Publication 800–39)[22] and is composed of four basic steps, each of which informs the other steps in the process:

1. *Frame risk.* That is, establish the context for risk-based decisions and your overall approach to risk management.

2. *Assess risk.* In other words, identify your exposures via an enterprisewide, comprehensive risk analysis.

3. *Respond to risk.* In this step, your organization focuses on making risk treatment decisions and executing risk treatment actions.

4. *Monitor risk on an ongoing basis.* Risk management is not a once-and-done proposition. It is a continuous process, which should include a feedback loop for process improvement.

Usage Example: "We need to make sure that we have established and documented an effective, enterprisewide ECRM process to ensure we execute ECRM consistently."

20. ECRM Maturity Model

A maturity model is a "tool that helps people assess the current effectiveness of a person or group and supports figuring out what capabilities they need to acquire next in order to improve their performance."[23] Another way of describing how a maturity model is used is that it helps the organization identify their current maturity level in relation to certain capabilities (for example, ECRM), facilitates the establishment of goals for performance improvement, and helps organizations set priorities for improvements aimed at achieving the desired maturity level.

A typical approach to the maturity process is to use the four-step management model sometimes referred to as the Deming Cycle. The four steps in this model are: Plan, Do, Check, Act.[24] The maturity model provides a mechanism for determining whether your ECRM program is improving over time. Based on my work with healthcare organizations, I recommend focusing your ECRM maturity model on improving five key capabilities:

1. *Governance* (and Awareness of the Benefits and Value of ECRM)

2. *People* (Skills, Knowledge, and Experience)

3. *Process* (Discipline and Repeatability)

4. *Technology* (Standards, Technology Tools, and Scalability)

5. *Engagement* (including Delivery and Operations)

Usage Example: "As we mature our ECRM program, I would like to see more focus on both governance and engagement. In our current program, those are two areas where I am seeing the most deficiencies."

Bringing It All Together

How do these terms and concepts work together? Figure 5.4 illustrates many of the key terms and concepts related to risk and their relationship to each other.

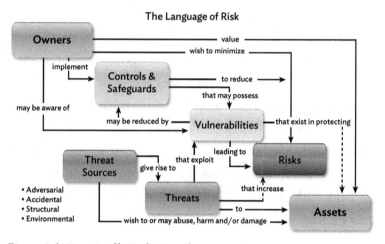

Figure 5.4 *How It All Works Together*
Source: Bob Chaput, Executive Chairman, Clearwater.

As C-suite executives and board members, you are the de facto "owners" of your organization's assets. And as I discussed in Chapter 1, with that responsibility comes a requirement that you exercise *duty of care*. That responsibility includes understanding your organization's unique cyber risks and providing the leadership and oversight to manage those risks to below your risk appetite. Your role is to understand your organization's unique risk profile well enough to enable informed decision-making about implementing controls and safeguards to protect the CIA of all of your organization's healthcare data, systems, and devices.

Risk Analysis Rigor and Comprehensiveness

Organizations that don't understand the breadth and depth of an OCR-Quality® Risk Analysis can easily underestimate the scope of the task. Now that you understand the terminology, think of what this means in terms of your organization's risk analysis. Remember that risk has three components: an asset + a threat + a vulnerability. A typical healthcare organization has thousands, if not tens of thousands, of assets (data, systems, and devices). There are typically hundreds of risk scenarios for each asset, because of multiple associated threats and vulnerabilities. For argument's sake, consider an overly simplified world where there are only 10 assets in an organization and there are only 10 threat sources to consider with 10 different threat events, 10 possible vulnerabilities, and only 10 possible controls one needs to consider. In this simplified world, the risk analysis team would need to consider $10 \times 10 \times 10 \times 10 \times 10 = 10^5 = 100,000$ risk scenarios.

You might ask, "Does OCR really expect our risk analysis to be that comprehensive?" The answer is "Yes." The dozens of OCR Resolution Agreements and Corrective Actions published on the OCR website are a testament to that fact.[25] The approximately $128 million (and counting) in negotiated-settlement amounts and civil money penalties that OCR has collected to date is also a testament to the rigor and comprehensiveness OCR expects from a risk analysis.[26] Time and time again, OCR has found inadequate risk analysis to be among the core failings of organizations that experience data breaches. Case in point: in 2018, health insurer Anthem paid OCR a record $16 million settlement for HIPAA violations.[27] Among other violations, Anthem was cited for its failure to conduct enterprisewide risk analysis.[28]

It's important to remember that the primary reason for conducting a rigorous and comprehensive risk analysis is not just to avoid HIPAA violations and OCR penalties. The primary reason for conducting a comprehensive risk analysis is to collect the information you need to manage your organization's unique risks appropriately. If you do not have a thorough and complete inventory of your assets and their associated threats and vulnerabilities, and therefore a complete picture of your unique risks, how can you even begin to treat them?

Risk Treatment Completeness

It is also important to remember that conducting a comprehensive, enterprisewide OCR-Quality® Risk Analysis is not the end of the story. In addition to requiring risk analysis, the HIPAA Security Rule also explicitly requires risk management, specifying that organizations must "implement security measures sufficient to reduce risks and vulnerabilities to a reasonable and appropriate level."[29]

This means that, once you've completed your risk analysis, you need to take the next step of deciding how to manage each risk and documenting those decisions. As I explained above (see definition #14), risk management uses the results of your risk analysis—the risk register—to make an explicit decision to accept, avoid, mitigate, or transfer each risk. All risks must be treated; not all risks need to be mitigated.

You Might Not Want to Do This Yourself! (At Least Not the First Time)

The data on completing comprehensive, enterprisewide OCR-Quality® Risk Analysis and risk management is very compelling.

It is simply not being performed very well at all. As of this writing, a Clearwater analysis of 58 OCR enforcement actions involving ePHI found that 90 percent of the cited organizations had not completed a comprehensive, enterprisewide risk analysis acceptable to OCR.[30] In addition, 81 percent of the organizations had adverse findings related to risk treatment.[31] Unfortunately, many organizations are caught off guard, believing they have conducted an adequate risk analysis or that they have an adequate ECRM program in place, only to find out that OCR doesn't agree.

Why is this the case? One reason is that most organizations simply don't have a good handle on their information assets. Many healthcare organizations are unable to confidently and *completely* identify and locate their assets in every line-of-business, in every facility, at every location. Another reason is that, although the risk analysis and treatment process is understandable, the sheer volume of the task can be overwhelming. It's not something you can address with a homemade Excel spreadsheet or a simple controls checklist. (Note that there are automated tools available to facilitate the overall ECRM process, specifically including the ongoing risk analysis and risk treatment steps required by HIPAA.)

Furthermore, the HIPAA Security Rule (at 45 CFR §164.306(e)) underscores the point I continue to make that ECRM is not a once-and-done proposition:

> Maintenance. A covered entity or business associate must review and modify the security measures implemented under this subpart as needed to continue provision of reasonable and appropriate protection of electronic

protected health information, and update documentation of such security measures in accordance with §164.316(b)(2)(iii).[32]

This requirement makes it even more important for organizations to implement a solution that supports not only initial ECRM efforts but also ongoing ECRM activities. (See *Appendix B: Enterprise Cyber Risk Management Software [ECRMS]* for more information about automated ECRM solutions). I encourage C-suite executives and board members to seek outside assistance in establishing, implementing, and maturing their organization's ECRM program. ECRM is typically not among most healthcare organizations' core competencies. Healthcare organizations often engage outside partners to assist with functions outside the organization's core activities. ECRM is one such area. Partnering with an experienced, reputable organization can help your organization establish, implement, and mature your ECRM program efficiently and effectively and help you achieve your cyber risk management goals.

Discussion Questions for Your C-suite and Board

After reading this chapter, I hope you understand that C-suite executives and board members do not need to be cybersecurity experts in order to provide meaningful and effective oversight and guidance for their organization's ECRM program. You simply need to have a good set of working definitions of key terminology and ensure that everyone is using the terminology consistently throughout your organization. The following questions will help you think about the terms and concepts defined in this chapter and how they might be applied in your organization.

1. Has your organization's C-suite and/or board discussed and agreed upon a common set of definitions related to cyber risk and cyber risk management?

2. Have these definitions been documented in your organization's ECRM strategy documents and communicated throughout your organization, via ECRM training?

3. Do you believe your organization has already, or is currently, conducting ongoing, rigorous, comprehensive, enterprisewide risk analysis that would meet OCR's expectations?

4. Has your organization produced an enterprisewide risk register like the sample excerpt illustrated in figure 5.3?

5. As C-suite executives and board members, have you discussed, debated, and established your cyber risk appetite?

6. If your organization has conducted a risk analysis, are you using the results of that analysis to inform your cyber risk treatment decisions?

7. Do you believe your C-suite and board are fully exercising their leadership, oversight, and fiduciary responsibilities with respect to ECRM?

8. Do you think it would be valuable to engage an experienced, reputable ECRM partner to establish, implement, and/or mature your organization's ECRM program?

CHAPTER 6

Set ECRM
Strategic Objectives

Culture eats strategy for breakfast.

~ ATTRIBUTED TO PETER DRUCKER[1]

As C-suite and board members, your responsibility is to enable and facilitate a *strategic* approach to ECRM at your organization and to create a cyber-risk-aware culture by showing your involvement in your program. An effective ECRM program does not begin with operational details (e.g., how many attack attempts have occurred in the last month? Do we have an intrusion-detection system in place?) but with an intentionally designed, business-aligned, enterprisewide strategic approach to cyber risk management.

One of the first steps in establishing your ECRM program is to frame your overall approach. As part of this task, I encourage you to develop an ECRM Framework and Strategy document which not only frames your organization's approach to ECRM but also documents your organization's ECRM strategic objectives.

The NIST approach (which I have referenced throughout this book and which I address in further detail in Chapter 10), encourages organizations to build their cybersecurity strategies and objectives around their unique business vision, mission, strategy, values, and services.[2] There is no such thing as a cookie-cutter, one-size-fits-all ECRM program. Your business objectives are not the same as your competitors' business objectives; therefore, your ECRM strategies won't be the same, either. Likewise, your information assets (data, systems, and devices) are not the same as your competitors' assets; therefore, your ECRM program will not be the same as your competitors' programs.

If your ECRM program to going to be relevant and effective, it must be aligned with your organization's business vision, mission, strategy, values, and services. Figure 6.1 illustrates a model for creating this alignment.

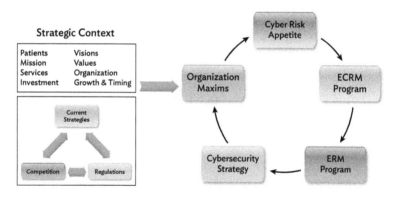

Figure 6.1 *Model for Driving Alignment in Cybersecurity Strategy*
Source: Bob Chaput, Executive Chairman, Clearwater.

I could write an entire book on the topic of aligning your organization's business and cybersecurity strategies as per the model above. My purpose in presenting this concept here is simply to underscore the importance of this alignment and to encourage you to keep asking questions about how your cybersecurity strategy supports your organization's vision, mission, strategy, values, and services. For example, if your CISO's team requests funding for a new mobile device management (MDM) solution, insist that they show how this solution will manage risks that support your organization's vision, mission, strategy, values, and services. Make sure your top cybersecurity projects align with your top business strategies.

The C-suite and Board's Strategic Role

As C-suite and board members, your role is to provide the leadership and oversight your organization needs in order to execute the three basic steps of ECRM that I introduced in the first chapter of this book:

1. Identify, and then prioritize, all of your organization's unique cyber risks.

2. Discuss, debate, and settle on your appetite for cyber risk, i.e., determine what level of risk your organization is prepared to accept.

3. Manage each risk, making informed decisions about which risks you will accept and which you will treat (avoid, mitigate, or transfer), and then execute on that plan.

However, execution of these steps does not occur in a vacuum. Another aspect of your role as a C-suite executive or board member is to prepare your organization to successfully execute these steps. You can do that by articulating strategic objectives that begin to build your cyber-risk-aware culture. To be more specific: the C-suite and board need to establish strategic objectives that address five critical core capabilities of your organization: governance, people, processes, technology, and engagement. Focusing on this specific and finite set of capabilities keeps it high level and sets the stage for the ECRM transformation your organization is about to undertake.

Metaphorically, it's the difference between planting the seeds of your ECRM program in sterile ground or planting your program in ground that has been tilled and enriched with compost. As Peter Drucker says in the quote that opened this chapter, "Culture eats strategy for breakfast." Establishing and working toward strategic objectives in the following five areas will help your organization grow and mature a cyber-risk-aware culture that supports your ECRM program.

1. Establish Appropriate Governance

The first critical core capability centers on *governance*. Governance can be defined as a system of processes and controls that ensures that stakeholder needs, conditions, and options are evaluated to determine balanced, agreed-upon enterprise objectives to be achieved, setting direction through prioritization and decision-making, and monitoring performance and compliance against agreed-upon direction and objectives.[3]

With respect to ECRM governance, the role of the board is to set direction and provide ongoing oversight. In other words, the board establishes and communicates, "This is where we are going (with respect to ECRM), and this is why we are going there." C-suite executives and their teams are then responsible for execution.

Sample Strategic ECRM Objective: Governance

A sample strategic ECRM objective around governance would be:

- Incorporate ECRM into strategic decision-making and ongoing business planning.

Sample Enabling Objectives

A sample enabling objective would be: set the ECRM framework, process, and maturity model by which ECRM will be performed consistently throughout your organization. This means the C-suite and board would consult with internal and external subject matter experts to understand the alternatives for a framework, a process and a maturity model, respectively. Establishing the framework, process, and maturity model by which your organization will conduct its ECRM work enables the incorporation of ECRM into ongoing strategic decision-making and business planning.

Another enabling objective could be: set your organization's cyber risk appetite (see Chapter 5, Definition #16), and require that cyber risks be rated when new business initiatives or programs are planned. For example, if your organization is planning to implement a new ambulatory surgery software application to support your new ASC line-of-business, you will want to conduct a risk analysis to determine the cyber risks associated with this new application. If you determine this initiative will create risks above your risk appetite that you are not currently able to treat (avoid, mitigate, or transfer), you may want to delay this initiative until you are in a position to treat the associated risks. Or, on the other hand, if this is a critical business initiative, you may want to increase your investment amount to ensure the associated cyber risks are managed below your risk appetite.

Sample Key Performance Indicators (KPIs)
    KPIs associated with this objective might include:

- Extent of alignment of your cybersecurity strategy with your business strategy and objectives. For example, if one of your key business initiatives this year is establishing a new ASC line-of-business, but all of your cybersecurity resources and projects are focused on securing the hospital-based EHR system, it demonstrates a lack of alignment between your cybersecurity strategy and your business strategy.

- Number/percentage of information assets without assigned business owners. For example, in most hospitals, the CMO would typically "own" the EHR; the head of accounting would "own" the business/accounting information system, and so on. But when you conduct an inventory of your organization's information assets (data, systems, and devices) you may find that some information assets do not have assigned business owners. "Orphaned" information assets can be particularly vulnerable to exploitation, due to the fact that no single individual is accountable for the exposures and risks of those particular assets. That is why an important aspect of governance is to assign committed business owners to 100 percent of your organization's information assets.

C-suite and board members set the tone for the entire organization's cyber risk management program through good governance practices. Good governance is the starting point of the five capabilities your organization needs to create an effective ECRM culture.

2. Resource Skilled People

The second critical core capability focuses on *people*. The success of any business program or initiative requires employing the right number of people with the right skills, knowledge, experience, and passion about the subject matter. I'm using "employing" in a generic sense here—as I pointed out in Chapter 4, lack of cybersecurity talent is one of the challenges impacting cyber risk management programs at healthcare organizations. As a result, many organizations are turning to outside experts to provide ECRM services.

Appropriately resourcing your ECRM program means putting the right people in place at every level of your organization, from the leadership level, to the tactical, front-line user. Fitting your ECRM program with the right number of people often requires organizations to leverage a combination of internal and external resources. Leveraging internal resources includes not only hiring skilled ECRM staff but also creating a risk-aware culture throughout your organization. As C-suite executives and board members, part of your leadership responsibility is to build understanding of the value and benefits of your ECRM program in order to justify resources assigned.

Sample Strategic ECRM Objective: People

A strategic ECRM objective around people would be:

- Establish a high degree of knowledge of your chosen ECRM framework, process, and maturity model among the people throughout your organization responsible for execution.

Sample Enabling Objectives

A sample enabling objective would be: establish clear delegation of program responsibility. For example, to support board oversight, establish a cross-functional executive committee and a subordinate, cross-functional working group, to help establish, implement, execute, and mature your organization's ECRM program (I discuss how to do this in more detail in Chapter 7).

Another sample enabling objective would be: hold line managers responsible for building your cyber-risk-aware culture in your organization. Most organizations have already implemented perfunctory "annual trainings" on cyber risks. But progressive organizations go beyond this to create an active cyber-risk-aware culture. Examples include:

- Holding regular, open "Lunch and Learn" events on cyber risk and cybersecurity

- Taking advantage of teachable moments, when peer organizations experience a cyber event, to review cyber risk management policies and practices with employees

- Deputizing workforce members as "privacy officers" and "security officers"

These types of activities will occur only if line managers are incentivized to lead their teams in ECRM engagement efforts.

Sample KPIs

Sample KPIs associated with this objective include:

- Performance on social engineering tests designed to measure security and risk awareness levels. For example, in a phishing test, employees are sent mock phishing emails. The percentage of employees who are successfully "phished" can provide a baseline measure. Subsequent training can target the most vulnerable employees, based on the results of the testing.

- Percentage of employees who have completed relevant professional training. For example, appropriate training at the C-suite and board level could include the Cyber Risk Oversight Certificate offered by the National Association of Corporate Directors (NACD).[4] Participants who complete the course and pass a series of exams earn the CERT Certificate in Cybersecurity Oversight, issued by the CERT Division of the Software Engineering Institute at Carnegie Mellon University.[5]

Organizations need people with the right ECRM skill sets to perform foundational and ongoing ECRM work, such as inventorying all information assets, anticipating threats and vulnerabilities, and assessing risk, based on likelihood and impact. Organizations must resource the right amount of expertise—either by hiring and training inside staff, by contracting with outside experts, or a combination of the two strategies—to build this critical capability.

3. Adopt Industry-Standard Processes

The third critical core capability is *process*. At the most basic level, a process is a specific way of doing something. A more complex definition of "process", from the *Business Dictionary*, is "[A] sequence of interdependent and linked procedures which, at every stage, consume one or more resources (employee time, energy, machines, money) to convert inputs (data, material, parts, etc.) into outputs. These outputs then serve as inputs for the next stage until a known goal or end result is reached."[6]

Organizations with a mature ECRM process have formal, well-documented, and consistently followed policies, procedures, and practices around risk management. These policies and procedures help ensure a risk management process that is predictable, measurable, and controlled and which aligns with the principles of continuous process improvement (CPI).

As with other core capabilities, healthcare organizations can benefit by referencing standards-based guidance on cyber risk management processes, rather than trying to create their own from scratch. OCR's guidance on risk management frequently references NIST resources. For example, OCR's publication "Guidance on Risk Analysis Requirements under the HIPAA Security Rule" refers to processes detailed in two NIST publications: NIST-SP 800–39 *Managing Information Security Risk* and NIST SP 800–30 *Guide for Conducting Risk Assessments.*[7]

As I have mentioned throughout this book, NIST is an excellent resource. All of NIST's resources on cyber risk management have been developed by experts from across industry verticals, have been vetted, and are freely available to the public.

Sample Strategic ECRM Objective: Process

A strategic ECRM objective around process would be:

- Adopt NIST-based ECRM processes (as described in NIST SP 800–39 *Managing Information Security Risk* and NIST SP 800–30 *Guide for Conducting Risk Assessments*).[8]

Sample Enabling Objective

With respect to process, NIST recommends four steps (see "process" definition in Chapter 5): (1) Frame your approach to ECRM; (2) Assess your risks; (3) Respond to risks; and (4) Monitor your risks. A sample enabling objective would be: complete the first of these four steps, i.e., Frame your approach to ECRM. This step involves deciding upon and recording your approach to ECRM in an overarching Framework and Strategy document. This document will include your chosen approach (e.g., NIST-based), define your key terms (e.g., "likelihood," "impact," "risk rating"), specify your risk appetite, and articulate your current-year strategic objectives. The Framework and Strategy document should also serve as the basis of your ECRM training program.

Sample KPIs

C-suite or board-level KPIs associated with this objective include:

- Progress toward the development of your organization's ECRM Framework and Strategy document (Version 1.0) as measured against your specified production schedule and final delivery date

- The number/percent of your line-of-business, process, and functional leaders who have completed training on your organization's chosen ECRM framework and strategy

A well-documented process, including developing an ECRM Framework and Strategy document and supporting policies and practices, is key to the success of your ECRM program.

4. Employ Relevant Technology

The fourth critical core capability is *technology*. Nearly all healthcare industry organizations already employ technology tools and automation to streamline clinical, administrative, and operational processes. Technology tools can also enable ECRM workflows and efficiency. More importantly, technology tools are essential for the scalability of your ECRM program.

As I noted in Chapter 5, a typical healthcare organization has thousands, if not tens of thousands, of information assets (data, systems, and devices). Multiply that by the other variables that comprise the risk scenario {asset-threat-vulnerability}, and a typical healthcare organization may be looking at more than 100,000 different risk scenarios that must be analyzed in order to complete an OCR-Quality® Risk Analysis.

It is simply not possible to complete—and maintain—an updated OCR-Quality® Risk Analysis without using an appropriate technology and automation solution. And since the results of your risk analysis serve as the foundation for your ECRM strategy, it is critical to have the right ECRM technology solution in place. That means using standards-based technology. The advantage of using standards-based technology is that standards (such as the NIST Cybersecurity Framework) have been developed, vetted, and successfully deployed across multiple organizations in multiple industries. Standards-based technology delivers consistent, predictable, repeatable, and measurable results, with the added benefit of explicit recognition (in the case of NIST) by OCR as a valid approach to ECRM.

Ultimately, the technology and automation tools you use to support your ECRM program will range from strategic-level solutions (such as an ECRMS solution) to operational-level solutions (such as a security information and event management [SIEM] system). The technology with the greatest relevance to the C-suite and board is the ECRMS solution. The ECRMS solution provides the foundation for the ECRM program and should include appropriate C-suite and board-level dashboards and reporting that provide the C-suite and board with the information you need to execute your ECRM leadership and oversight responsibilities.

Sample Strategic ECRM Objective: Technology

A strategic ECRM objective around technology would be:

- Implement technology and automation tools to support strategic, tactical, and operational aspects of your ECRM program

Sample Enabling Objective

Given this book's focus on the C-suite and board, an obvious enabling objective would be: oversee the implementation of a standards-based ECRMS solution to operationalize your organization's approach to ECRM. As I have suggested throughout this book, I strongly recommend implementing a solution aligned with NIST standards.

Sample KPIs

C-suite or board-level KPIs associated with this objective include:

- The number/percent of your organization's total information assets (data, systems, and devices) under the management of your chosen ECRMS solution

- The number/percent of organizational entities (i.e., lines of business, functional areas, or process areas) using your chosen ECRMS solution

The right technology tools are critical to implementing and maturing your ECRM program. The wrong ECRMS solution—or, alternately, the deployment of different ECRMS solutions in different areas of your organization—will seriously undermine the effectiveness of your ECRM program.

5. Ensure Organizational Engagement

The fifth and final core capability is *engagement*. The success of your ECRM program depends on the extent to which the entire organization is actively engaged in ECRM. As I have emphasized throughout this book, ECRM is not "just an IT problem." Nor is it "just a compliance problem" or "just a chief risk officer problem." Cyber risk management is an enterprise risk management issue with consequences that can impact your patients and every stakeholder in your organization. It follows, then, that everyone in your organization has a role to play in your ECRM program.

Even if your C-suite and board are providing appropriate leadership and oversight, if your organization's other executives, managers, and workforce members are not engaged in your ECRM program, it will fail. Without engagement and ownership of risks by line-of-business, process, and functional leaders, risk-related decisions will be made by people without the full strategic business view. This is why engagement is so critical.

All organizations have (or should have) an enterprisewide risk management plan that describes the broad, strategic objectives to be pursued. At the same time, requiring departments to develop their own ECRM plans (within the context of your organization's overall ECRM framework and strategy) can help enforce accountability for risk management throughout the entire organization.

Sample Strategic ECRM Objective: Engagement

A strategic ECRM objective around engagement would be:

- Ensure line-of-business, process, and functional leaders are engaged in the ECRM program

Sample Enabling Objectives

An enabling objective would be: include specific ECRM performance goals in all line-of-business, process, and functional leaders' annual objectives. Depending on the ECRM maturity of your organization, in your first-quarter goals, you might explicitly require that each leader complete an inventory of all information assets for which they have responsibility. If your organization is further along in maturity, your objective for all line-of-business, process, and functional leaders might be to complete an OCR-Quality® Risk Analysis for *the most critical information assets* under their purview. The ultimate objective would be for all line-of-business, process, and functional leaders to conduct an OCR-Quality® Risk Analysis for *all of the information assets* under their purview and to update the analysis on a regular basis (for example, whenever there are changes in information assets, technology assets, or personnel).

Sample KPIs

C-suite or board-level KPIs associated with this objective include:

- (Quarter One) The number/percent of line-of-business, process, and functional leaders who have completed an inventory of all information assets for which they have responsibility

- (Quarter Two) The number/percent of line-of-business, process, and functional leaders who have completed an OCR-Quality® Risk Analysis for the most critical information assets under their purview

- (Quarter Three) The number/percent of line-of-business, process, and functional leaders who have completed an OCR-Quality® Risk Analysis for all of the information assets under their purview

Clearly defining ECRM accountability at the line-of-business, process, and functional-leadership levels is an important step that can help create a culture of engagement around ECRM. In a McKinsey Working Paper on Enterprise Risk Management, the authors stated:

> . . . it is altogether too easy for human beings to fall into several behavioral traps that lead to poor decision-making in situations where risk and reward have to be weighted. Such behaviors can become a threat to an organization when they become the norm—that is, when they become engrained in the company's risk culture.[9]

The point of enabling a culture of engagement is to ensure that decisions and behaviors that support ECRM become the norm across all levels of your organization. Building the right level of engagement and a cyber-risk-aware culture is a key C-suite and board responsibility, as it sets the tone for the entire enterprise.

Discussion Questions for Your C-suite and Board
As C-suite executives and board members, it is your responsibility to provide strategic direction to your organization's ECRM efforts and to create a cyber-risk-aware culture. One way to do that is by establishing strategic objectives around the five core capabilities your organization needs in order to establish, implement, and mature your ECRM program. Those core capabilities are governance, people, process, technology, and engagement. The examples provided in this chapter are intended to be thought-starters for you and your colleagues to consider. The following questions will help you think about the maturity level of your organization with respect to these five critical ECRM capabilities.

1. How well aligned is your organization's cybersecurity strategy with your organization's vision, mission, strategy, values, and services? Do you have a process in place to ensure alignment?

2. Does your organization have a good governance structure in place, one that clearly articulates *who* makes *what* ECRM decisions, and *how* and *when*, using what data and facts?

3. Does your organization have the right number of people, with the right skills, to establish, implement, and mature your ECRM strategy?

4. Is your organization using a proven industry standard and up-to-date ECRM processes to manage cyber risks?

5. Has your organization adopted technology and automation tools to make your ECRM program more consistent, repeatable, and scalable?

6. Are your organization's line-of-business, process, and functional leaders all fully engaged in managing your organization's cyber risks?

CHAPTER 7

Take Six Initial Actions to Establish or Improve Your ECRM Program

Action expresses priorities.

~ MAHATMA GANDHI

Establishing and articulating objectives, like the examples I gave in the previous chapter, will help to provide strategic direction for your organization's ECRM program. But, of course, it's not enough to simply establish strategic objectives. Your organization will need to take action, in the context of those objectives, to establish a new ECRM program or to improve your existing program.

In this chapter, I describe six specific, tangible initial actions your organization can take to jump-start a new ECRM program or reinvigorate an existing one. The actions I recommend align with the NIST approach to cyber risk management. As I have emphasized throughout this book, I highly recommend the guidance and resources available from NIST. NIST offers an industry-recognized approach that is technology-agnostic, and NIST resources are available at no cost. (See Chapter 10 for more detail about the advantages of using the NIST Cybersecurity Framework).

As you consider taking these actions within your organization, it is important to remember that establishing, implementing, and maturing your ECRM program should be thought of as a long-term, ongoing, iterative initiative—not a short-term project with a start date and an end date. Think journey, not destination.

Action Item #1: Conduct Ongoing Enterprisewide OCR-Quality® Risk Analysis

The first action I recommend is to conduct an OCR-Quality® Risk Analysis. The reason to start with a risk analysis is simple: before you can make wise decisions regarding cyber risk management investments and take meaningful action to manage your organization's cyber risks, you must first *identify* and *prioritize* your unique risks. Risk identification begins with conducting a comprehensive inventory of your healthcare data, systems, and devices, followed by an analysis of the risks associated with each asset.

Prioritization requires both identifying high-risk areas and defining your risk appetite, so that you can tailor your risk management measures to align with the level of risk involved. As former National Security Advisor McGeorge Bundy once observed, "If we guard our toothbrushes and diamonds with equal zeal, we will lose fewer toothbrushes and more diamonds."[1]

Beginning with an OCR-Quality® Risk Analysis is also important because of OCR's continuing focus on risk analysis and risk management. Risk analysis and risk management have been required since February 2003, when the HIPAA Security Rule was published in the Federal Register. OCR enforcement actions, along with increasing negotiated settlement amounts and civil money penalties, underscore the continuing importance OCR places on risk analysis.

OCR is responsible for issuing guidance on the provisions of the HIPAA Security Rule. To that end, OCR published guidance on its expectations for organizations working to meet the risk analysis requirement.[2] OCR's guidance identifies nine essential elements an OCR-Quality® Risk Analysis must include:

1. *Scope of the Analysis*: The scope of the risk analysis encompasses "the potential risks and vulnerabilities to the confidentiality, availability, and integrity of **all e-PHI** [emphasis added] that an organization creates, receives, maintains, or transmits."[3] This means including every piece of data, every device, and every system, from a single thumb drive to a cloud-based EHR. All of an organization's e-PHI must be accounted for "regardless of the particular electronic medium in which it is created, received, maintained, or transmitted, or the source or location of its e-PHI."[4]

2. *Data Collection*: Organizations must identify and document "where the e-PHI is stored, received, maintained, or transmitted."[5] This means creating and maintaining a complete, up-to-date inventory of all e-PHI and all systems and devices that create, receive, maintain, or transmit e-PHI.

3. *Identify and Document Potential Threats and Vulnerabilities*: Organizations must "identify and

document reasonably anticipated threats to e-PHI," including threats that may be unique to the organization. In addition, organizations must "identify and document vulnerabilities, which, if triggered or exploited by a threat, would create a risk of inappropriate access to or disclosure of e-PHI."[6]

4. *Assess Current Security Measures*: Organizations must "assess and document the security measures an entity uses to safeguard e-PHI, whether security measures required by the Security Rule are already in place, and if current security measures are configured and used properly."[7] OCR also notes here that it expects security measures to vary by organization—a clear indication that a "checklist" approach is not what OCR has in mind.

5. *Determine the Likelihood of Threat Occurrence*: "Likelihood," as I defined in Chapter 5, is the chance or probability that a potential threat will exploit or trigger a given vulnerability (see figure 5.1 in Chapter 5 for an example of a Risk Likelihood Scale). OCR specifies that the output of this element of the risk analysis should be "documentation of all threat and vulnerability combinations with associated likelihood estimates that may impact the confidentiality, availability and integrity of e-PHI of an organization."[8]

6. *Determine the Potential Impact of Threat Occurrence*: In addition to likelihood, organizations must assess and document the "criticality," or impact, of potential

risks. OCR specifies that the output of this element of the risk analysis should be "documentation of all potential impacts associated with the occurrence of threats triggering or exploiting vulnerabilities that affect the confidentiality, availability and integrity of e-PHI within an organization."[9]

7. *Determine the Level of Risk*: Ultimately, organizations must identify the level of (i.e., rate) each potential risk, based upon factors that include the likelihood and impact. Again, OCR requires documentation of the output of this element, including "assigned risk levels and a list of corrective actions to be performed to mitigate each risk level."[10]

8. *Finalize Documentation*: Per the HIPAA Security Rule, the entire risk analysis must be documented. OCR's Guidance specifies that "the risk analysis documentation is a direct input to the risk management process."[11] Bringing it all together, this risk analysis documentation must include a risk register. (See figure 5.3 in Chapter 5 for a Sample Excerpt from a Risk Register).

9. *Periodic Review and Updates to the Risk Assessment*: Finally, OCR emphasizes that "the risk analysis process should be ongoing."[12] Per the HIPAA Security Rule, organizations should update and document its security measures "as needed."[13] OCR recommends conducting continuous risk analysis to identify when updates are needed. OCR Guidance states, "A truly integrated risk

analysis and management process is performed as new technologies and business operations are planned, thus reducing the effort required to address risks identified after implementation . . . Performing the risk analysis and adjusting risk management processes to address risks in a timely manner will allow the covered entity to reduce the associated risks to reasonable and appropriate levels."[14]

On the basis of these nine elements, it is clear that OCR's expectations for risk analysis are rigorous and comprehensive. You cannot simply walk through your organization with a clipboard and checklist to complete a rigorous and comprehensive risk analysis. Organizations often find it helpful to engage a partner with expertise in conducting an OCR-Quality® Risk Analysis in order to complete this task in accordance with OCR's expectations.

Action Item #2: Establish Board and Executive Team Governance
A simple way to think about governance is to pose it as a set of interrelated questions: Who makes what decisions? How and when do they make those decisions? And what data and facts do they use to make those decisions?

In my experience working with organizations to establish, implement, and mature ECRM programs, I have found that a three-tiered ECRM governance model is most effective, although the model will vary by the size and resources of each organization. The three tiers in this governance model include:

> ***Tier 1:*** *The full board or designated board committee (e.g., Audit & Compliance Committee or a specific ECRM Oversight Council or Committee)* sets direction and provides oversight.

Tier 2: An ECRM Executive Steering Committee (including the CEO and his/her full team) ensures execution of the ECRM program.

Tier 3: An ECRM Cross-Functional Working Group (depending on your organization, may include representatives from legal, risk management, finance, HR, audit, compliance, privacy, IT, clinical engineering, security, quality, and/or others as appropriate) executes the steps to establish, implement, and mature the ECRM program.

A small organization might use a simplified version of this model, for example, by combining Tier 2, the ECRM Executive Steering Committee with Tier 3, the Cross-Functional Working Group. On the other hand, a large, complex organization with multiple lines of business might add additional tiers or establish the three-tiered model within each line-of-business. In any case, it is also important to assign your internal audit organization with overall assurance responsibility to provide an independent opinion on the ECRM program to the board. Figure 7.1 illustrates how the three-tiered ECRM governance model might work in a large organization.

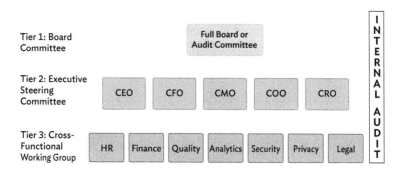

Figure 7.1 *Example of Three-Tiered ECRM Governance Structure*
Source: Bob Chaput, Executive Chairman, Clearwater.

Each of the three tiers should have a formal, written charter that delineates the group's decision-making authority, structure, scope of responsibilities, work processes to be followed, etc. If your organization has a Project Management Office (PMO), the PMO can help with chartering and facilitating the groups. As I pointed out in Chapter 6, resourcing skilled people is one of the key capabilities needed to make an ECRM program work. That plays out in the governance structure by ensuring that each governance group has appropriate training, as well as access to ECRM expertise, sourced internally or externally. The NACD publication *Cyber-Risk Oversight 2020: Key Principles and Practical Guidance for Corporate Boards* is a great resource for those participating in governance at the board level.[15]

Once these three tiers of governance are in place, an appropriate starting point is the development of your organization's ECRM Framework and Strategy document (introduced in Chapter 6). The ECRM Cross-Functional Working Group would be responsible for drafting the ECRM Framework and Strategy document, covering: ECRM Strategic Objectives, Scope of the ECRM Strategy, Responsibility for and Governance of the ECRM Strategy, ECRM Framework, ECRM Process, Risk Appetite, ECRM Framing Guidance, ECRM Constraints, ECRM Risk Assessment Guidance, ECRM Risk Response Guidance, ECRM Risk Monitoring Guidance, ECRM Automation Tools, Records, and Reporting, Summary of ECRM Roles and Responsibilities, and ECRM Budget by Line-of-business. The Executive Steering Committee would review and revise the document as needed and then ultimately recommend it to the Board Committee for approval.

Action Item #3: Adopt the NIST Cybersecurity Framework
As described above, the ECRM Framework and Strategy document is very broad in scope, covering everything from strategic objectives, to ECRM roles and responsibilities, to the ECRM budget by line-of-business. Think of the NIST Cybersecurity Framework as a tool—an architectural blueprint, as it were—that will inform your ECRM Framework and Strategy document.[16]

The NIST Cybersecurity Framework, Version 1.1, is industry-vetted, nonproprietary and technology-agnostic. All of the supporting resources for the NIST Cybersecurity Framework are freely available at: https://www.nist.gov/cyberframework. The NIST Cybersecurity Framework is described in detail in a 55-page document available at the URL noted above. I will briefly describe the NIST Cybersecurity Framework approach here, but, for more detail, please consult the source document.

The Framework provides a risk-based approach to managing cybersecurity risk. It is composed of three parts:

- The *Framework Core*

- The *Framework Profile*

- The *Framework Implementation Tiers*

The *Framework Core* "consists of five concurrent and continuous Functions—Identify, Protect, Detect, Respond, Recover. When considered together, these Functions provide a high-level, strategic view of the lifecycle of an organization's management of cybersecurity risk."[17] The five Functions are further broken down into Categories, which are broken down into Subcategories.

For example, the "Identify" Function breaks down into six Categories of outcomes. An example of one of these Categories is:

1. Asset Management (ID-AM): The data, personnel, devices, systems, and facilities that enable the organization to achieve business purposes are identified and managed consistent with their relative importance to organizational objectives and the organization's risk strategy.

Each Category then breaks down into Subcategories. The Category "Asset Management," for example, breaks down into six subcategories, including:

- ID.AM-1: Physical devices and systems within the organization are inventoried.

- ID.AM-2: Software solutions and applications within the organization are inventoried.

- ID.AM-3: Organizational communication and data flows are mapped.

- ID.AM-4: External information systems are catalogued.

- ID.AM-5: Resources (e.g., hardware, devices, data, time, personnel, and software) are prioritized based on their classification, criticality, and business value.

- ID.AM-6: Cybersecurity roles and responsibilities for the entire workforce and third-party stakeholders (e.g., suppliers, customers, partners) are established.

The statements at the Subcategory level describe desired outcomes in understandable English. As a C-suite executive or board member, you do not need to become an expert on the Framework Core; you need only to understand that the Core is going to be used to articulate your desired cybersecurity outcomes in priority order. As a quick example, at a very high level, among Identify, Protect, Detect, Respond, and Recover, you may decide that your top priority at this time is around your organization's resilience in the event of a cyber attack, and, therefore, you would prioritize work in the Respond Function above others.

A *Framework Profile* "represents the outcomes based on business needs that an organization has selected from the Framework Categories and Subcategories. The Profile can be characterized as the alignment of standards, guidelines, and practices to the Framework Core in a particular implementation scenario."[18] In other words, the Framework Profile represents your desired outcomes based on your organization's unique vision, mission, strategy, values, and services, as well as your risk appetite. You can use profiles to take stock of where your organization is today (current profile) versus where your organization wants to be (target profile/desired outcomes).

The *Framework Implementation Tiers* "provide context on how an organization views cybersecurity risk and the processes in place to manage that risk. Tiers describe the degree to which an organization's cyber risk management practices exhibit the characteristics defined in the Framework (e.g., risk and threat aware, repeatable, and adaptive)."[19]

The NIST Cybersecurity Framework document includes a detailed, seven-step process for how your organization can use the Framework to create a new cybersecurity program or improve an existing program.[20] Briefly, these steps include:

Step 1: Prioritize and Scope. Identify business objectives and priorities to inform decision-making around cybersecurity implementation and scope

Step 2: Orient. Identify systems and assets, regulatory requirements, and overall risk approach

Step 3: Create a Current Profile. Use the Framework Core to document which Category and Subcategory outcomes are currently being achieved

Step 4: Conduct a Risk Assessment. See *Action Item #1: Conduct Ongoing OCR-Quality® Risk Analyses,* in the first part of this chapter

Step 5: Create a Target Profile. Use the Framework Core to document which Category and Subcategory outcomes are desired

Step 6: Determine, Analyze, and Prioritize Gaps. Compare the Current Profile to the Target Profile to determine gaps—and then create a prioritized action plan to address those gaps

Step 7: Implement Action Plan. Take action to address gaps

NIST further recommends repeating these steps as needed to continuously assess and improve your ECRM program.

The NIST Cybersecurity Framework is designed to encompass your organization's unique assets and risks. It is not designed to be a "one-size-fits-all" checklist of things to do, nor is it a controls checklist. It's not a process description (See *Action Item #4*, next), and it is not a maturity model (See *Action Item #6*, below). However, used properly, the NIST Cybersecurity Framework provides the basis for a business-driven conversation designed to facilitate how you will conduct ECRM in your organization and serves as a tool for articulating your organization's desired cybersecurity outcomes.

Action Item #4: Implement the NIST "Managing Information Security Risk" Process

Adopting a *framework* (*Action Item #3*) helps you articulate WHAT you wish to achieve with your ECRM program, whereas implementing a *process* provides HOW you are going to achieve your desired outcomes. Consistent with my recommendations throughout this book, I encourage you to reference the resources NIST has developed with respect to managing information security risk.

NIST Special Publication 800–39, "Managing Information Security Risk," gives a detailed description of NIST's recommended risk management process.[21] According to NIST SP 800–39:

> Risk management is a comprehensive process that requires organizations to: (i) frame risk (i.e., establish the context for risk-based decisions); (ii) assess risk; (iii) respond to

risk once determined; and (iv) monitor risk on an ongoing basis using effective organizational communications and a feedback loop for continuous improvement in the risk-related activities of organizations. Risk management is carried out as a holistic, organization-wide activity that addresses risk from the strategic level to the tactical level, ensuring that risk-based decision-making is integrated into every aspect of the organization.[22]

As indicated in this description, the NIST process includes four components: frame, assess, respond, and monitor. I briefly describe each of these components below. For a more detailed description of each process component, please consult the source document.

1. *Frame*: Think of this process step as creating your organization's ECRM Framework and Strategy document as discussed in Action Item #2. NIST states, "The purpose of the risk framing component is to produce a risk management strategy that addresses how organizations intend to assess risk, respond to risk, and monitor risk—making explicit and transparent the risk perceptions that organizations routinely use in making both investment and operational decisions."[23] In addition, documenting your risk management strategy in your ECRM Framework and Strategy document provides your organization with a shared vocabulary to talk about risk. Having a shared vocabulary helps to move cyber risk management out of the IT department and into the wider organization—which is essential to the success of your ECRM program.

2. *Assess*: Throughout this book, I have emphasized the importance of risk assessment in establishing your ECRM program. Risk assessment enables the identification of your organization's unique assets and risks. The critical nature of risk assessment is emphasized in HIPAA laws and regulations and in OCR's enforcement actions. You simply cannot implement an effective ECRM program without first conducting an OCR-Quality® Risk Analysis. (See *Action Item #1*, earlier in this chapter).

3. *Respond*: The third component of NIST's recommended information security risk management process is to respond. After your organization has completed an OCR-Quality® Risk Analysis, your organization will need to respond to those risks. As I introduced in Chapter 5, risk response entails one of four choices: accept, avoid, mitigate, or transfer. *Acceptance* will be the response when the particular risk's rating is within your organization's risk appetite. *Avoidance* means discontinuing certain practices or shutting down certain services that have risk ratings above your risk appetite and for which there is not a return on investment to justify additional countermeasures. *Mitigation* involves implementing tools, techniques, controls, and methods to lower the likelihood or impact of a threat exploiting a vulnerability. *Transfer* refers to shifting the liability for risk, for example, by using insurance to transfer risk from your organization to an insurance company. Each of the risks identified in the assessment process requires one of these four responses.

4. *Monitor*: The fourth component of the NIST process is to monitor the program over time. Monitoring enables organizations to verify whether risk management measures have been adequately implemented and whether those measures are effective. Monitoring is also important because of the dynamic nature of risk management. Internal environments change (e.g., information assets, people, technologies, policies, procedures), and external environments change (e.g., changes in the nature of external threats or regulatory requirements). An ECRM program will not be effective if it does not include continuous monitoring of the effectiveness of your organization's cyber risk management strategies.

Action Item #5: Engage Your Executive Risk Insurance Brokers

One of the four possible responses to treating risk is to *transfer* risk. This is where your organization's liability insurance may come into play, as an example. But what factors determine appropriate cyber risk coverage? And how do insurance carriers price cyber risk insurance? The art—or science—of underwriting cyber risk is still evolving. Recent research published in the *Journal of Cybersecurity* set out to determine: (i) what losses are covered by cyber insurance policies, and which are excluded?; (ii) what questions do carriers pose to applicants in order to assess risk?; (iii) how are cyber insurance premiums determined—that is, what factors about the firm and its cybersecurity practices are used to compute the premiums?[24]

Among the findings of the research, the authors noted ". . . a surprising variation in the sophistication (or lack thereof) of the equations and metrics used to price premiums."[25] But even given the current uncertain and evolving state of cyber risk insurance, there are several proactive strategies your organization can undertake to position yourself appropriately in this area:

1. *Acknowledge that your organization is at risk.* The 2019 HIMSS Cybersecurity Survey found that 82 percent of hospitals, 64 percent of non-acute care facilities, 68 percent of vendors, and 76 percent of other types of healthcare organizations (physician practices, ambulatory surgery centers, etc.) experienced one or more "significant security incidents" over a 12-month period.[26]

2. *Perform a thorough review of your organization's various liability policies.* I recommend that healthcare organizations conduct a thorough review of their respective liability policies to identify gaps, conflicts, and redundancies. The policies that should be reviewed include, but are not limited to: General Liability, Errors & Omissions (E&O), Directors & Officers (D&O), Cyber Liability, Medical Professional Liability, and Hospital Professional Liability. Cyber and privacy risks are increasingly impacting patient safety and, by extension, medical professional liability. That is why it is important to examine every policy that touches on your organization's liability, in order to ensure that your organization has appropriate coverage. Among the questions you will want to investigate as you review your organization's liability insurance coverage are the following:[27]

   ✓ What are the terms of your cyber policy?

✓ What exclusions are included?

✓ What is the wording around cybersecurity controls?

✓ Does your cyber policy contain a clause related to extortion (e.g., ransomware attacks or other types of cyber extortion)? If yes, what limits, sub-limits, and deductibles are associated with the extortion clause?

✓ Does your cyber policy include language related to social engineering schemes and related fraud and losses?

✓ What additional coverages may be included in your E&O or D&O policy language?

3. *Partner with your liability insurance brokers.* Collaborate with your liability insurance brokers as you conduct a comprehensive review of your various liability policies. Have open conversations with them, and work to partner with them to share your ECRM efforts and understand their pricing mechanism for cyber liability. Clearwater clients have found that demonstrating that they have a robust ECRM program and plans to make it even stronger will result in lower premiums in multiple liability policy areas, not just cyber.

4. *Proactively manage your risk—using the guidance offered throughout this book.* Taking action—and communicating the seriousness of your intent to better manage cyber risks—have the potential to positively impact your

insurer's calculation of your cyber risk and associated premium costs.

5. *Pay attention to the details.* In insurance, the devil is in the details. Many organizations have believed they had adequate coverage in place, only to discover that their claim was denied due to policy terms or exclusions they hadn't considered. Two examples:

- ✓ Cottage Health System suffered a data breach in 2013. A class-action lawsuit, resulting in a $4.1 million settlement, was approved by the court. The insurer, Columbia Casualty, argued they were not obligated to fund the settlement because of a policy exclusion that precludes coverage for "failure to follow minimum required practices."[28] Among other deficiencies, the insurer alleged that the data breach was caused by Cottage's ". . . failure to regularly re-assess its information-security exposure . . ."[29]

- ✓ Biopharmaceutical giant Merck & Co., Inc., was impacted by the 2017 NotPetya cyberstrike.[30] However, when the U.S. government stated that Russia was behind the NotPetya attack, it gave insurers an out: the war exclusion contained in the policies. As Joshua Gold reported in *Risk Management,* "The suspected role of nation-state actors has raised the possibility that insurance companies may attempt to invoke war risk exclusions to escape paying cyber-related insurance claims."[31] As of this writing, the case is still under active litigation.[32]

Cyber insurance (an example of risk transfer) is an important component of your overall ECRM program, but it is not a panacea. The most effective ECRM programs include all four types of risk responses: acceptance, avoidance, mitigation, and transfer.

Action Item #6: Measure the Maturity of Your ECRM Program

In Chapter 5, I introduced the concept of using a maturity model to evaluate and improve your ECRM program. Because ECRM is a continuous process, not a once-and-done, there must be a mechanism in place for continuous process improvement. Adopting and using a maturity model provides a means for ensuring that ongoing improvements will keep your ECRM program moving forward. Cyber risks keep evolving; so must your ECRM program.

Recent research by the Deloitte Center for Health Solutions underscored the importance of having a maturity model in place.[33] Deloitte interviewed 18 CISOs, CIOs, and C-suite executives from biopharma companies, medical device manufacturers, health plans, and health systems who are involved in making decisions around cybersecurity.[34] All of the interviewees—without exception—use maturity models in their presentations to boards and leadership.[35]

What does an appropriate maturity model for ECRM look like? First, it is important to point out what is *not* a maturity model. For example, the tiers detailed in the NIST Cybersecurity Framework are not intended to be used for maturity modeling. The NIST Cybersecurity Framework tiers describe the degree to which your organization's ECRM practices exhibit the characteristics defined in the Framework (for example, whether processes are repeatable and adaptive). A maturity model goes beyond the "tiers" concept to formalize ongoing process-improvement efforts which enhance your ECRM program's effectiveness over time.

The ECRM Maturity Model I recommend assesses program maturity by evaluating your organization's standing vis-à-vis the five key capabilities introduced in Chapter 5 and which form the basis for the strategic objectives outlined in Chapter 6, that is: governance, people, processes, technology, and engagement.

In this model (developed and used by Clearwater), the five core capabilities are broken down into 17 practice areas, which, in turn, are supported by 104 best-practice statements. For example, the *governance* capability is composed of four practice areas:

1. Board Oversight and Expertise

2. Oversight Council Strategic Alignment

3. Oversight Council Operational Alignment

4. Oversight Council Planning and Process

Each of these practices areas is supported by detailed best-practice statements. In this example, the practice area "Board Oversight and Expertise" is supported by six practice statements. These practice statements include:

✓ A Board, Governance, or Oversight Council focused on ECRM exists

✓ Oversight Council members are actively engaged in ECRM matters

✓ And so on . . .

ECRM program maturity can be evaluated based upon the extent to which specific best practices are in place in each practice area. The maturity assessment should be conducted annually, by stepping through each capability, each practice area, and each practice statement. The following three questions should be answered for each practice statement:

1. Does your organization have written policies, procedures, practices, standards, or other appropriate documentation pertaining to the Practice Statement?

2. Does your organization consistently follow its policies, procedures, practices, and standards pertaining to the Practice Statement?

3. Is your organization assessing its performance against this Practice Statement and creating plans to improve, when necessary?

The maturity level of your organization can be defined based on your organization's answers to these questions. Figure 7.2 gives an example of levels of maturity that can be used in conjunction with the Practice Statements and the three questions above to define your organization's maturity level in each practice area.

Discussion Questions for Your C-suite and Board

The six specific actions described in this chapter are designed to help you launch a new ECRM program or strengthen an existing

Maturity Level	Description
Immature	Not adopted or minimally adopted, not implemented or achieved, and not measured
Defined	Partially adopted, implemented, or achieved and measured
Managed	Largely adopted, implemented, or achieved and measured
Established	Almost fully adopted, implemented, or achieved and measured
Optimized	Fully adopted, implemented, or achieved and measured

Figure 7.2 *ECRM Levels of Maturity*
Source: Bob Chaput, Executive Chairman, Clearwater.

one. At the very minimum, you can use the actions described in this chapter as the basis for a critical review of your existing program. Optimally, however, your organization can use these specific actions as a guide for ECRM activities you can begin to engage in immediately. The following questions will help you think about where your organization stands in relationship to the foundational ECRM actions described in this chapter.

1. Would your organization's current risk analysis/risk management work products meet OCR's expectations?

2. Does your organization have a formal ECRM governance structure in place? Does it clearly define who makes what decisions, how and when those decisions are made, and what data and facts are used to inform those decisions?

3. What ECRM framework, if any, has your organization adopted? How is it being used?

4. What ECRM process, if any, has your organization adopted? Is it an industry-standard approach, such as that advanced by NIST?

5. What is the likelihood that your liability insurance portfolio contains gaps, conflicts, and/or redundancies? How would your coverage work in the "hacked CT scan" case cited in Chapter 1?

6. Is your ECRM program improving over time? Is your organization proactively measuring program improvement?

CHAPTER 8

Fund Your
ECRM Program

*Cybersecurity isn't a black hole of funding unless you let it
be treated that way . . . You should ensure that cybersecurity status is framed similarly to how other business risks
are managed, in terms of the impacts potential security
incidents have on the business assets.*

~ MICHAEL GABRIEL, IN CIO[1]

At this point, it should be clear that ECRM is not optional. It
should also be clear that investment in ECRM is a necessary
part of enterprise risk management. ECRM investment is about
protecting your organization's reputation, revenue, and margin,
and ensuring the survival of your organization. It is not about IT.

Consider the words of Jamie Dimon, Chairman and Chief
Executive Officer of JPMorgan Chase. In his April 2019 Letter
to Shareholders, on the topic of cybersecurity, Dimon wrote:

I have written in previous letters about the enormous
effort and resources we dedicate to protect ourselves
and our clients—we spend nearly $600 million a year

on these efforts and have more than 3,000 employees deployed to this mission in some way. Indirectly, we also spend a lot of time and effort trying to protect our company in different ways as part of the ordinary course of running the business.[2]

My point is not that healthcare organizations should try to match this spending benchmark. The point is that Dimon understands that investing in cybersecurity is "part of the ordinary course of running the business." This is the same way healthcare organizations should be looking at their cybersecurity investments.

Allocating Resources for Something That May Not Happen

For most organizations, funding their ECRM program will require a shift in thinking. Investing in cybersecurity is different from the traditional types of investing that healthcare organizations undertake. Hospitals and health systems are used to investing in new lines of service or new facilities that promise a significant and measurable ROI, such as buying or creating a joint venture with an ambulatory surgery center, for example.

Investing in ECRM, on the other hand, is about investing to prevent something bad from happening. To return to the home metaphor for a moment, investing in cyber risk is *not* like redoing your kitchen to realize a greater return when you sell your home; investing in ECRM is more like buying heat and smoke detectors for your home. It's a cost of doing business that you must take on, despite the fact you don't really know whether your house will catch fire—or whether your organization will be hit by a cyber attack. (Although, based on the data I shared in Chapter 3, the likelihood of your healthcare organization experiencing a cyber attack is substantial—and increasing over time. In other words, investing in ECRM is more about "when" than "what if . . .")

Investing in ECRM is more about cost avoidance and minimizing losses rather than revenue generation. There are few visible business rewards for stopping a phishing attack or a hacking attack. At the same time, experiencing a cyber event can severely impact your organization's revenue and margin, and can even put a healthcare organization out of business. Recall the case of the American Medical Collection Agency (AMCA), which I mentioned in Chapter 3. Between 2018 and 2019, AMCA experienced a system hack that exposed the data of up to 20 million patients.[3] In 2019, AMCA's parent company filed for Chapter 11 protection, noting in the court filing that the company had incurred "enormous expenses that were beyond the ability of the debtor to bear."[4]

The fact is that your organization will spend money on cybersecurity one way or another. The question is: would you rather make those spending and allocation decisions proactively, with your organization's best interests as the driver? Or will your spending occur reactively, in response to a cybersecurity incident? In 1735, Benjamin Franklin famously wrote, "An Ounce of Prevention is Worth a Pound of Cure." At the time, Franklin was writing about fire prevention, but his axiom is equally applicable to cybersecurity investment today.

Estimating Your Organization's Costs if a Data Breach Were to Occur
In an ideal world, it would be great to be able to quantify the return on ECRM program investments. Clear ROI examples

within ECRM are rarely possible, however. This is due, in part, to the unpredictable nature of cyber events, along with the breadth of the potential impacts on your organization. While the ROI of ECRM investments is not readily accessible, another approach is to consider the costs of NOT investing in your ECRM program.

The compromise of the CIA of your organization's healthcare data, systems, or devices has the potential for significant cost repercussions. Categories of costs include, but are not limited to, reputational, investigative, financial, legal and regulatory, operational, and clinical costs. As I discussed in Chapter 1, these costs are increasingly likely to include expenses associated with a medical professional liability lawsuit in the future. In addition, you must consider the consequences to your organization's vision, mission, strategy, values, and services if you fail to fund your ECRM program to address these loss exposures.

The potential costs of a cybersecurity incident—specifically a data breach—are more accessible than specific ROI data. Many resources are available to help you obtain a rough estimate of the potential costs of a data breach for your organization. As a C-suite executive or board member, you should have a rough estimate. For example, the Ponemon Institute conducts an annual data breach study, sponsored by IBM Security, to calculate data breach costs. The 2020 Cost of a Data Breach Report found that the average cost of a data breach (globally) was $3.86 million.[5] The study also found that:

- The average global cost per lost or stolen record is $150.

- The United States is the most expensive country with respect to data breach costs, with an average cost of $8.64 million per incident.

- Healthcare is the most expensive industry with respect to data breach costs, with an average cost (globally) of $7.13 million per incident.

- Data breach costs carry over for years. While 61 percent of costs occur in the first year, 24 percent of costs occur in the second year, and 15 percent of costs occur after two years.[6]

While the results of the Ponemon analysis are interesting, global averages are not especially helpful when it comes to estimating your organization's unique loss exposures. The Ponemon analysis and other similar studies do not address your organization's unique set of information assets, threat sources, threat events, likelihood, and other factors that must be considered when estimating loss exposures.

There is, however, a publicly available resource that can help you calculate your unique loss exposures. In 2012, I participated with the American National Standards Institute (ANSI), The Santa Fe Group, the Internet Security Alliance (ISA), and leaders from many other healthcare organizations to develop a report entitled, "The Financial Impact of Breached Protected Health Information." The report was designed to assist organizations in the healthcare sector to build a strong business case for the benefits of investing in PHI protection and for turning compliance with privacy and security laws to their market advantage.

The report was updated in 2017 and released as "The Financial Impact of Breached Protected Health Information: 2017 Update," along with an updated version of an Excel model (Cost of a Data Breach Excel Model) designed to help organizations estimate their own, unique loss exposures.

The updated report and the Excel model address a broad range of potential cost repercussions, including reputational, financial, legal and regulatory, operational, and clinical (figure 8.1).

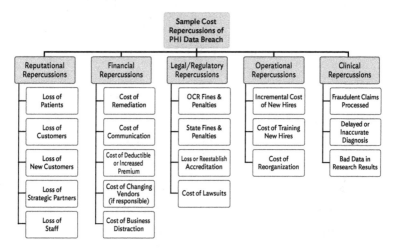

Figure 8.1 *Sample Cost Repercussions of PHI Data Breach*
Source: Bob Chaput, Executive Chairman, Clearwater. Adapted from *The Financial Impact of Breached Protected Health Information: A Business Case for Enhanced PHI Security.* March 2012. Accessed April 30, 2020. https://clearwatercompliance.com/wp-content/uploads/2014/07/1-6.-The-Financial-Impact-of-Breached-Protected-Health-Information.pdf.

In the reputational repercussions section, loss of current and new revenues, loss of insurer/health plans, and loss of strategic partners and staff are quantified and estimated. Estimated financial repercussions include remediation costs, notification costs, and cyber insurance and third-party business associate switching costs. The model estimates various legal and regulatory costs, including

OCR fines and penalties, state fines and penalties, and lawsuits. The costs of corrective actions are also considered. Operational repercussions include the potential costs of adding new staff and reorganization to strengthen your organization's compliance and ECRM posture. Finally, in the category of clinical repercussions, the costs considered are focused on professional liability exposures from a cyber-driven medical or hospital malpractice lawsuit.

Using this model may help you develop a more accurate estimate of your organization's unique loss exposures, which can help you justify the investment in your ECRM program. The "Cost of a Data Breach Excel Model" can be downloaded from the *Stop the Cyber Bleeding* resource page at https://www .clearwatercompliance.com/stopthecyberbleeding.

This model will give you a more customized result than simply calculating exposures based on an average, global, cost-per-record number. However, it is important to note that no single study or model will capture all of the costs associated with a data breach. In addition to tangible costs, there may be additional, intangible, difficult-to-quantify costs, such as management distraction costs. Customer churn is another cost that can be hard to quantify. The 2019 Cost of a Data Breach Report found that, "Healthcare, financial services, and pharmaceuticals had more trouble than other industries retaining customers after a breach."[7] That report noted that the global average of abnormal customer turnover following a data breach was 7 percent for health organizations, well above the average of 3.9 percent across all industries.[8]

The Costs of a Data Breach Are NOT Merely Theoretical

The Excel model mentioned above can help you calculate the potential costs of a data breach for your organization. But I want to assure you that this is not just a theoretical exercise. Two real-world examples illustrate the size and scope of costs that can be triggered by a data breach.

St. Joseph Health: Data Breach Leads to More Than $37 Million in Associated Costs

St. Joseph Health (SJH) is a nonprofit, integrated, Catholic healthcare delivery system which includes acute care hospitals, home health agencies, hospice care, outpatient services, skilled nursing facilities, community clinics, and physician groups. In February 2012, SJH reported to OCR that files containing ePHI for 31,800 individuals had been publicly accessible on the internet for the prior 12 months. A new server had been purchased to store the files, and the server included a file-sharing application whose default settings permitted file access to anyone with an internet connection.[9]

OCR identified the following alleged violations of HIPAA Rules:

- From February 1, 2011, to February 13, 2012, SJH potentially disclosed the PHI of 31,800 individuals

- Evidence indicated that SJH failed to conduct an evaluation in response to the environmental and operational changes presented by implementation of a new server for its meaningful use project, thereby compromising the security of ePHI

- Although SJH hired a number of contractors to assess the risks and vulnerabilities to the CIA of ePHI held by SJH, evidence indicated that this was conducted in a patchwork fashion and did not result in an enterprisewide risk analysis, as required by the HIPAA Security Rule[10]

In the press release HHS issued about the settlement, then-OCR Director Jocelyn Samuels said, "Entities must not only conduct a comprehensive risk analysis but must also evaluate and address potential security risks when implementing enterprise changes impacting ePHI. The HIPAA Security Rule's specific requirements to address environmental and operational changes are critical for the protection of patient information."[11]

SJH incurred the following costs as a result of the data breach:

- $2.14 million OCR settlement

- $7.5 million cash payment to participating settlement class members

- $7.5 million for identity theft protection

- $13 million to implement policies to bring SJH into compliance with federal and state requirements

- $7.4 million in attorneys' fees[12]

All told, this incident led to more than $37 million in direct settlement costs and associated expenses for SJH.[13] Only SJH knows its indirect and intangible costs.

Anthem: Data Breach Leads to More Than $424 Million in Associated Costs

Anthem, Inc., an independent licensee of the Blue Cross and Blue Shield Association, is one of the nation's largest health benefits companies. In 2015, Anthem reported to OCR that a series of cyber attacks exposed the ePHI of nearly 79 million people.[14] OCR noted that in January 2015, Anthem "discovered cyber attackers had gained access to their IT system via an undetected continuous and targeted cyber attack for the apparent purpose of extracting data, otherwise known as an advanced persistent threat attack."[15]

OCR's investigation alleged that Anthem:

- Failed to conduct an enterprisewide risk analysis

- Had insufficient procedures to regularly review information system activity

- Failed to identify and respond to suspected or known security incidents

- Failed to implement adequate, minimum access controls to prevent the cyber attackers from accessing sensitive ePHI, beginning as early as February 18, 2014[16]

In the press release HHS issued about the settlement, OCR Director Roger Severino said, "We know that large healthcare entities are attractive targets for hackers, which is why they are expected . . . to monitor and respond to security incidents in a timely fashion or risk enforcement by OCR."[17]

As of January 2017, Anthem had incurred the following costs as a result of the data breach:

- $16 million OCR settlement

- $2.5 million to engage expert consultants

- $115 million to implement security improvements

- $31 million to provide initial notification to the public and affected individuals

- $112 million to provide credit protection to breach-impacted consumers[18]

More than 100 lawsuits were filed in the wake of the Anthem data breach.[19] In 2018, an additional $115 million settlement was approved in U.S. District court in a consolidated settlement that addressed these lawsuits.[20]

Anthem's annual reports, as filed with the Securities and Exchange Commission, have not detailed the full cost of the data breach; however, based on the costs listed above, as well as other costs reported in the press, Anthem's estimated total costs, to date, exceed $424 million.[21]

How Much Should You Spend on Cybersecurity?

According to the 2018–19 EY Global Information Security Survey (GISS), "Half of healthcare and Government & Public Sector organizations say they have increased spending on cybersecurity over the past 12 months, while 66% plan to spend more over the next 12 months."[22] The bad news is that the same survey found that 87 percent of organizations "do not yet have a sufficient budget to provide the levels of cybersecurity and resilience they want."[23]

But what does a "sufficient" cybersecurity budget look like? Research shows that the healthcare industry lags behind other industries with respect to information security spend. A Gartner study found that banking and financial services companies spent 7.3 percent of their total IT budgets on security; retail and wholesale spent 6.1 percent; insurance spent 5.7 percent; and healthcare providers spent about 5 percent.[24]

The 2019 HIMSS Cybersecurity Survey found the percent of IT spending dedicated to information security varied greatly among healthcare organizations (figure 8.2).

Budget Allocation	N	Percent
1 to 2 percent	17	9%
3 to 6 percent	45	25%
7 to 10 percent	20	11%
More than 10 percent	19	10%
No specific carve out	47	26%
No money is spent on cybersecurity	1	1%
Don't Know	34	19%

Figure 8.2 *Percentage of Organizations' Current IT Budget Allocated to Cybersecurity*

Source: 2019 HIMSS Cybersecurity Survey, https://www.himss.org/sites/hde/files/d7/u132196/2019_HIMSS_Cybersecurity_Survey_Final_Report.pdf

While this information is interesting, it's not proscriptive. For one thing, why should your cybersecurity spend be measured as a percentage of your already fiscally challenged IT budget? As I have emphasized throughout this book, cyber risk management is a business risk management issue: it is not an IT line item.

The second reason that benchmarking against peer organizations is not especially helpful is that these percentages tell you nothing about that organization's unique assets, risks, threats, and risk appetite. Your organization's cybersecurity challenges are unique: it stands to reason that your ECRM investment will be unique to your organization as well.

Someone once asked U.S. President Abraham Lincoln how long he thought a man's legs should be. He famously answered, "Long enough to reach from his body to the ground."

The same could be said of funding your ECRM program. Your organization's spending on cyber risk management should reflect your organization's unique assets, threat sources, threat events, likelihood, and other factors, including your organization's specific risk appetite. You can't base your spending on somebody else's spending benchmarks any more than you can base your ECRM program on somebody else's controls checklist.

Meaningful Use of Meaningful Use Dollars

One of the reasons the healthcare industry continues to lag behind other industries with respect to funding ECRM is because of the rush to digitize that followed the rollout of CMS's EHR Incentive Program, also known as Meaningful Use (MU). The Meaningful Use program (now subsumed into CMS's Promoting Interoperability [PI] Program) offered billions of dollars in incentives to hospitals and clinicians to digitize clinical records and then to use that digitized information in meaningful ways.[25] Incentive payments began in 2011, and through October 2018 (as last reported on HHS website), more than $30 billion in payments has been made to more than 546,644 eligible professionals, eligible hospitals (EHs), and critical access hospitals (CAHs), including 5,007 EHs and CAHs.[26]

But for better or for worse, the MU program emphasized clinical applications and data interoperability over information security. In Stage 1 of the Meaningful Use program, eligible hospitals were required to measure and report on 14 Core Objectives.[27] Objective 14 (of 14) was "protect electronic health information."[28] CMS later elaborated on this objective in Stage 2, with some focus on encryption, as follows:

Stage 1 Objective: Protect electronic health information created or maintained by the Certified EHR Technology through the implementation of appropriate technical capabilities.

Stage 1 Measure: Conduct or review a security risk analysis per 45 CFR §164.308(a)(1), implement security updates as necessary, and correct identified security deficiencies as part of its risk management process.

Stage 2 Objective: Protect electronic health information created or maintained by the Certified EHR Technology through the implementation of appropriate technical capabilities.

Stage 2 Measure: Conduct or review a security risk analysis in accordance with the requirements under 45 CFR §164.308 (a) (1), including addressing the encryption/security of data at rest and implement security updates as necessary and correct identified security deficiencies as part of its risk management process.²⁹

In 2016 CMS issued additional, detailed guidance for meeting the objective related to security risk analysis.³⁰ But even though CMS clearly spelled out a requirement for conducting a security risk analysis (which aligns with the HIPAA Security Rule), many organizations somehow overlooked this requirement. As healthcare providers rushed to attend to the other objectives in time to qualify for incentive payments, issues of information security fell through the cracks.

I remember speaking to the CIO of a large health system who was overseeing a $50 million Cerner EHR implementation project. He proudly described the scope of the project and the positive outcomes he expected for the health system. But when I asked him how much of those funds he had allocated to cyber risk management, he looked puzzled for a moment and then said, "None!"

This is what I refer to as "ECRM debt." As healthcare organizations complete massive digital transformations, every program, project, or initiative a hospital or health system undertakes should include not only an examination of the cyber risk implications, but also a budget for addressing those implications. By and large, this did not happen during the race to collect Meaningful Use incentive money. This has left the healthcare industry with a huge ECRM debt—dollars that should have been spent on managing cyber risk *at the same time* that implementation of EHRs and related systems was happening. Those cyber risk management dollars weren't allocated at the time—and the cyber risk implications of those projects now need to be addressed.

Now that the EHR Incentive/MU program has been sub-sumed into CMS's Promoting Interoperability program, the program's focus has shifted away from incentives for EHR use in favor of a new focus on interoperability. The 2020 Medicare PI program requirements include four objectives (Electronic Prescribing, Health Information Exchange, Provider to Patient Exchange, Public Health and Clinical Data Exchange).[31] While submitting a "yes" to the Security Risk Analysis measure is a base requirement for attestation, none of the *scored* measures under these four objectives specifically address cyber risk management.[32]

While it may be true that the bulk of Meaningful Use incentive dollars has come and gone and that cyber risk management is not a scored measure in the PI program, this does not mean that healthcare organizations can ignore the cybersecurity risks they incurred while building out the digital side of their enterprises. The point I've made throughout this book is that ECRM is a business imperative for healthcare organizations. Compliance with applicable regulations, such as the HIPAA Security Rule, is definitely a compelling reason to manage cybersecurity risks. But the most compelling reasons are to protect your patients from loss or harm and to protect your enterprise from the same—that is, to facilitate your organization's ability to continue to deliver on its vision, mission, strategy, values, and services.

Funding Your ECRM Program Going Forward

As I noted in the introduction, Jamie Dimon, Chairman and Chief Executive Officer of JPMorgan Chase, discussed cybersecurity as "part of the ordinary course of running the business." He has the right perspective.

Along with addressing your organization's ECRM debt (all the cybersecurity spending you didn't do when you were digitizing), you also need to put practices in place to ensure proper funding for ECRM going forward. Rather than thinking of ECRM as a line item in your IT budget, I recommend thinking of your ECRM spend in terms of a percentage of *each* line-of-business, process, and functional leader's *revenue* budget. Several organizations with whom I have worked to address ECRM debt have treated the establishment, implementation, and maturity of their overall ECRM program as a CapEx project (rather than OpEx), which allows them to amortize costs over the life of their program. Depending on your accounting practices and current state of ECRM in your organization, you may consider the same treatment.

The best way to ensure that you don't incur additional ECRM debt going forward and that you help stop the cyber bleeding is to withhold approval of any initiatives, projects, or programs involving healthcare data, systems, or devices, unless and until specific and appropriate funding has been designated for cyber risk management. In fact, NIST suggests that, before a new system can be deployed, there should be an "authorization to operate" or an "authorization to use" issued by senior management (authorizing official), contingent on the assessment of security and privacy risks.[33]

Successful ECRM outcomes can best be achieved by building ECRM into business programs and initiatives—following the principle of "security-by-design"—rather than trying to add ECRM after the fact. This approach may also offer budgeting flexibility, depending on your organization's accounting practices.

The following three sections provide potential sources of funding for your ECRM program (figure 8.3).

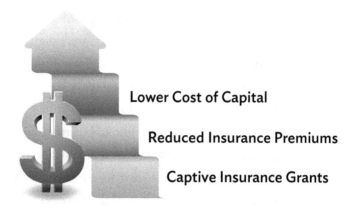

Figure 8.3 *Three Specific Sources of ECRM Funding*
Source: Bob Chaput, Executive Chairman, Clearwater.

Realizing Lower Cost of Capital

Although investing in your ECRM program will not produce a new revenue stream (although it can serve as a differentiator in marketing), there are other ways in which implementing a strong ECRM program can positively impact your organization's bottom line. One of those ways is by helping your organization maintain access to capital at a competitive cost.

Access to capital is vital for all types of healthcare organizations, including for-profit and not-for-profit hospitals and health systems. Without capital, healthcare organizations would be unable to acquire new technologies, start new lines of business for alternative sources of revenue, renovate facilities, or offer new programs. In order to stay competitive, healthcare organizations have to maintain access to capital at low rates.

ECRM is playing an increasingly important role in this arena. Credit-rating agencies—including Standard and Poor's, Moody's, and Fitch Group—have all implemented or signaled consideration of the financial impact of a cyber attack on an organization's credit rating.

In 2018, Moody's named Derek Vadala (Moody's CISO) to a newly established role as Head of Cyber Risk for Moody's Investors Service.[34] In a press release announcing the appointment, Rob Fauber, President of Moody's Investors Service (MIS), said, "As with environmental, social, and governance risks, we see cyber risk as an area of increasing relevance to issuers, investors, counterparties, and government authorities as it impacts operational and credit risk. Moody's has a unique perspective that can help enhance market understanding of the ways credit and cyber risk intersect."[35]

Four months later, in February 2019, Moody's Investors Service released a research report in which they assessed the cyber risk of 35 industry sectors, including healthcare.[36] The report classified high-risk, medium-high risk, medium-low risk and low-risk sectors. The healthcare sector—including hospitals, pharmaceutical companies, and medical device manufacturers—was classified as high risk.[37] Of all 35 sectors rated, only three others (banks, securities firms, and financial market infrastructures) were found to be at "high risk."[38]

The February Research Announcement indicated one of the key factors in Moody's credit analysis could include ". . . the extent of an entity's investment in cyber defenses before an event . . ."[39] The announcement went on to say:

> When assigning a credit rating, we consider cyber risks in the context of all other risks an issuer faces. A significant cyber event could lead to lower scoring for factors such as cost structure, market position, profitability, coverage, and leverage. When we believe an emerging risk is highly likely to weaken a company's credit quality, we

incorporate these expectations into our ratings. Consistent with this long-standing approach, we expect to incorporate the credit effects of cyber risk as our understanding of issuer-level exposures and mitigation strategies evolves and well before the effect of a significant cyber event is fully evident in financial and operating results.[40]

Three months after Moody's published this research announcement, it became a reality when Moody's downgraded the ratings outlook for Equifax from "stable" to "negative" based on the immense data breach the company experienced in 2017.[41] Among the reasons cited for the downgrade were "incremental debt associated with the announced potential global litigation and regulatory investigation settlement, expected minimal revenue and margin growth in Equifax's core business through 2019, and higher than expected information technology costs stemming from the breach."[42]

In other words, a robust ECRM program may positively impact your credit rating and help your organization obtain more competitive rates for capital. This benefit can be viewed as an indirect source of funding for your ECRM program.

Leveraging Reduced Insurance Premiums

In Chapter 7, I recommended six initial strategic actions you can take to establish or improve your ECRM program. Action Item #5 was to "Engage Your Executive Risk Insurance Brokers." This is another area—like cost of capital—you can leverage to help fund your ECRM program.

It is a common insurance practice to lower premiums when the insured takes actions to reduce risk. For example, years ago, when you installed a sprinkler system or fire-suppression system in your healthcare facilities, you realized a discount on your fire insurance policy. Similarly, your organization may receive more competitive rates for medical professional liability insurance premiums when your organization is able to demonstrate the implementation of training, quality, and patient-safety programs.

The same thing is beginning to happen with cyber liability insurance. Beginning in 2012, the Cybersecurity & Infrastructure Security Agency (CISA), part of the U.S. Department of Homeland Security, held a series of sessions with insurers and other key stakeholders to discuss the relationship between cyber risk management and cybersecurity insurance.[43] CISA has suggested that:

> A robust cybersecurity insurance market could help reduce the number of successful cyber attacks by: (1) promoting the adoption of preventative measures in return for more coverage; and (2) encouraging the implementation of best practices by basing premiums on an insured's level of self-protection.[44]

Through conversations with stakeholders, CISA hoped to expand the cybersecurity insurance "market's potential to encourage businesses to improve their cybersecurity in return for more coverage at more affordable rates" and to develop "new cybersecurity insurance policies that 'reward' businesses" for adopting and enforcing best practices—such as implementing a robust ECRM program.

In fact, this concept is beginning to play out in the marketplace. As one security expert wrote:

While it's pretty straightforward that you can get a safe driving deduction on vehicle insurance or cut the cost of healthcare premiums by signing a non-smoking certification, there is no widely advertised fee reduction structure for cyber insurance. Yet, implementing cybersecurity best practices and remaining compliant with industry standards will lower your premiums with many carriers.[45]

I've seen this approach work firsthand. I worked with a $2 billion health system that was faced with the challenge of very high cyber insurance premiums. Part of the problem was that the health system treated ECRM in a siloed manner: it was not part of their overall enterprise risk management program. As a result, there were both redundancies and gaps in their liability insurance portfolio. When they first came to me, they were working with two different carriers to secure sufficient cyber liability coverage.

This client worked in a collaborative manner to streamline and mature their approach to cyber risk management. The system CISO brought together the chief risk officer, chief financial officer, other internal stakeholders, and their executive risk broker. First, they brought ECRM into their overall ERM program. Then they identified some initial savings in their overall liability portfolio premiums. They used the savings to establish, implement, and mature a NIST-based ECRM program. They followed best practices, including:

- Adopting the NIST Cybersecurity Framework

- Implementing the NIST ECRM process for conducting risk analyses and risk management

- Using an ECRMS solution that enabled them to complete (and regularly update) a comprehensive OCR-Quality® Risk Analysis

- Measuring and developing their ECRM program maturity on an ongoing basis

The results of their efforts included doubling of their cyber liability coverage limit, expanding coverage to include business interruption coverage (which they previously could not afford), building enough confidence in their ECRM program to enable management to accept higher risk retention, reducing premiums on other policies that overlapped with cyber, and moving to a single cyber carrier who was confident enough in their efforts to take on the entire cyber policy coverage—all while holding their overall liability insurance portfolio premiums flat.

Together with their broker and carrier, they collaborated to ensure that all ECRM program elements were incorporated into their ERM framework, so that the program receives ongoing C-suite and board visibility. Monies saved on what could have been higher premiums (for the enhanced cyber coverage they negotiated) have been used for additional investments in the ECRM program.

The key to reducing your insurance premiums as a way to help fund your ECRM program is to collaborate with internal executive colleagues, your cyber risk broker, and carrier underwriter. Get advance buy-in from the underwriter that they will work with you to review your ECRM program and take it into account when pricing your cyber liability premiums. Working together, you can create a win/win scenario that keeps your premium costs down and, at the same time, mitigates the insurer's risk of a large payout.

Captive Insurance Program Grants

As risk management and insurance models continue to evolve, more healthcare organizations are turning to a captive insurance model. Captive insurance is a type of self-insurance, offering organizations an alternative to commercial carriers. Captive insurance programs have long been a source of innovative risk financing for many industries.

The captive insurance model gives organizations more control over the risk management process. By using a captive insurance model, organizations are able to customize coverage, maintain predictable premium costs, leverage flexibility in deciding whether to settle claims or pursue litigation, and encourage the engagement of the organization in risk management.

In the captive model, risks are not transferred to a third-party insurance company. Instead, the organization makes strategic decisions about risk management and self-insures accordingly. Thus, the captive insurance model promotes executive ownership of risk management.

The captive insurance model was pioneered within the Harvard medical community in the mid-1970s to address rising medical professional liability insurance premiums. Now the captive model is being used in a number of different ways within the healthcare industry, including for medical malpractice, employee benefit stop loss, provider excess stop loss, and general liability for patient risk.[46] In addition, organizations are increasingly turning to the captive model to cover cyber risk.[47] According to a 2019 report on captives by Marsh, a global leader in insurance broking and risk management, "the number of captives writing cyber liability coverage over the past five years has grown by 95%."[48]

You may be able to use your captive as a source of funds for your ECRM program even if your captive insurance company does not currently have a cyber liability line. The lines separating medical professional liability, privacy risk, and cyber risk have become blurred. Case in point: in 2014, CRICO, a leader in medical professional liability, provided $2.4 million in grants to six member institutions to conduct risk assessments in order to better understand its cyber exposures.[49]

The costs associated with privacy risk and cyber risk can easily exceed the cost associated with an individual instance of medical professional liability. Because of this, the captive insurance model is beginning to be a model that many other healthcare organizations are exploring as they consider enterprisewide cyber risks.

It is outside the scope of this book to explore the captive insurance model in depth. However, the captive insurance model is one that healthcare organizations would do well to consider when they are examining cyber risk and exploring how to fund an enterprisewide ECRM program.

Discussion Questions for Your C-suite and Board

You can't rely on external spending benchmarks to establish your ECRM investments any more than you can rely on somebody else's one-size-fits-all checklist to establish your ECRM program. At the end of the day, the right level of spending will be the level that supports your vision, mission, strategy, values, and services while operating below your risk appetite. As you think about your

ECRM spending, it is important to address both *past* ECRM debt (ECRM funding you need to allocate now to make up for past omissions) and *future* ECRM spending. Adopting a "security-by-design" approach will help you build ECRM into all of your new initiatives, projects, and programs going forward. You may be able to use strategies such as leveraging CMS incentive funds, reducing your cost of capital, reducing your cyber insurance premiums, and using captive insurance to realize additional funds for your ECRM program. The following questions will help you think about your organization's ECRM funding.

1. Do you have an accurate understanding of how much a data breach could cost your organization? Does your estimate include reputational, financial, legal and regulatory, operational, and clinical costs, as well as intangible costs?

2. Is your organization's current level of ECRM funding adequate to address the ECRM debt your organization has built up over the past 10 years? What "critical" or "high" legacy risks need to be treated as soon as possible?

3. Is your organization prepared to implement a policy to limit funding of programs, projects, and initiatives (involving healthcare data, systems, or devices) to only those that include an ECRM line-item as part of their budget?

4. What is your organization's current cost of capital? Is it being affected by your organization's current ECRM

posture? Can your organization reduce the cost of capital by investing in ECRM?

5. Could your organization reduce the total premium cost of your liability insurance portfolio by developing a stronger ECRM program?

6. What are the possibilities for using grants from your organization's captive insurance program to jump-start or strengthen your ECRM program?

SECTION THREE:

Outcomes

CHAPTER 9

Experience the Ideal
ECRM Board Meeting

*The superior man, when resting in safety, does not forget
that danger may come. When in a state of security,
he does not forget the possibility of ruin. When all is
orderly, he does not forget that disorder may come.*

~ CONFUCIUS

For your ECRM program to be effective, it needs to be integrated into every part of your organization. This includes integrating ECRM into the *governance* of your organization by including it as a regular part of your board meeting agenda. Remember that, in Chapter 6, the sample strategic ECRM objective I suggested, on the topic of governance, was "Incorporate ECRM into strategic decision-making and ongoing business planning." You cannot achieve this objective without integrating ECRM into your entire governance structure, up to and including the full board.

The NACD publication *Cyber-Risk Oversight 2020: Key Principles and Practical Guidance for Corporate Boards* supports the idea that cyber risk be given attention at the board level.[1] One of five key principles identified in *Cyber-Risk Oversight 2020* is, "Boards should have adequate access to cybersecurity expertise, and discussions about cyber risk management should be given regular and adequate time on board meeting agendas."[2]

Board involvement in ECRM is necessary in order for the board to execute its *duty of care*, as I discussed in Chapter 1. In addition, the IBM/Ponemon studies on the cost of a data breach, referenced earlier, noted that "board-level involvement" is one of the factors that is associated with a *decrease* in the average cost of a data breach—one more reason it is essential to have board involvement in your ECRM program.[3]

If possible, your organization should establish a three-tiered ECRM governance structure as described in Chapter 7. Ideally, the third ECRM governance tier—the ECRM Cross-Functional Working Group—will meet several times monthly in order to execute its responsibility to establish, implement, and mature your organization's ECRM program. The ECRM Executive Steering Committee should meet monthly to ensure execution of the ECRM program. The full board or designated committee should discuss ECRM at least quarterly.

With this governance structure in place, information should flow naturally between the tiers, and be distilled from the Cross-Functional Working Group, to the ECRM Executive Steering Committee, and from there, on to the full board or designated committee. Figure 9.1 illustrates the meeting schedule I recommend, according to each respective governance body.

Too often, the first ECRM meetings in which a board becomes involved occur only as the result of a cyber crisis. If your organization has not yet had a board meeting focused on

ECRM, now is the time to do so, even if it is a special, separate kickoff meeting. Remember, most organizations have some ECRM debt to repay, and now is a great time to get started. If your organization has experienced a cyber crisis, don't squander it. Seize the opportunity to educate your board and to begin initiating the recommendations on formalizing your ECRM program that I have included throughout this book.

Tier	Governance Body	Members	Function	ECRM Meeting Frequency
1	*Full board* or designated board committee (e.g., *Audit & Compliance Committee* or a specific *ECRM Oversight Council*)	Full board or designated committee	Sets direction and provides oversight.	Quarterly
2	*ECRM Executive Steering Committee*	CEO + his/her full team	Ensures execution of the ECRM program.	Monthly
3	*ECRM Cross-Functional Working Group*	May include representatives from legal, risk management, finance, HR, audit, compliance, privacy, IT, clinical engineering, security, quality, and/or others.	Executes the steps to establish, implement, and mature the ECRM program.	Several times per month

Figure 9.1 *Recommended ECRM Meeting Schedule by Governance Body*
Source: Bob Chaput, Executive Chairman, Clearwater.

ECRM as a Board Agenda Item

In this chapter, I will focus on ECRM as a *board* agenda item. I've identified three key subtopics that should be covered in each board discussion of ECRM:

1. ECRM Risks and Treatment

2. ECRM Program Advancement

3. ECRM Relevant Current Events and Board Education

Of course, these three subtopics should also be addressed in the Tier 2 and Tier 3 ECRM governance bodies, but at a level of detail appropriate for ECRM establishment and implementation, rather than oversight.

Who Should Present the Information?

If, as recommended, ECRM has been integrated into your organization's Enterprise Risk Management program, it would be appropriate for your Chief Risk Officer (or most trusted risk management executive) to lead the ECRM discussion at the board meeting. If ECRM has not been integrated into your ERM program, I recommend you do so. (I briefly discussed this integration in connection with figure 6.1, Business Strategy/Cybersecurity Strategy Alignment, in Chapter 6.) Historically, healthcare CROs have focused on medical malpractice. However, security research and demonstrations are serving as harbingers of that first cyber-driven medical professional liability lawsuit. It's appropriate for other leaders, such as the CIO, CISO, CFO, CCO, CAE, and CMO, to be present during the ECRM discussion. However, if your CIO or CISO is currently leading the ECRM discussion, it is time to make the change to the CRO. Assigning the role of ECRM discussion leader to the CIO or CISO perpetuates the idea that cyber risk is just an IT problem, rather than an enterprise risk problem.

How Should the Information Be Presented?

Board members often receive ECRM reporting that is too detailed, too technical, and too difficult to interpret. Technical details may be appropriate for the ECRM Cross-Functional Working Group, but, at the board level, ECRM information needs to consist of succinct summaries and actionable insights.

I have frequently seen a CISO or CIO attempt to deliver stacks of detailed operational data from vulnerability scans, penetration tests, and security information and event management (SIEM) tools that are irrelevant to the C-suite and board. Often the information is difficult to read and interpret, providing little strategic insight. This is not a helpful strategy.

A useful resource in developing board-appropriate presentation materials can be found in NACD's *Cyber-Risk Oversight 2020: Key Principles and Practical Guidance for Corporate Boards.*[4] The handbook includes "Guiding Principles for Board-Level Metrics." The Guiding Principles state that metrics for the board should:

- Be relevant to the audience (full board; key committee)

- Be reader-friendly: use summaries, callouts, graphics, and other visuals, and avoid technical jargon

- Convey meaning: communicate insights, not just information

✓ Highlight changes, trends, and patterns over time

✓ Show relative performance against peers, against industry averages, against other relevant external indicators, etc. (e.g., maturity assessments)

✓ Indicate impacts on business operations, costs, market share, etc.

- Be concise: Avoid information overload

- Above all, enable discussion and dialogue[5]

The *Stop the Cyber Bleeding* resource page (https://www.clearwatercompliance.com/stopthecyberbleeding) also includes examples of board-appropriate presentation slides and handouts that you can use as a template for your own reporting.

How Much Time Should Be Devoted to the ECRM Agenda Item?

The three ECRM subtopics I cited above and outline further below are each substantial in their own right. In order to cover this material adequately, I recommend allocating 30 minutes to each subtopic, for a total of 90 minutes dedicated to ECRM at each of the quarterly board meetings in which this topic is addressed. That will seem like a great deal of time to most C-suite executives and board members. As your ECRM program matures, and, as it becomes more integrated into your business strategies and plans, this time can likely be reduced. No matter the amount of time allocated, keep ECRM as an agenda item and three key subtopics prominently visible on your board meeting agenda.

ECRM Subtopic 1: ECRM Risks and Treatment

The first subtopic that should be addressed during each and every quarterly board ECRM discussion is ECRM risks and risk treatment. This subtopic should naturally involve an ongoing discussion of your organization's risk appetite. The three parts of this discussion include:

Risk Analysis

As I have emphasized throughout this book, the first and most important task your organization must accomplish is to identify and prioritize your organization's unique cyber risks. Your organization cannot develop an effective ECRM program without first understanding what data, systems, and devices comprise your organization's unique assets and what reasonably anticipated threats and vulnerabilities jeopardize those assets.

I have observed—and OCR findings have validated—that the single biggest ECRM challenge organizations face is the identification of their unique risks. Healthcare organizations are not conducting enterprisewide, comprehensive risk analysis (OCR-Quality® Risk Analysis) that meets the HIPAA Security Rule Risk Analysis standard and OCR guidance and expectations. Therefore, it is very important that the board be educated and informed on the status and scope of your organization's risk analysis, in order for them to be able to provide oversight for this important task.

Thus, this subtopic should include discussion about your organization's current approach to identifying all of your information assets and the status of your inventory and classification of information assets. It may also include a discussion of whether your organization has the internal resources to conduct an OCR-Quality® Risk Analysis, or whether it would be more effective to identify an independent, objective, third-party vendor who offers expertise and supporting software tools for this task.

Examples of questions that should be included under this risk analysis discussion item are:

- How many total risks (number) have been identified in your risk register?

- What percentage of the risks you have identified have been given risk ratings?

- What is your categorization of risk, from most serious to least serious—(i.e., what are the respective percentages of critical risks, high risks, medium risks, and low risks?)?

- What does your risk rating look like when broken down by media/asset-component group (e.g., laptops, electronic medical devices, desktops, servers, etc.)? Which of these media/asset-components show the highest average risk rating?

- What are the top five vulnerabilities identified in your risk analysis?

- Has your organization completed a risk analysis that will be acceptable to OCR?

Discussion of risks is an evergreen topic for the ECRM agenda. That is, the discussion of risk is never finished. Risks evolve; assets change as facilities, data, systems, and devices are added and retired. Risk analysis is an ongoing process and, therefore, an item of continuing importance for the board.

Risk Appetite

The second critical task of your organization is to discuss, debate, and settle on your organization's appetite for risk. After all risks have been identified, rated, and prioritized, your organization needs to determine how risks identified will be treated. As a quick reminder, risk treatment typically means accepting risks below your risk appetite and avoiding, mitigating, and/or transferring risks at or above your risk appetite. (See Definition #16 in Chapter 5 for more on this topic).

Therefore, this topic should include a discussion about what your process is (or will be) for setting and communicating your risk appetite and what your current risk appetite is (if it has been established). Additional questions that would be important to discuss include:

- What is the *percentage* of risks above your risk appetite?

- What is the *number* of risks above your risk appetite?

- Which of your entities/facilities are showing the largest number of risks above your organization's risk appetite?

- Which of your media/asset-component groups are showing the largest number of risks above your risk appetite?

The right Enterprise Cyber Risk Management Software (ECRMS) solution will make it easy for your organization to capture, report, and discuss this data. The right ECRMS solution will also offer visual, "at-a-glance" style dashboards that make it simple to compile and present this information to the board (and other stakeholders).

Just as with the discussion of risk analysis, the discussion of risk appetite is an evergreen topic. It never loses its relevance. Your organization's risk appetite may well change as your risk profile changes, as your ECRM resources change, and as your business vision, mission, strategy, values, and services change. So, risk appetite is always an appropriate topic of discussion at the board level.

Risk Treatment

The final critical discussion item in the risk analysis/appetite/treatment subtopic is risk treatment or risk response. Each identified risk requires a response. Typically, as we've discussed, your organization will *accept* risks that are rated below your risk appetite. Risks rated at or above the risk appetite will need to be treated by either *avoiding* them, *mitigating* them, or *transferring* them (for more detail, revisit Definition #17 in Chapter 5).

Among the questions to address on the risk treatment discussion item are:

- What is your current process for conducting risk treatment?

- Who is authorized to make what risk treatment decisions, using what data and facts?

- Have you documented your current risk treatment plan?

- Would it be advantageous to contract with a third party to develop a risk treatment plan?

- If you have already contracted with a third party for this task, what are the highlights of the current risk treatment plan of which the board should be aware?

- Has your organization developed a risk treatment or risk management plan that will be acceptable to OCR?

These three discussion items—risks, risk appetite, and risk treatment—will continue to have relevance regardless of how new or how mature your ECRM program is.

ECRM Subtopic 2: ECRM Program Advancement

The second subtopic that should be addressed during the board's quarterly ECRM discussion is ECRM program advancement. At the board level, ECRM program advancement should be reviewed within the context of your organization's strategic ECRM objectives, as discussed in Chapter 6. In that chapter, I said that, in order for your ECRM program to be relevant and effective, it must be aligned with your organization's business vision, mission, strategy, values, and services.

Your organization's strategic ECRM objectives should also address the five critical core capabilities: Governance, People, Process, Technology, and Engagement. (These core capabilities are also discussed in Chapter 6). When developing presentation materials for this agenda item, it is important to remember that C-suite executives and board members need enough actionable insight to be able to execute their oversight responsibilities. At the same time, it is not helpful to overwhelm C-suite executives and board members with in-the-weeds details that are more relevant to implementation and execution than oversight.

One way to attain the balance between actionable insight and extraneous detail is to limit presentation materials (whether they be printed handouts or presentation slides) to one page for each strategic ECRM objective. In the presentation slide or one-page handout dedicated to each strategic objective, you should include the following information:

1. The strategic ECRM objective description, including costs and expected benefits

2. Enabling objectives, including target completion date, expected completion date, and current status

3. Key accomplishments toward achieving this objective during the last reporting period

4. Planned accomplishments for the next reporting period

5. Key issues, risks, and barriers that require board attention

6. Key discussion areas for this update

It can be helpful to develop a consistent template for reporting this information. (When you are evaluating ECRMS solutions, check to make sure your solution includes an executive-level reporting dashboard that makes it easy to compile and display this information for quarterly reporting to the board.) A consistent presentation template—one that incorporates graphic elements, such as color-coding to identify the status of objective metrics—will help C-suite executives and board members comprehend the information quickly and at the level they need to provide informed oversight. Strategic objectives for Governance, People, Process, Technology, and Engagement will change over time, of course, but the reporting format should be consistent. (For an example of the presentation format I have outlined above, please visit the *Stop the Cyber Bleeding* resource page at https://www.clearwatercompliance.com/stopthecyberbleeding.)

It is also important to remember that the presentation format I have outlined above is specific to board-level program updates (Tier 1 Governance). The project management plans used by the ECRM Executive Steering Committee (Tier 2 Governance) and ECRM Cross-Functional Working Group (Tier 3 Governance) will include much more detail.

ECRM Subtopic 3: ECRM-Relevant Current Events and Board Education

The third subtopic that should be addressed during the board's quarterly ECRM discussion has two components: (a) ECRM-relevant current events and (b) board education.

ECRM-Relevant Current Events

The overall objective of addressing current events is to keep your board apprised of both internal and external relevant events that may affect your risk posture. The board should be informed in a timely manner (not waiting until the quarterly ECRM agenda item) about any internal incidents related to the compromise of the CIA of your assets. Bad news doesn't age well: a board meeting should not be the first time your board is hearing about the hacked CT scan image that resulted in a misdiagnosis and a patient's death.

It's also important to make the board aware of any high-profile external events, such as data breaches in peer organizations or OCR enforcement actions that have been taken against other similar healthcare organizations. Cite lessons learned from these external incidents or enforcement actions. Discuss your organization's risk analysis findings and risk treatment plans in the context of these events. In addition to discussing external breaches and OCR actions, the relevant current events discussion should also include:

- Reporting on any significant global, federal, state, or local regulatory changes that may affect your ECRM program, including actions your organization is taking to address these changes. (An example would be discussion of the 2018 implementation of the GDPR or the 2020 implementation of California Consumer Privacy Act [CCPA] and the new regulations' specific impact[s] on your organization).

- ECRM-related moves on the part of your competitors that may impact your organization's competitive positioning. (For example, has your competitor begun to tout its ECRM program as part of its marketing/branding strategy? How does your ECRM program position you with respect to competitive advantage?)

- Significant changes to the threat landscape, including new threat sources or new safeguards, that affect your organization's risk posture. (An example of a change in threat sources would be in 2017 when WannaCry, Petya, and NotPetya hit healthcare in a very visible way.[6] The discussion would have included whether these new threat sources impacted your organization and how they were being addressed).

Board Education

Board education in ECRM is a continuing process. Over time, as the right subject matter experts deliver the right content, board members will become more fluent in ECRM topics and therefore better equipped to execute their duty of care. In this respect, ECRM fluency is similar to financial fluency: not all board members are Certified Public Accountants. However, all board members understand enough to engage in a meaningful discussion of your organization's P&L, balance sheet, and cash-flow statement.

Board education does not have to be limited to the quarterly ECRM board agenda item, but some element of board education should always be included as part of the ECRM agenda. Board education can be accomplished both within the ECRM agenda and in separately scheduled internal/external events. Remember that board member education is NOT the same as workforce member training. Board member education is designed specifically to strengthen board members' abilities to exercise their duty of care with respect to ECRM. Workforce member training focuses on topics such as good cyber hygiene practices at the front lines, e.g., how to recognize phishing attempts and how to avoid falling for them.

Examples of appropriate and effective board member educational activities/subjects include:

- Hiring outside experts to brief the board on ECRM 101

- Having internal advisors, such as your chief audit executive or general counsel, provide in-depth briefings

- Engaging outside counsel to discuss the legal implications of a breach

- Engaging your organization's executive risk insurance broker to discuss potential gaps, clashes, and redundancies in your liability policy portfolio

- Engaging outside and inside experts to provide a forecast of the cyber risk landscape, one, three, and five years out

- Inviting external advisors, such as FBI representatives or OCR staff, to discuss the healthcare cyber risk environment

- Providing a briefing on the NACD Cyber-Risk Oversight Certificate (https://www.nacdonline.org) to validate the importance of ECRM and encourage board members to pursue continuing education in cyber risk

- Providing a briefing on the NIST Cybersecurity Framework, including information on how adoption of the Framework encourages integration of ECRM into the overall business strategy

Additional Considerations When Addressing ECRM in Your Board Meeting

A final point to remember is that your organization should maintain a record of board discussions related to ECRM. All key discussion topics and ECRM program decisions should be documented. Likewise, all risk treatment decisions (accept, avoid, mitigate, or transfer) should be explicitly documented, including those decisions to accept risk. Minutes and presentation materials should be retained and secured. Diligent recordkeeping of the board's ECRM discussions and decisions creates important documentation that the board is exercising duty of care and reasonable diligence.

Discussion Questions for Your C-suite and Board

My long-term vision for your organization, consistent with the Strategic ECRM Objectives related to Governance and Engagement, is that ECRM should become so embedded in the fabric of your organization's business strategy and planning processes that it is discussed as a part of all board meeting agenda items. This vision reflects the principle of "ECRM-by-design." The following questions will help you evaluate whether your organization has integrated ECRM into your governance structure in a way that supports your board in exercising their duty of care and reasonable diligence.

1. Has your organization established a hierarchy of ECRM governance as described in Chapter 7 and revisited here?

2. Is your organization allocating an appropriate amount of time to ECRM discussions at the board level?

3. Is the ECRM information presented to the board appropriate for the audience? Is the information concise,

relevant, and meaningful enough to encourage the right dialogue?

4. Does your board's ECRM agenda include a discussion of your organization's risks, risk appetite, and risk treatment?

5. Does your board's ECRM agenda include a discussion of your organization's program advancement? In other words, is the board monitoring progress on establishing, implementing, and maturing the ECRM program so that they are able to assess whether it is working?

6. Does your board's ECRM agenda include a discussion of relevant current cyber events?

7. Does your board's ECRM agenda include an educational component for the board? What topics would be best for your organization, given the current state of your ECRM program?

8. Is your organization adequately documenting and recording board discussions and decisions related to ECRM?

9. Does your organization facilitate educational opportunities on the topic of ECRM for the board outside of board meetings?

CHAPTER 10

Realize the Benefits of a NIST-Based ECRM Approach

We always talk about there's a lack of funding, a lack of support, a lack of tools and gadgets or gizmos, but when I look back at the 19 years I've been doing this and see where are the real [information security] weaknesses, it's usually a lack of strategy. It's that we have all this stuff in place, but we don't have a head coach who's seeing the whole playing field, who understands where all the pieces fit together, and who has devised a strategy to make it all work.

~ SHAWN TUMA, CYBERSECURITY AND DATA PRIVACY ATTORNEY AT SPENCER FANE LLP[1]

Cyber risks are real, they are here now, and, if you work in or with the healthcare industry, your organization has a target on its back. The best way to address cyber risk is to establish, implement, and mature an ECRM program. Your organization's ECRM program begins with you. As C-suite and board members, you have a fiduciary responsibility and duty of care to take actions (such as establishing an ECRM program) that

protect your organization and its clients (patients). More importantly, as C-suite and board members, you have the big-picture
perspective and powers of oversight that enable you to provide
the leadership and guidance necessary to establish, implement,
and mature an effective ECRM program.

The Benefits of Implementing an ECRM Program

In order to provide effective leadership for your organization,
C-suite and board members must understand the value and
benefits of ECRM. In addition, C-suite and board members
must communicate this value throughout your organization.
This includes communicating the value of ECRM to internal and
external stakeholders (employees, patients, business associates,
outside counsel, risk insurers, etc.).

I have emphasized the value and benefits of ECRM throughout this book. In Chapter 1, I described the very real possibility
of a cyber-based medical malpractice scenario. In Chapter 2, I
detailed how ECRM can help your organization address many of
the significant challenges healthcare organizations are currently
facing. In the first part of this chapter, I want to refresh your
memory as to some of the key benefits your organization will
realize by implementing an effective ECRM program.

An Effective ECRM Program Protects Your Patients

The highest priority of healthcare organizations is to protect
their patients from harm (i.e., "First, do no harm."). An effective
ECRM program protects patients from harm by protecting the
CIA of their health information. Equally importantly, such a
program also protects the growing number of healthcare IoT
devices, many of which are attached to or implanted in your

patients, creating direct patient-safety issues. An ECRM program does this by identifying risks to your organization's data, systems, and devices; prioritizing those risks; and treating them.

An Effective ECRM Program Aligns with Your Duty of Care Responsibilities

As I detailed in Chapter 1, healthcare organization board members and C-suite executives are fiduciaries of your organization. As fiduciaries, you have a duty of care—that is, a legal responsibility—to act in a reasonable manner toward the people you are responsible for (e.g., patients). Implementing and maturing an effective ECRM program helps to establish that the board and C-suite executives are taking their fiduciary responsibilities seriously and acting in a manner that addresses those responsibilities.

An Effective ECRM Program Helps Your Organization Comply with Diverse Regulatory Requirements

As I described in Chapter 2, healthcare organizations must ensure compliance in the context of an extremely complex regulatory environment. Federal legislation, policies, and regulations; state legislation, policies, and regulations, and even global policies and regulations (think GDPR) impact the way healthcare organizations do business. A common requirement of many of these regulations and standards is that organizations must conduct a comprehensive risk analysis. For example, an academic medical center serving patients from around the world may be subject to HIPAA, FERPA, GLBA, PCI DSS and GDPR—all of which require risk assessments. Because a comprehensive and effective ECRM program meets the risk assessment (and risk management) requirements of many different mandates, it can simplify and enhance the effectiveness of your organization's compliance activities.

An Effective ECRM Program Positions You for Legal Action Should an Incident Occur

As I noted in Chapter 2, C-suite executives and board members can be found personally liable for having inadequate protections in place in the case of a cyber incident. In the publication "Avoiding Personal Liability: A Guide for Directors and Officers," global law firm DLA Piper stated:

> A board that fails to implement any reporting or information system or fails to correct a system it "knows" is not working, may face liability for bad faith. Similarly, having implemented such a system, directors can face liability if they consciously fail to monitor or oversee the system, thereby disabling themselves from being informed and being deemed to be "asleep at the switch."[2]

However, when members of the C-suite and board are actively engaged in the oversight of your organization's efforts to establish, implement, and mature an ECRM program, it can demonstrate the opposite of being "asleep at the switch."

I am not a lawyer, and, as indicated in the disclaimer at the beginning of this book, I do not offer legal advice or guidance. That being said, there is a concept called "affirmative defense" that may also have relevance here. "Affirmative Defense" is "a defense in which the defendant introduces evidence, which, if found to be credible, will negate criminal liability or civil liability, even it if is proven that the defendant committed the alleged acts."³ In November 2018, the state of Ohio enacted Senate Bill 220, known as the Ohio Data Protection Act (DPA).⁴ Among the provisions of the DPA:

> Importantly, the DPA now provides Ohio businesses with an affirmative defense to some forms of data breach claims where the business has in place reasonable security measures at the time of the breach. In enacting the DPA, Ohio became the first state in the nation to implement a law that affords a data breach safe harbor for business entities.⁵

Furthermore, the Act requires that organization's cybersecurity program must "reasonably conform" to "an industry recognized cybersecurity framework."⁶ The Act specifically cites the NIST Cybersecurity Framework (including NIST Special Publications 800-53, 800–53a, and 800–171) as the first example of "an industry recognized cybersecurity framework."⁷

An Effective ECRM Program Facilitates M&A Activity

Consolidation continues to be a significant factor in the healthcare industry. Whether your organization is acquiring another organization, or whether your organization is the target of an acquisition effort, it is extremely important to have your cyber risk management house in order. An inadequate ECRM program can derail M&A negotiations. As a seller, your organization may be subjected to a rigorous cybersecurity due diligence review. In order to maintain your sales price and, potentially, shareholder value, you want to show a strong ECRM position, with cyber risks well understood and managed. On the other hand, as a buyer, you may be acquiring substantial cyber risk. If you have a strong ECRM position, your organization will be able to conduct a more rigorous due diligence on your target, allowing you to factor weaknesses into your purchase price. A number of private equity firms I have worked with requested an ECRM assessment as part of their diligence work when considering new portfolio-company investments.

An Effective ECRM Program Can Be a Market Differentiator

As data breaches continue to make headlines, consumers have become increasingly aware of data privacy and security issues. Organizations that experience data breaches risk losing consumer trust and driving them to other providers. Proactively establishing an ECRM program can serve as a market differentiator by engaging consumer trust. Or, if your organization has already experienced a breach, the establishment of an effective ECRM program can help to rebuild consumer trust in your organization.

The Benefits of Implementing a *NIST-Based* ECRM Program

Throughout this book, I have also emphasized the point that, for your ECRM program to be effective, it must be risk-based. It cannot be controls-checklist-based. The best, most comprehensive risk-based approach is the approach developed by the National Institute of Standards and Technology (NIST). I have alluded to the superiority of this approach throughout this book. In this section, I offer a more in-depth look at why a NIST-based ECRM program is the best choice for your organization.

The NIST Cybersecurity Framework Was Developed Using an Open, Inclusive Process

The NIST Cybersecurity Framework development process was designed to be as open and inclusive as possible. The genesis of the Framework was Presidential Executive Order 13636, which was issued on February 12, 2013.[8] The goal of the order was to share cybersecurity threat information across industries in order to develop a framework for reducing risks to critical U.S. infrastructure. The initial framework development and subsequent updates included the participation of more than 2,000 people across a wide range of impacted industries. The strength, relevance, and effectiveness of the NIST Cybersecurity Framework is directly related to the open, inclusive, process that has been used to develop and update it.

The NIST Cybersecurity Framework Uses Accessible Language That All Stakeholders in Your Organization Can Understand

The NIST Cybersecurity Framework is built around five core functions: Identify, Protect, Detect, Respond, Recover. These five words encompass the entire scope of cybersecurity. They are also intentionally accessible words, so that all stakeholders in any organization—from board members to clinicians to hospital volunteers—can understand and contribute to your organization's cybersecurity efforts.

The NIST Cybersecurity Framework Facilitates Information Governance

The NIST Cybersecurity Framework has governance built into it, because it outlines both a "top-down" and a "bottom-up" response. Per the Framework, your organization's technical people may be collecting data and identifying what is working and what is not working. At the same time, it is up to the leadership—including C-suite executives and board members—to look at that data and decide how it will change your organization's approach to security. The NIST model includes people at every level of governance: from the front-line technical people operating your organization's Security Operations Center (SOC), to mid-management (including your ECRM Cross-Functional Working Group), to the ECRM Executive Steering Committee, to the board. It encompasses all levels of ECRM activity, from tactical, to policy and procedures, to oversight.

The NIST Cybersecurity Framework Leverages Current Standards, Guidelines, and Best Practices from a Number of Internationally Recognized Sources

Although security controls, in and of themselves, don't constitute a cybersecurity framework, they can provide important guidance in the tactical implementation of safeguards once your unique risks are identified. The NIST Cybersecurity Framework includes cross-references to other industry and, in some cases, global, standards related to cybersecurity (e.g., COBIT 5, ISA 62443, ISO/IEC 27001, NIST SP 800–53) which provide the safeguards to be considered for a more robust security program.[9]

The NIST Cybersecurity Framework Is Directly Aligned with HIPAA Requirements

In February 2016, OCR released a document entitled, "HIPAA Security Rule Crosswalk to NIST Cybersecurity Framework."[10] The 35-page document maps the administrative, physical, and technical standards and implementation specifications in the HIPAA Security Rule to the relevant categories in the NIST Cybersecurity Framework. OCR's publication of this document provides further validation that adopting the NIST approach to ECRM can assist your organization with HIPAA compliance and reduce regulatory compliance risk.

The NIST Cybersecurity Framework Has Been Endorsed by Healthcare Industry Heavyweights, Including the Healthcare Information Management and Systems Society (HIMSS)

In September 2016, the HIMSS North America Board of Directors approved a HIMSS Cybersecurity Position Statement. HIMSS stated that the framework adopted by the health sector should align with Section 405 of the Cybersecurity Act of 2015, specifically addressing the "voluntary, consensus-based, and industry-led guidelines, best practices, methodologies, procedures, and processes." In light of those criteria, HIMSS recommended the NIST Cybersecurity Framework as the best fit for the health sector.[11]

A Majority of Healthcare Organizations Have Adopted the NIST Cybersecurity Framework

A security survey conducted by HIMSS showed that nearly 6 of 10 healthcare organizations (57.9 percent) have adopted the NIST Cybersecurity Framework.[12] The advantage of using the same cybersecurity framework as your peers is that it makes it easier to share information about threats and problems. Because all of the organizations using the NIST Cybersecurity Framework share a common language and common tools, it makes it possible, for example, for the CISO at Hospital A to call the CISO at Hospital B and talk about what to do about a particular cybersecurity problem. Using the NIST Cybersecurity Framework also facilitates third-party cyber risk management. It enables hospitals and health systems (HIPAA's "covered entities") to place requirements on vendor business associates (BAs) using a common framework.

The NIST Cybersecurity Framework Has Become the Standard for the U.S. Government

The NIST Cybersecurity Framework as originally released in 2014 was voluntary. An Executive Order issued in May 2017 by the President changed that. All agencies of the U.S. government are now required to use the NIST Cybersecurity Framework to manage cybersecurity risk. That includes programs administered by CMS (Medicare, Medicaid). Healthcare organizations talk a lot about the benefits of digital interoperability—scalability, efficient use of resources. The benefits of "interoperability" can similarly be applied to your organization's cybersecurity framework. For example, using the same cybersecurity framework as peers and partners can facilitate cyber intelligence sharing across information systems and expedite collaborative approaches to threat analysis and response.

The NIST Cybersecurity Framework Is Emerging as a National Standard Across Industries

According to a 2019 survey by Gartner, Inc., a research and advisory firm, 73 percent of organizations around the world have implemented and currently use the NIST Cybersecurity Framework.[13] This is important for healthcare organizations because the healthcare sector is dependent on other sectors, including the energy sector, the financial services sector, the information technology sector, and the emergency services sector. Communication about cybersecurity needs to be precise and efficient not only within sectors, but across sectors. As different sectors adopt the NIST Cybersecurity Framework, it will continue to enhance cross-sector communications about cybersecurity.

The NIST Cybersecurity Framework Is Customizable

The NIST Cybersecurity Framework provides a template for your organization's own framework. It is neither one-size-fits-all nor rigidly prescriptive. It simply provides a foundation for the development of an ECRM program specifically suited to any particular organization's assets and risks.

The NIST Cybersecurity Framework Is Scalable

There are enormous variations in organization size within the healthcare industry, from one-physician practices to large, multi-national corporations. The NIST Cybersecurity Framework is flexible enough to accommodate organizations at both ends of the spectrum and every organization in between—e.g., one subcategory of the framework that requires your organization to establish and communicate its business objectives and business priorities. A well-resourced organization might fulfill that subcategory with a 100-page business plan, while a smaller organization might capture that in a page or a paragraph. The extent to which each organization fulfills a given subcategory is not prescribed, and that is what makes the NIST Cybersecurity Framework scalable.

The NIST Cybersecurity Framework Is Affordable

Unlike commercial frameworks, all of the resources your organization needs to adopt and implement the NIST Cybersecurity Framework are available for free. The Framework itself, as well as supporting documentation, video presentations, FAQs, industry-specific resources and implementation guides, are available at: https://www.nist.gov/cyberframework. Some organizations may choose to hire an outside vendor to assist in implementing the framework across a large, complex enterprise, but this is not required.

The NIST Cybersecurity Framework Does Not Require Certification

Some cybersecurity framework vendors offer "certification" services for a fee. The implication is that "certification" will protect a healthcare organization in the event of a cybersecurity breach or incident. But in fact, OCR has published guidance indicating that external "certification" does not ensure compliance with the HIPAA Security Rule. OCR's guidance states: "It is important to note that HHS does not endorse or otherwise recognize private organizations' 'certifications' regarding the Security Rule, and such certifications do not absolve covered entities of their legal obligations under the Security Rule. Moreover, performance of a 'certification' by an external organization does not preclude HHS from subsequently finding a security violation."[14]

The NIST Cybersecurity Framework Is Designed to Accommodate Changes in Technology and Changes in the Threat Landscape

A preliminary version of the first Framework was released on July 1, 2013.[15] After a comprehensive, inclusive development process, Version 1.0 of the NIST Cybersecurity Framework was released on February 12, 2014. But the development of the Framework did not end with its initial release. After additional stakeholder input was incorporated, Version 1.1 was released on April 16, 2018. Per the original directive, NIST continues to develop the framework through active dialogue and community outreach.[16]

In addition, irrespective of version number, the NIST Cybersecurity Framework is intentionally designed to accommodate changes in technology and in the threat landscape. It is designed to be agile and adaptable over time, to keep pace with the ever-changing risk landscape.

For additional perspectives/testimonials on the value of the NIST Cybersecurity Framework, from experts across a variety of industries, visit: https://www.nist.gov/cyberframework/general-perspectives

Real-World Examples

Deploying a NIST-based ECRM program is an effective way to address cyber risk management challenges across a broad range of organization types and cyber risk circumstances. These five examples, from my own experience, demonstrate the benefits of a NIST-based ECRM program in real-world scenarios. Please note that, in most of these examples, I have not disclosed the name of the client organization, given the sensitive nature of an organization's cybersecurity posture.

Example 1: Post-Acute Healthcare Services Firm Proactively Establishes ECRM

Challenge: A post-acute healthcare services firm decided to proactively establish a NIST-based ECRM program. This large, multi-billion-dollar enterprise offers both facility-based and home-based post-acute services across the U.S. Because of the scope and distribution of their information assets (healthcare data, systems, and medical devices), they needed to implement an effective, efficient, and scalable ECRM solution.

Action: I met with the CIO and CISO and subsequently fielded a Clearwater team that worked with this organization using a rapid, agile approach. The organization undertook a series of initiatives to establish its ECRM program by adopting the NIST Cybersecurity Framework, implementing the NIST approach to cyber risk management and creating a continuous improvement process. Actions taken included:

- Establishing effective governance

- Recruiting skilled risk management professionals

- Standardizing ECRM policies, procedures, and practices

- Deploying ECRM technology, including an ECRM software (ECRMS) SaaS solution

- Engaging leaders and managers throughout the organization

Outcome: As a result of these efforts, enterprisewide, ongoing, comprehensive, OCR-quality risk management is being performed. The ECRM work is aligned with the organization's vision, mission, strategy, values, and services. The ECRMS solution enables the ECRM program to address the constantly evolving cyber risk environment. C-suite executives and board members have increased confidence in the accuracy, detail, timeliness, and scope of their ECRM program.

Example 2: Health System Responds to OCR Corrective Action Plan While Completing Merger

Challenge: A large Midwestern health system had experienced a major data breach involving millions of patient records. OCR imposed a Corrective Action Plan (CAP) on the organization, which included a requirement to complete an OCR-Quality® Risk Analysis within 180 days. The information assets to be analyzed included thousands of assets, located in hundreds of facilities, at dozens of locations across the Midwest region. At the same time, the organization was working through a merger with another large health system.

Action: The organization engaged Clearwater to help in addressing the challenges they were facing. They implemented the NIST ECRM approach using Clearwater's ECRMS solution. They also engaged Clearwater's ECRM subject matter experts to facilitate in-person and virtual sessions with OCR enforcement officials, as they worked through compliance with the OCR CAP. They leveraged the ECRMS solution and consulting expertise to complete a rigorous, comprehensive, OCR-Quality® Risk Analysis per the requirements of the CAP.

Outcome: The organization completed the risk analysis and made risk treatment decisions for tens of thousands of risks. They fully met all of OCR's CAP requirements, on time, and received a complete sign-off on CAP requirements from OCR. The merger was successfully completed—and the organization subsequently adopted a NIST-based ECRM approach across the entire combined entity. The organization's chief compliance officer observed, "I don't know how anyone can deliver the risk analysis OCR is expecting without using the ECRMS solution Clearwater developed."

Example 3: Global Rideshare Organization Proactively Meets HIPAA ECRM Requirements to Facilitate Expansion into Healthcare Vertical

Challenge: Uber, one of the nation's leading rideshare providers, wanted to expand services into the healthcare vertical. Previous studies have shown that millions of adults miss, or delay, nonemergency medical care each year due to transportation barriers.[17] Uber saw a way to address this gap by leveraging their network of rideshare services to provide cost-effective, non-emergency medical transportation (NEMT) to help patients and their caregivers get to medical facilities. Uber, being aware of the sensitive nature of patient information, wanted to proactively address issues related to patient privacy and confidentiality, and compliance with HIPAA, state, and local regulations.

Action: Uber worked with Clearwater to ensure that their new business, Uber Health, was in compliance with HIPAA and also grounded in ECRM best practices. Actions taken included:

- Conducted an OCR-Quality® Risk Analysis

- Developed risk treatment plan

- Established appropriate administrative processes

- Implemented appropriate technical controls (e.g., data encryption of rider information)

- Created a dedicated, HIPAA-trained healthcare team to better serve the healthcare market

- Established Business Associate Agreements (BAA) with healthcare partners, committing to safeguarding and protecting PHI

Outcome: Uber Health has experienced dynamic business growth, due in part to the fact that they proactively put ECRM and HIPAA safeguards in place, making them an attractive partner for large healthcare systems. Since Uber Health's initial launch in 2018, they have established more than 1,000 partnerships (most with healthcare systems) and have plans to double the size of their healthcare team in 2020.[18]

Example 4: M&A Target Meets OCR-Risk Analysis™ Requirements After Three Failed Attempts

Challenge: A growing health system in the Southwest was completing the acquisition of a smaller, six-hospital health system. The target system was the subject of an OCR investigation regarding impermissible disclosure of ePHI. As part of the investigation, OCR had requested a copy of the organization's most recent risk analysis and risk management plan. The organization initially submitted an internally prepared document, which they believed to be a risk analysis but which OCR rejected. The acquiring organization engaged a third-party firm to prepare a risk analysis. The work product was again rejected by OCR. A second vendor was engaged to perform a risk analysis, but once again, the final work product was rejected by OCR. With only 30 days left to meet OCR's request, the chief compliance officer of the acquiring organization called me and asked if we could help them conduct an OCR-Quality® Risk Analysis.

Action: I met with the CCO, CIO, CISO and GC to develop a plan to complete the project within the 30-day timeline. I fielded a team of ECRM and HIPAA experts and at the same time deployed Clearwater's ECRMS solution to facilitate the task. The organization, working in partnership with Clearwater, rapidly made and documented initial governance decisions, completed information asset inventory work, identified all reasonably anticipated threats and vulnerabilities, built the organization's risk register, and developed a risk treatment plan of action. An OCR-Quality® Risk Analysis and risk management plan were delivered to OCR within the 30-day timeline.

Outcome: OCR approved the risk analysis and risk management plan and closed the case. The C-suite executives recognized the value of the ECRMS solution and decided to adopt it as the enterprise solution for all of its ongoing ECRM work. The organization's general counsel observed, "I have never worked with an organization that has been so responsive and efficient while producing such high-quality work products."

Example 5: Top Five Integrated Delivery Network (IDN) Transforms ECRM Program from Siloed, Separated Systems to Standardized, Cohesive Enterprisewide Approach

Challenge: A large Integrated Delivery Network (IDN) had, over time, inadvertently developed a piecemeal approach to ECRM. A newly appointed CISO noted wide variations in

ECRM governance, staffing processes, technology, and management across the enterprise. At the operational level, regional information security officers were using a variety of risk analysis techniques. Most were labor-intensive, controls-focused, and based on spreadsheets developed by different CPA firms. The spreadsheet-based efforts made it impossible to roll up the data into an enterprisewide view of risk management efforts. The CISO knew that the existing approach to ECRM would not meet OCR standards with respect to risk analysis and risk management.

Action: The organization adopted the NIST Cybersecurity Framework and the overall NIST approach to ECRM. To facilitate implementation of more consistent risk analysis and risk management, the organization engaged Clearwater. Clearwater's experts trained and equipped corporate and regional information security staff to perform critical ECRM process steps, including frame, assess, respond, and monitor, per NIST ECRM processes. The organization also deployed Clearwater's ECRMS solution to facilitate and document the process across the organization.

Outcome: Over an 18-month period, the IDN accomplished the following:

- ECRM governance was established

- The approach to ECRM (including policies, procedures, and processes) was standardized across the organization

- The ECRMS solution was deployed across the enterprise

- Corporate and regional security staff were trained in the NIST-based ECRM approach

- The organization leveraged the NIST Cybersecurity Framework and ECRM SaaS solution to conduct an OCR-Quality® Risk Analysis and establish a risk management plan

- The organization leveraged the NIST Cybersecurity Framework to facilitate region-by-region ECRM maturity assessments, which were rolled up into enterprise views

The IDN now has a comprehensive, coordinated approach to ECRM across the entire organization. Furthermore, the use of the ECRMS solution has enabled C-suite and board engagement in ECRM by providing useful, real-time, enterprise-level insights into the ECRM program. The CISO said, "The information provided in the ECRMS dashboard is exactly what I need to take to my fellow C-suite executives and board in order to have a high-quality budget discussion about ECRM."

The real-world examples above show how ECRM can benefit organizations regardless of where they are in their ECRM journey—from proactively implementing ECRM to differentiate themselves in the healthcare market, to reactively implementing ECRM in response to a cyber breach incident and OCR sanctions. Think about where your organization fits within this range of scenarios. Is your organization just beginning to think proactively about ECRM? Is your organization engaged in M&A activity, either as an acquiring organization or an acquisition target? Has your organization already experienced a cyber incident? No matter what size your organization is or what stage of the ECRM journey your organization is in, *now* is the best time to establish, implement, and mature your ECRM program to protect your patients and your organization.

Discussion Questions for Your C-suite and Board

My goal in writing this book is to give you, as C-suite and board members, the information and understanding you need to provide knowledgeable and competent guidance and leadership in establishing, implementing, and maturing your organization's ECRM program. The following questions will help you think about how the cyber risk management concepts in this book apply to your organization.

1. Do you understand the business value and benefits of ECRM? Thinking specifically of your organization, which of the benefits of ECRM are most applicable to your situation (e.g., risk reduction, duty of care, regulatory compliance, legal positioning, M&A activity, market differentiation)?

2. Have you discussed the matter of personal liability as it relates to the robustness of your ECRM program?

3. Does your organization have a formal, structured ECRM program in place?

4. Do you know if your organization has adopted a cyber-security framework (any framework)?

5. Do you know if your organization has adopted an internationally recognized, risk-based standard, such as the NIST Cybersecurity Framework?

6. Can you articulate the specific benefits of adopting the NIST Cybersecurity Framework?

7. Do you understand your organization's ECRM program well enough to assess the maturity level of your ECRM program?

8. As a C-suite or board member, do you feel that the level of information you receive about your organization's ECRM program enables you to competently exercise your ECRM oversight responsibilities? If not, how could ECRM communications be improved?

9. Do you know whether your organization has conducted an OCR-Quality® Risk Analysis? If your organization has conducted a risk analysis, have the results of that analysis been communicated to the board and C-suite in an actionable way?

10. Does your organization have the internal resources to establish, implement, and mature an ECRM program that will meet all applicable regulatory expectations? If not, do you think it would be valuable to engage an experienced, reputable ECRM partner to establish, implement, and mature your organization's ECRM program?

11. Does your organization have a scalable software solution (e.g., ECRMS) in place that can support your ECRM program?

CHAPTER 11

The Upshot

The primary focus and responsibility of a board is governance, and broken down to its essence, governance is all about patient-safety and mitigation.

~ MIKE MYATT, AUTHOR OF *HACKING LEADERSHIP*[1]

As C-suite executives and board members, you have both the responsibility and the authority to provide your organization with leadership and oversight regarding enterprise cyber risk management. As you oversee your organization's ECRM efforts, I recommend you keep the following key points in mind:

Context

- First and foremost, cyber risk management is a business issue, not an "IT problem." In fact, a strong, proactive ECRM program can be a business enabler.

- Recognize that bad things related to cyber risks have happened to hundreds of healthcare organizations. They will continue to happen.

- Embrace the reality that cyber risks have evolved. Cyber risk management is no longer simply a matter of compliance or security; cyber risk has also grown to encompass matters related to patient safety and medical professional liability.

- Take action now! As of this writing, few healthcare organizations are conducting ECRM properly—now is the time to correct that.

Your Role

- As a C-suite executive or board member, remember that your role is to become an ECRM enabler, not necessarily an ECRM expert.

- Adopt and communicate strong governance principles.

- Emphasize the continuity of your ECRM program: your organization's vision, mission, strategy, values, and services should drive your ECRM program, which, in turn, feeds into your overall ERM program and determines your cybersecurity plan.

- Align your assets and ECRM work with your business strategy and objectives; prioritize everything.

- Engage your liability insurance broker(s) in your organization's conversations about ECRM.

- Make ECRM a "team sport." Insist on cross-functional engagement and accountability by lines-of-business, functional, and process owners.

- Be creative in funding your ECRM program. Consider reductions in your cost of capital, insurance premium savings and captive insurance grants as sources of funds.

Best Practices

- Critically evaluate your current ECRM situation. Would your current situation/program pass an OCR audit?

- Focus on your organization's unique assets and their exposures, not a third-party controls checklist.

- Insist on a risk-based approach to ECRM versus a controls-checklist-based approach.

- Require industry-standard methodology (such as NIST) rather than a closed or proprietary approach.

- Adopt the NIST Cybersecurity Framework.

- Implement the NIST ECRM Process.

- Ensure that your ECRM program covers every information asset, in every line-of-business, in every facility, in every location.

- Assess the extent to which you have ECRM debt, and plan to prioritize any catch-up ECRM work you may have to undertake.

- Require that all new healthcare data, systems, and devices include an ECRM budget line item before approval.

- Conduct ongoing risk analyses, and execute ongoing risk management plans; remember that risk analysis is not a once-and-done project.

- Monitor and measure your ECRM program maturity annually.

- Make certain that ECRM is integrated into your overall ERM program.

Last Words

My goal in writing this book was to provide you, as C-suite executives and board members, with the conceptual and foundational knowledge you need to provide effective cyber risk management oversight and leadership for your organization.

Although this book is geared toward C-suite executives and board members, it may also be helpful for you to share this information within your organization and with your organization's business partners, especially downstream business associates.

Additional resources are also available on the *Stop the Cyber Bleeding* resource page, at: https://clearwatercompliance.com/stopthecyberbleeding.

Obviously, one book cannot address all of the questions and concerns you might have. Please feel free to reach out to me at: bob.chaput@clearwatercompliance.com. I will answer your questions directly or point you to resources that can help you find the answers.

Appendices

What to Look for in an ECRM Company and Solution

In *Stop the Cyber Bleeding*, I outlined the key concepts C-suite executives and board members need to understand to provide leadership and oversight for their organization's ECRM efforts. I also provided specific, tangible, and actionable recommendations to get started. As C-suite executives and board members become more engaged in their organization's ECRM program, they often find that they need to augment their organization's internal resources with outside support, in order to establish, implement, and mature a comprehensive and effective ECRM program.

ECRM is a specialty area that requires expertise beyond what is typically found in most organizational IT, security, or risk management departments. Your organization's IT and/or risk management departments may be excellent at meeting the day-to-day tactical and operational needs of your organization but may not have the time, experience, or strategic expertise to establish an ECRM program.

If this is the case for your organization, you may want to consider hiring a third-party service provider to help you build your organization's ECRM program. Buyer beware, however, since ECRM consultants and service providers are not currently regulated or evaluated by a reliable, objective third party. This means that anyone can call themselves a "cyber risk management expert." Therefore, it is incumbent on your organization to exercise due diligence before contracting with a cyber risk management consultant or service provider.

The following considerations and questions will help you evaluate the depth of expertise, experience, and service you may expect from the prospective service providers you are considering.

Alignment with Your Organization's Strategic ECRM Objectives

An effective ECRM program begins with an analysis of your organization's unique vision, mission, strategy, values, and services. Next, you identify all of your information assets that enable you to achieve your mission. It is critically important to use the context of your organization's unique vision, mission, strategy, values, and services to identify your organization's "crown jewel" assets. This context—the identification of your organization's most valuable information assets—is critical to establishing an ECRM program that prioritizes the protection of those assets.

If a prospective service provider comes to you with a one-size-fits-all checklist, I recommend you look elsewhere for help. Likewise, if a prospective service provider does not offer a risk-based ECRM program approach tailored to your unique organization, keep looking. A one-size-fits-all checklist or a controls-based approach will not be effective in protecting your organization's unique assets, nor will it align with your organization's specific, strategic business objectives.

The following questions can help you determine whether a prospective provider is offering a cookie-cutter approach or an authentic, risk-based approach:

1. Will the prospective service provider's proposed ECRM solution be adaptable to, and aligned with, your organization's unique vision, mission, strategy, values, and services?

2. Is the prospective service provider proposing a *risk-based* ECRM approach or a *controls checklist*? If they are proposing a *controls checklist*, I suggest you walk away and keep looking!

3. Will the prospective service provider's proposed ECRM process result in the identification of *all* of your organization's electronic healthcare data, systems, and devices (i.e., all information assets used to create, receive, maintain, or transmit all sensitive data, including ePHI, as required by HIPAA)?

4. Is the prospective service provider proposing to conduct a comprehensive, asset-based, enterprisewide, OCR-Quality® Risk Analysis as an essential, foundational component of your organization's cyber risk management work? (This question is a canary-in-the-coal-mine question that must be answered affirmatively.)

5. Will the prospective service provider's proposed ECRM solution result in practical, tangible deliverables that your organization can use as evidence that you are exercising your fiduciary responsibility?

Competency and Expertise

Competency and expertise are essential table-stakes qualities in any prospective service provider. But how do you determine that a potential service provider has the skills, knowledge, and experience to successfully and efficiently establish, implement, and/or mature an effective ECRM program? Asking the following questions can help you determine the nature and depth of their competence and expertise:

6. Is the prospective service provider's ECRM methodology based on an industry-standard process and framework, such as NIST's *Managing Information Security Risk*[i] and the NIST *Cybersecurity Framework*[ii]?

7. Does the prospective service provider's specific risk analysis solution and methodology address the nine essential elements a risk analysis must incorporate, as outlined in the HHS/OCR *Guidance on Risk Analysis Requirements under the HIPAA Security Rule*[iii]?

8. Does the prospective service provider demonstrate deep industry experience in HIPAA compliance, other

---

i   Managing Information Security Risk. NIST Special Publication 800-39. National Institute of Standards and Technology. March 2011. Accessed April 12, 2020. https://nvlpubs.nist.gov/nistpubs/Legacy/SP/nistspecialpublication800-39.pdf

ii   Framework for Improving Critical Infrastructure Cybersecurity, Version 1.1. National Institute of Standards and Technology (NIST). April 16, 2018. Accessed April 12, 2020. https://nvlpubs.nist.gov/nistpubs/CSWP/NIST.CSWP.04162018.pdf

iii   Guidance on Risk Analysis Requirements under the HIPAA Security Rule. OCR/HHS. July 14, 2010. Accessed April 12, 2020. https://www.hhs.gov/sites/default/files/ocr/privacy/hipaa/administrative/securityrule/rafinalguidancepdf.pdf important and relevant compliance requirements, and ECRM implementation work?

9. What are the qualifications of the prospective service provider's cyber risk management professionals?
   a. What are their qualifications in terms of *expertise* (e.g., what industry-recognized certifications and credentials have they earned?)
   b. What are their qualifications in terms of *experience* (e.g., how many previous ECRM program implementation projects have they led? Have they established ECRM programs in similarly sized organizations as yours, in a comparable healthcare industry subsegment?)

10. Does the prospective service provider have evidence that work products for previous ECRM clients have been accepted by OCR during enforcement actions?

Capability and Capacity to Scale to Enterprise

Capability and capacity speak to the depth and power of the resources the prospective service provider has to offer to scale and extend to serve an organization of your size. Cyber risk management, to be effective, must be scalable across, and extensible to, your entire organization. Therefore, it is important that a prospective service provider has the capacity to facilitate enterprisewide deployment of your ECRM program.

11. Does the prospective service provider offer all of the tools and services needed to establish, implement,

and mature a comprehensive ECRM system (i.e., a proven methodology based on industry standards, comprehensive consulting services and a software solution)?

12. Does the prospective service provider offer a *scalable* software solution capable of facilitating and automating an ECRM program? [See *Appendix B* for more information about choosing an ECRM software solution.]

13. Does the prospective service provider's solution provide multiple levels of reporting and delegation of responsibility (e.g. by facility, by line-of-business, etc.) to enable engagement and accountability across your entire enterprise?

14. Does the prospective service provider's solution facilitate the continuous improvement (i.e., maturity) of your ECRM program?

15. Does the prospective service provider's solution facilitate ongoing monitoring and change management to adapt your ECRM program as your organization's vision, mission, strategy, values, and services evolve?

16. Does the prospective service provider's solution equip your organization to become self-sufficient in conducting ECRM, should your organization decide to proceed independently after an initial engagement?

Healthcare Industry Commitment

Cyber risk management is critical across all industries—from manufacturing, to financial services, to utilities, to education and healthcare. As such, there are common approaches and best practices (as articulated by NIST) that apply across all industries. Cyber risk management within the healthcare industry is, however, more nuanced due to healthcare's unique regulatory environment (e.g., HIPAA), distinctive ecosystem (millions of organizations and connected devices) and what's at stake (patients' lives). Therefore, it is important that any prospective service provider demonstrates specific expertise in, and commitment to, the healthcare industry.

17. How has the prospective service provider given back to the healthcare industry (e.g., through industry association participation, NIST collaboration and advocacy group support)?

18. What is the depth and breadth of the prospective service provider's healthcare industry ECRM experience?
    a. How many years have they worked within the healthcare industry?
    b. How many different healthcare clients have they served?

19. How has the prospective service provider been a thought leader, contributing to increased awareness of and education about cyber risk management within the healthcare industry? For example, does the provider educate, inform, and give back to the healthcare industry, above and beyond the commercial services they provide?

Reputation

Henry Ford once said, "You can't build a reputation on what you are going to do." The reputation of your prospective service provider matters, because it represents what the company has already accomplished. That is, reputation speaks to promises kept, not promises made.

20. Do your peers in the industry have any experience with the service provider you are considering? If so, was their experience a good one?

21. Has the prospective service provider earned any significant industry recognition, endorsements or awards?

22. How long has your prospective service provider been working in the cyber risk management field? Do they have years of experience, or are they a brand-new company with little history?

23. If the prospective service provider has a history of working with organizations like yours, what has been their ECRM track record with those organizations? That is, have the client companies of the prospective service provider suffered any serious data breaches since the engagement of the prospective provider's cyber risk management services?

Customer Service

An effective service provider will have an established process not only for implementation, but also for measuring customer satisfaction. ECRM is a journey, not a destination, so you will want to engage the services of a provider whose methodology indicates a collaborative, long-term partnership rather than a once-and-done approach.

24. Has the prospective service provider offered a clear and measurable description of the tangible ECRM work products your organization will receive as a result of the engagement?

25. Has the prospective service provider offered a timeline, including benchmarks and a transparent process for communication, so that your organization will be fully informed about every step in the ECRM implementation process and every milestone achieved?

26. Has the prospective service provider identified the specific individuals who will lead the partnership with your organization and identified the means of communication with those individuals?

27. Is the prospective service provider well-known in the industry for customer satisfaction? What is the evidence? For example, have they been recognized and rewarded by KLAS, Black Book, or other independent evaluators? If they have been so recognized, what kinds of customer comments have they garnered?

28. Does the prospective service provider have a formal customer feedback process established to track customer

satisfaction? For example, do they conduct annual or periodic surveys or reviews to collect customer feedback? How do they incorporate that feedback into their solutions and services?

29. Can the prospective service provider provide you with independently verifiable customer references? Are they willing to provide you with contact information for previous and/or existing customers?

I advise finding out the answers to all of these questions *before* your organization contracts with a cyber risk management services provider. Executing due diligence at the front end will help to ensure that the resulting engagement with a cyber risk management solutions provider will result in an ECRM program that optimizes risk management for your organization's unique vision, mission, strategy, values, and services and that advances your organization's strategic ECRM goals.

Enterprise Cyber Risk
Management Software (ECRMS)

The right software can simplify and facilitate the task of conducting enterprisewide risk analysis and cyber risk management. The wrong software—or worse, no cyber risk management software solution at all—makes it nearly impossible to establish, implement, and mature an effective ECRM program.

I've seen organizations try to use office software suites—word processors, presentation software, or spreadsheets—to try to establish, implement and mature an ECRM program. These solutions are typically dead-on-arrival, as by the time these generic tools have been customized enough to accept the data, and all of the data entered, they are no longer relevant. The data is outdated by the time the document is complete. Likewise, governance, risk management, and compliance (GRC) platforms are equally unsuited to ECRM. GRC platforms aren't architected to provide the conceptual infrastructure, address assets, threats, and vulnerabilities or drive risk management workflows needed to support an ECRM program.

As I've addressed in *Stop the Cyber Bleeding*, ECRM in the healthcare industry is complex and multi-layered. Risk analysis and risk management must not only protect your organization but must also align with HIPAA and meet the expectations of OCR and CMS, among others. It simply isn't possible to conduct and document an OCR-Quality® Risk Analysis and implement an ECRM program without an appropriate software solution in place. Trying to establish and manage an ECRM program without the appropriate software tool would be like to trying to use an Excel spreadsheet to track inpatient care at a hospital, instead of using an EHR. It just doesn't work.

There are a growing number of competing vendors offering software purported to simplify and document the tasks of risk analysis and risk management. These vendors include GRC vendors, who typically deliver an open platform on which you must build your own solution. To be clear, a platform—GRC or otherwise—means that your organization will be doing a lot of additional work, designing and 'programming' the solution, before the actual work of cyber risk analysis and cyber risk management can begin. Therefore, before you make a commitment to purchase a specific software package, it's important to exercise due diligence to ensure that the solution you choose will support compliance risk management *and* cyber risk management, out-of-the-box, and in a manner that protects your patients, protects your organization, and aligns with OCR's expectations.

A comprehensive ECRMS solution must include all of the components of an ECRM program in order to serve your organization. That means functionality that supports not only comprehensive risk analysis but also security assessments, compliance with the HIPAA Privacy, Security, and Breach Notification Rules, and adoption of the NIST Cybersecurity Framework. In addition, like any useful solution designed for enterprisewide use, the solution should be user-friendly, include accessible dashboards, offer actionable reporting capabilities, facilitate enterprisewide ECRM collaboration and provide for C-suite and board governance.

The following questions will help you evaluate whether the ECRMS solution you are considering is comprehensive enough to support your organization's ECRM program.

Risk Analysis Features and Functionality

As I emphasized throughout *Stop the Cyber Bleeding*, the only effective means of establishing an ECRM program is to take a risk-based approach. That means inventorying all of your organization's information assets (i.e., electronic healthcare data, systems, and devices, including all information assets used to create, receive, maintain, or transmit sensitive data, including ePHI). This typically involves categorizing tens or hundreds of thousands of information asset-components (e.g., from desktops, servers, and laptops to wireless IV infusion pumps, heart monitors, and insulin pumps) and then identifying and rating the specific risks associated with each asset-component category. As an example, an asset-component category might be laptops used by home health clinicians or wireless IV pumps used in post-op.

Important questions to ask about risk analysis features and functionality include:

1. Does the ECRMS solution facilitate establishment of your organization's risk appetite?

2. Does the ECRMS solution support enterprisewide risk analysis by offering:

a. The scalable capacity to inventory all ePHI assets and components across your enterprise?

b. The ability to associate specific, reasonably anticipated threats and vulnerabilities with each asset-component category? (Note that this functionality should include both pre-populated threats and vulnerabilities associated with particular assets as well as the ability to catalogue unique-to-your-organization threats and vulnerabilities.)

3. Does the ECRMS solution provide an enterprisewide view of top exposures?

4. Does the ECRMS solution provide the functionality to manage risk remediation at the individual asset or asset-component level?

5. Does the ECRMS solution facilitate ongoing, continuous ECRM work with version control?

Security Rule Assessment Features and Functionality

A good ECRM program includes compliance risk management as well as cyber risk management. In addition to comprehensive risk analysis, the HIPAA Security Rule also requires that organizations conduct periodic nontechnical evaluations of their compliance with the Security Rule.[iv] Your ECRMS solution should be able to support these nontechnical evaluations (sometimes referred to

---

iv   Evaluation Standard. 45 CFR §164.308(a)(8) (Security Standards for the Protection of Electronic Protected Health Information, Administrative Safeguards), *available at* https://www.ecfr.gov/cgi-bin/text-idx?SID=1d634f7427981e7ae8b181f7649bb85 9&node=45:1.0.1.3.78&rgn=div5#se45.2.164_1308

as compliance gap assessments) in a manner that aligns with the HIPAA Security Rule standards and implementation specifications.

6. Does the ECRMS solution enable you to assess your organization's compliance posture against *all* of the standards, implementation specifications, and requirements in the HIPAA Security Rule?

7. Does the ECRMS solution enable you to identify the gaps in your compliance with the HIPAA Security Rule standards, implementation specifications, and requirements?

8. Does the ECRMS solution enable you to manage remediation actions with respect to compliance with the HIPAA Security Rule?

Privacy and Breach Notification Rule Assessment Compliance Features and Functionality

HIPAA's Privacy and Breach Notification Rules are separate from the HIPAA Security Rule. Covered entities and business associates must also be compliant with the HIPAA Privacy Rule and Breach Notification Rule, which include different standards and implementation specifications which must be addressed. Your ECRM program should enable your organization to separately assess your compliance with the HIPAA Privacy and Breach Notification Rules in order to manage these compliance risks.

9. Does the ECRMS solution enable you to assess your organization's compliance posture with respect to the HIPAA Privacy and Breach Notification Rules?

10. Does the ECRMS solution enable you to identify the gaps in your compliance with the HIPAA Privacy and Breach Notification Rules?

11. Does the ECRMS solution enable you to manage remediation actions with respect to compliance with the HIPAA Privacy and Breach Notification Rules?

Cybersecurity Framework Support

For reasons that I outlined in Chapter 10, I highly recommend the adoption of the National Institute of Standards and Technology (NIST) Cybersecurity Framework. A comprehensive ECRMS solution should support your organization's efforts to adopt the NIST Cybersecurity Framework.

12. Does the ECRMS solution support the operationalization and adoption of the NIST Cybersecurity Framework?

13. Does the ECRMS solution incorporate all aspects of the structure and language of the NIST Cybersecurity Framework?

14. Does the ECRMS solution enable you to assess and document the current state of your organization's adoption of the NIST Cybersecurity Framework?

15. Does the ECRMS solution enable you to set your desired, future state of your organization's adoption of the NIST Cybersecurity Framework and assess the gaps?

16. Does the ECRMS solution enable you to define your specific goals with respect to NIST Cybersecurity Framework adoption (e.g., to set your desired tier, as articulated in the Framework)?

17. Does the ECRMS solution enable you to manage and document your progress toward your NIST Cybersecurity Framework adoption goals?

General Additional Features and Functionality

In addition to offering support for compliance risk management and cyber risk management, and supporting the adoption of a cybersecurity framework, your ECRMS solution should also enable efficient ECRM by offering the following features and functionality:

18. Does the ECRMS solution provider offer unlimited, complimentary training in the use of their solution?

19. Does the ECRMS solution offer accessible, user-friendly dashboards that provide actionable insight into:
    a. Your organization's progress on risk analysis?
    b. Your organization's most serious and likely threats?
    c. Your organization's most critical vulnerabilities?
    d. Your organization's control deficiencies?
    e. Your organization's real-time remediation/risk mitigation efforts?

20. Does the ECRMS solution offer dashboards and reporting functionality that supports leadership-level ECRM

governance and oversight (i.e., dashboards and reporting that provides information useful to C-suite executives and board members)?

21. Does the ECRMS solution offer dashboards and reporting functionality that supports tactical-level ECRM program activities (i.e., dashboards and reporting that provides information useful to other managers and professionals engaged in ECRM at the facility, division, or department level)?

22. Does the ECRMS solution include dashboards that feature:
    a. Configurable views?
    b. Configurable reporting capabilities?
    c. Real-time analytics capabilities?

23. Does the ECRMS solution facilitate enterprisewide collaboration via the following functionalities and workflow tools:
    a. The ability to assign tasks (e.g., control evaluations, risk mitigation action items, etc.)?
    b. The ability of users to view and update work performed toward the completion of assigned tasks?
    c. The ability of risk managers to monitor users' progress toward task completion via real-time reports?

24. (For large health systems) Does the ECRMS solution provide for cascading/inheritance of data capabilities,

so that parent entities can share information with child entities, thus reducing duplicative data entry and analysis?

A Word About Cloud-Based Software Solutions, Software-as-a-Service (SaaS)

Cloud-based software solutions (also known as Software-as-a-Service, or SaaS) offer many advantages over on-premise software systems. They typically entail a lower total cost of ownership (TCO), because organizations do not have to purchase and maintain the hardware to host them. ECRMS is particularly well suited to be a cloud-based solution. Using a cloud-based solution shortens implementation time—your organization can put the solution to work soon after signing a contract. Considering the urgency with which ECRM needs to be implemented, this is a plus. In addition, the cyber threat landscape is changing constantly. A cloud-based solution can be updated (with overall feature and functionality upgrades, as well as risk-related data and algorithms) regularly and automatically. For these reasons, a cloud-based, SaaS solution makes more sense for ECRMS.

25. Is the ECRMS solution offered as software-as-a-service (SaaS) to enable you to realize lower TCO, faster implementation and updates, anytime-anywhere access, and other SaaS benefits?

26. Is the ECRMS solution accessible through multiple browsers and devices?

Reputation

The software industry is replete with stories of so-called vapor-ware: software products that are billed as offering every feature and functionality your organization might desire. However, after implementation, it becomes clear that some of those claims were aspirational, and those features and functions aren't actually in place yet. That's why it is important to verify a vendor's reputation as part of the due diligence process.

27. Do your peers in the industry have any experience with the ECRMS solution you are considering? If so, was their experience a good one?

28. Has the specific ECRMS solution you are considering earned any significant industry recognition, endorsements, or awards?

29. How long has the ECRMS solution you are considering been on the market? Has it been used in industry long enough to have proven its value? Or is it a beta version, which may be riddled with unresolved problems?

30. Can the vendor provide you with independently verifiable customer references? Are they willing to provide you with contact information for previous and/or existing customers?

Customer Service

It is a truism that even the most carefully designed, so-called turnkey software solutions require more than the flip of a switch to be implemented effectively. This is especially true if you acquire a GRC platform. With a true out-of-the-box ECRMS solution, you will need excellent support but not a development team to create a solution. By now it should be clear that establishing an ECRM program requires much more than simply populating a database or ticking off boxes on a controls checklist. Therefore, it is important that your ECRMS solution vendor provides strong customer service support.

31. Is the vendor of the ECRMS solution well-known in the industry for customer satisfaction? What is the evidence? For example, has the vendor been recognized and rewarded by KLAS, Black Book, or other independent evaluators? If they have been so recognized, what kinds of customer comments have they garnered?

32. Does the ECRMS solution vendor have a formal customer feedback process and metrics established to track customer satisfaction with the product? For example, do they conduct annual or periodic surveys or reviews to collect customer feedback? How do they incorporate that feedback into their ECRM solution?

33. Sometimes an organization will determine that they require more than just customer services support for an ECRMS solution. If this is the case, it is important to know whether the vendor provides services above and beyond the provision of an ECRMS solution. For example, in addition to the software, does the vendor provide:

a. A documented methodology for implementing the ECRMS solution?

b. Consulting services to support the implementation of the solution?

c. Consulting services to assist your organization in actually conducting the risk analysis on your organization's behalf, conducting a security assessment, managing the adoption of the NIST Cybersecurity Framework, etc.?

The Benefits of Using an ECRMS Solution

With software solutions, the wrong tool or an inadequate tool is just as useless as no tool at all. Make sure you acquire a true *solution* and not just a vacant platform. Asking these questions listed above before you contract with an ECRMS solution provider will help ensure that you invest in a solution that provides the breadth of functionality you need to establish, implement, and mature an effective ERCM program across your organization.

The right ECRMS solution offers many benefits to your organization:

- Enables consistent cyber risk management across the entire enterprise, eliminating redundant, non-interoperable, and siloed tools that may have previously been used for risk management.

- Enables leadership to make informed decisions about where to deploy controls to achieve the best outcomes. Because these decisions are based on accurate information about where risks exist, and the likelihood and impact of those risks, it helps your organization with the cost-efficient application of limited ECRM resources.

- Enables leadership to make informed risk treatment decisions (e.g., accept, avoid, mitigate, or transfer) based upon real-time information about your organization's unique information assets, risks to those assets, priorities, gaps, and your organization's risk appetite.

- Promotes cross-functional risk management collaboration across all stakeholders, by providing a "single source of truth" for enterprisewide risk management efforts.

- Provides ECRM documentation for auditors, such as your outside audit firm, OCR, or CMS.

- Provides ECRM documentation for insurers, which may result in lower insurance premiums (see Chapter 8).

- Provides ECRM documentation for credit-rating agencies, which may improve your credit ratings and lower your cost of capital (see Chapter 8).

The right ECRMS solution can facilitate the establishment, implementation, and maturation of your organization's ECRM program. But beyond that, the right ECRMS solution can also enhance the results of your organization's ECRM efforts by making it easier to make more informed, strategic decisions about ECRM investments; increasing efficiency; and enabling ECRM efforts across your organization to work toward the achievement of the same, strategic ECRM goals.

For more information, please visit the *Stop the Cyber Bleeding* resource page at https://www.clearwatercompliance.com/stopthecyberbleeding.

Acknowledgments

First, I would like to thank our Clearwater customers for all their great feedback that enabled us to continuously improve our solutions and make our value proposition stronger. We built our solutions around your compliance and cyber risk management challenges, goals, and objectives.

Without the opportunity to work with my brilliant leadership team at Clearwater since 2010, this book would not have been possible. They afforded me the opportunity to be challenged, to think, to teach, to deliver services, and to write on the subject of enterprise cyber risk management, about which I remain deeply passionate. I extend my special thanks to Mary Chaput, our CFO, fellow consultant, and my dear spouse; to Kathy Ebbert, our totally-keep-the-trains-running-on-time COO; to Jon Stone, our Product Innovation leader for his creativity and energy to bring the vision of Clearwater to life; and, last but not least, to Dan Pruyn for his tireless work assisting our customers in understanding their challenges, our solutions and value proposition, and, ultimately, engaging Clearwater to assist them.

Finally, I wish to thank the team at Altaris Capital Partners for allowing me to have the time to write this book.

About the Author

Bob Chaput is a leading authority on healthcare compliance, cybersecurity, and enterprise cyber risk management. He is passionate about helping healthcare organizations and their business associates safeguard protected health information and patient health through the establishment of strong, proactive privacy and cyber risk management programs.

Chaput is the Founder and Executive Chairman of Clearwater, an award-winning provider of healthcare compliance and cyber risk management solutions. Chaput has worked with board members and C-suite executives at dozens of healthcare organizations, including Fortune 100 organizations and agencies within the federal government.

In addition to his work on behalf of Clearwater clients, Chaput is dedicated to providing education about cyber risk management to healthcare industry leaders through articles, presentations, and webinars. He was a contributing author to two books: Wolters Kluwer's *Health Law and Compliance Update* and the American Society of Healthcare Risk Management (ASHRM)'s *Health Care Risk Management Fundamentals*. His insights about cyber risk management have also been published in dozens of periodicals, including *Modern Healthcare*, *CISO Mag*, the Health Care Compliance Association's *Compliance*

Today, *HealthITSecurity*, *HealthcareInfoSecurity* (Information Security Media Group), and *The Wall Street Journal (WSJ) Pro Cybersecurity*.

Chaput has given presentations on the topic of cybersecurity and cyber risk management at the National HIPAA Summit, the Health Care Compliance Association (HCCA) Managed Care Compliance Conference, HCCA's Healthcare Enforcement Compliance Conference, the Association of Healthcare Internal Auditors' (AHIAs') Annual Conference, the College of Health Information Management Executives (CHIME) CIO Summit, the Association of Executives in Healthcare Information Security (AEHIS) Annual Conference, and for the American Hospital Association (AHA).

Beyond his more-than 35 years of experience in the field, Chaput also holds numerous risk management, privacy, and security professional certifications, including: Certified Information Systems Security Professional (CISSP), Health Care Information Security and Privacy Practitioner (HCISPP), Certified in Risk Information Security Controls (CRISC), Certified Information Privacy Professional/US (CIPP/US), Certified Ethical Hacker (C|EH) and NACD CERT Certificate in Cybersecurity Oversight.

Chaput served on the HealthCare's Most Wired™ Survey Governance Board and as a board member of the Association of Executives in Healthcare Information Security (AEHIS). He is also a member of the National Association of Corporate Directors (NACD), the American College of Healthcare Executives (ACHE), the College of Healthcare Information Management Executives (CHIME), the Healthcare Information and Management Systems Society (HIMSS), the Health Care Compliance Association (HCCA), (ISC)², ISACA, and ISSA.

About Clearwater

Clearwater is the leading provider of Enterprise Cyber Risk Management and HIPAA compliance software and consulting services for the healthcare industry. Clearwater's solutions enable organizations to gain enterprisewide visibility into cybersecurity risks and more effectively prioritize and manage those risks. By helping organizations improve their security postures, Clearwater helps organizations ensure compliance with industry regulations, as well as protect the privacy and security of patient data.

Today, with more than 400 customers using Clearwater's software and services, Clearwater has become the Gold Standard in healthcare cyber risk management and HIPAA compliance solutions. The foundation of these solutions is Clearwater's IRM|Pro®, an Enterprise Cyber Risk Management Software (ECRMS) that facilitates a NIST-based risk management process. When IRM|Pro® is combined with Clearwater's wide range of consulting services and the company's proven methodology, organizations gain an effective and scalable approach to developing and maturing their cyber risk management programs.

Clearwater's customers include more than 70 of the nation's largest health systems and integrated delivery networks (IDNs), as well as leading law firms, medical device manufacturers, private equity firms, and other companies that work with or within the healthcare industry.

Clearwater's award-winning cyber risk and compliance solutions have been voted Best in KLAS for Cybersecurity Advisory Services in 2018 by its customers, and have received a top rating for Compliance and Risk Management Solutions in Black Book for three years in a row: 2017, 2018, and 2019.

For more information about Clearwater, please visit https:// clearwatercompliance.com/.

Notes

CHAPTER 1: *When Something "Cyber" Happens*

1. Yisroel Mirsky, Tom Mahler, Ilan Shelef and Yuval Elovici. "CT-GAN: Malicious tampering of 3D medical imagery using deep learning." 28th USENIX Security Symposium (USENIX Security 19), 461–478. 2019. Accessed July 25, 2019. https://arxiv.org/abs/1901.03597 See the video demonstration at: https://www.youtube.com/watch?v=_mkRAArj-x0&feature=youtu.be

2. Kim Zetter. "Hospital viruses: Fake cancerous nodes in CT scans, created by malware, trick radiologists." *The Washington Post.* April 3, 2019. Accessed July 25, 2019 https://www.washingtonpost.com/technology/2019/04/03/hospital-viruses-fake-cancerous-nodes-ct-scans-created-by-malware-trick-radiologists/?utm_term=.8baffe081d2b

3. 2019 Data Security Incident Response Report. BakerHostetler. Accessed July 25, 2019 http://e.bakerlaw.com/rv/ff00498db267a11ce4182d53934889997a36f6d4/p=8213342

4. Jaliz Maldonado. "The biggest data breach of 2017 and why it matters to even the smallest law firms." *The National Law Review.* March 20, 2018. Accessed July 26, 2019. https://www.natlawreview.com/article/biggest-data-breach-2017-and-why-it-matters-to-even-smallest-law-firms

5. "What is medical malpractice?" American Board of Professional Liability Attorneys (ABPLA). Accessed July 27, 2019. https://www.abpla.org/what-is-malpractice

6. "Negligence". *Wex Legal Dictionary and Encyclopedia*. Legal Information Institute (LII). Cornell Law School. Accessed July 27, 2019. https://www.law.cornell.edu/wex/negligence

7. "What is medical malpractice?" American Board of Professional Liability Attorneys (ABPLA). Accessed July 27, 2019. https://www.abpla.org/what-is-malpractice

8. Gerald and Kathleen Hill. "fiduciary" definition. *The People's Law Dictionary*. Fine Communications. Accessed July 27, 2019. https://dictionary.law.com/Default.aspx?typed=fiduciary&type=1

9. Larry Walker. "The board's fiduciary responsibility: Putting the community's trust into action." *Board Brief.* The Walker Company Health Care Consulting. October 3, 2008. Accessed July 28, 2019. https://www.mnhospitals.org/Portals/0/Documents/Trustees/briefs-resources/board-fiduciary-responsibility.pdf

10. Larry Walker. "The board's fiduciary responsibility: Putting the community's trust into action." *Board Brief.* The Walker Company Health Care Consulting. October 3, 2008. Accessed July 28, 2019. https://www.mnhospitals.org/Portals/0/Documents/Trustees/briefs-resources/board-fiduciary-responsibility.pdf

11. Gerald and Kathleen Hill. "Duty of care" definition. *The People's Law Dictionary*. Fine Communications. Accessed July 27, 2019. https://dictionary.law.com/Default.aspx?typed=duty%20of%20care&type=1

12. Kevin McCoy. "Target to pay $18.5M for 2013 data breach that affected 41 million consumers." *USA Today*. May 23, 2017. Accessed July 28, 2019. https://www.usatoday.com/story/money/2017/05/23/target-pay-185m-2013-data-breach-affected-consumers/102063932/

13. Craig Newman. "Lessons from the war over the Target data breach." *NACD Board Talk*. July 27, 2016. Accessed July 29, 2019. https://blog.nacdonline.org/posts/lessons-from-the-war-over-the-target-data-breach

14. Craig Newman. "Lessons from the war over the Target data breach." *NACD Board Talk*. July 27, 2016. Accessed July 29, 2019. https://blog.nacdonline.org/posts/lessons-from-the-war-over-the-target-data-breach

15. Freya K. Bowen. "Recent developments in Yahoo and Equifax data breach litigation suggest increased risk of personal liability for directors and officers for cybersecurity incidents." *Perkins Coie Tech Risk Report*. February 6, 2019. Accessed July 29, 2019. https://www.techriskreport.com/2019/02/recent-developments-yahoo-equifax-data-breach-litigation-suggest-increased-risk-personal-liability-directors-officers-cybersecurity-incidents/

16. Freya K. Bowen. "Recent developments in Yahoo and Equifax data breach litigation suggest increased risk of personal liability for directors and officers for cybersecurity incidents." *Perkins Coie Tech Risk Report*. February 6, 2019. Accessed July 29, 2019. https://www.techriskreport.com/2019/02/recent-developments-yahoo-equifax-data-breach-litigation-suggest-increased-risk-personal-liability-directors-officers-cybersecurity-incidents/

17. "Equifax to pay $575 million as part of settlement with FTC, CFPB, and States related to 2017 data breach." Federal Trade Commission. July 22, 2019. Accessed July 29, 2019. https://www.ftc.gov/news-events/press-releases/2019/07/equifax-pay-575-million-part-settlement-ftc-cfpb-states-related

18. Freya K. Bowen. "Recent developments in Yahoo and Equifax data breach litigation suggest increased risk of personal liability for directors and officers for cybersecurity incidents." *Perkins Coie Tech Risk Report*. February 6, 2019. Accessed July 29, 2019. https://www.techriskreport.com/2019/02/recent-developments-yahoo-equifax-data-breach-litigation-suggest-increased-risk-personal-liability-directors-officers-cybersecurity-incidents/

19. Freya K. Bowen. "Recent developments in Yahoo and Equifax data breach litigation suggest increased risk of personal liability

for directors and officers for cybersecurity incidents." *Perkins Coie Tech Risk Report*. February 6, 2019. Accessed July 29, 2019. https://www.techriskreport.com/2019/02/recent-developments-ya-hoo-equifax-data-breach-litigation-suggest-increased-risk-person-al-liability-directors-officers-cybersecurity-incidents/

20. 45 CFR § 160.103 https://www.ecfr.gov/cgi-bin/text-idx-?SID=2db3954737dfe4336ece42185b0d17d7&mc=true&node=se45.2.160_1103&rgn=div8

21. 45 CFR § 160.401 https://www.ecfr.gov/cgi-bin/text-idx-?SID=2db3954737dfe4336ece42185b0d17d7&mc=true&node=se45.2.160_1401&rgn=div8

Chapter 2: *Your Organization's Top Challenges (And How ECRM Can Help)*

1. Ginni Rommety, quoted in "Phrases to help us think about cyber attacks." The Cyber Rescue Alliance. Accessed September 18, 2019. https://www.cyberrescue.co.uk/library/quotes

2. National Health Expenditure Projections 2018–2027, Forecast Summary. Centers for Medicare & Medicaid Services. CMS. gov. 2019. Accessed August 9, 2019. https://www.cms.gov/Research-Statistics-Data-and-Systems/Statistics-Trends-and-Reports/NationalHealthExpendData/Downloads/ForecastSummary.pdf

3. Kelly Gooch. "The 10 most concerning issues for hospital CEOs in 2018." *Becker's Hospital CFO Report*. January 28, 2019. Accessed August 9, 2019. https://www.beckershospitalreview.com/finance/no-1-community-hospital-ceo-worry-in-2018-money.html

4. Derek Thomson. "Health care just became the U.S.'s largest employer." *The Atlantic*. January 9, 2018. Accessed August 8, 2019. https://www.theatlantic.com/business/archive/2018/01/health-care-america-jobs/550079/

5. Unemployment Rate. Labor Force Statistics from the Current Population Survey. Bureau of Labor Statistics, United States Department of Labor. Accessed September 8, 2020. https://data.bls.gov/timeseries/LNS14000000

6. Martha Gimbel and Tara Sinclair. "Larger skills gap in healthcare than in overall economy." Indeed Hiring Lab. March 20, 2019. Accessed August 8, 2019. https://www.hiringlab.org/2019/03/20/healthcare-skills-gap/

7. "Trends in hospital inpatient drug costs: Issues and challenges." American Hospital Association. October 11, 2016. Accessed August 8, 2019. https://www.aha.org/system/files/2018-01/aha-fah-rx-report.pdf

8. Maria Clemens. "Technology and rising health care costs." *Forbes*. October 26, 2017. Accessed August 8, 2019. https://www.forbes.com/sites/forbestechcouncil/2017/10/26/technology-and-rising-health-care-costs/#700ed748766b

9. Jeff Lagasse. "EHR investments slowing down as hospitals cite high costs, study finds." *HealthcareFinance*. September 10, 2018. Accessed August 8, 2019. https://www.healthcarefinancenews.com/news/ehr-investments-slowing-down-hospitals-cite-high-costs-study-finds

10. HHS Press Office. "OCR concludes all-time record year for HIPAA enforcement with $3 million Cottage Health settlement." February 7, 2019. HHS.gov. Accessed August 9, 2019. https://www.hhs.gov/about/news/2019/02/07/ocr-concludes-all-time-record-year-for-hipaa-enforcement-with-3-million-cottage-health-settlement.html

11. HHS Press Office. "Tennessee diagnostic medical imaging services company pays $3,000,000 to settle breach exposing over 300,000 patients' protected health information." May 6, 2019. Accessed August 28, 2019. https://www.hhs.gov/about/

news/2019/05/06/tennessee-diagnostic-medical-imaging-services-company-pays-3000000-settle-breach.html

12. HHS Press Office. "Tennessee diagnostic medical imaging services company pays $3,000,000 to settle breach exposing over 300,000 patients' protected health information." May 6, 2019. Accessed August 28, 2019. https://www.hhs.gov/about/news/2019/05/06/tennessee-diagnostic-medical-imaging-services-company-pays-3000000-settle-breach.html

13. Clearwater analysis of data publicly available at: Resolution Agreements and Civil Money Penalties. Health Information Privacy. U.S. Department of Health and Human Services. (n.d.) Accessed April 20, 2020. https://www.hhs.gov/hipaa/for-professionals/compliance-enforcement/agreements/index.html

14. Clearwater analysis of data publicly available at: Resolution Agreements and Civil Money Penalties. Health Information Privacy. U.S. Department of Health and Human Services. (n.d.) Accessed April 20, 2020. https://www.hhs.gov/hipaa/for-professionals/compliance-enforcement/agreements/index.html

15. "State of the industry." *Managed Healthcare Executive.* December 10, 2018. Accessed August 9, 2019. https://www.managedhealthcareexecutive.com/state-industry/managed-care-state-industry-2018

16. Kelly Gooch. "The 10 most concerning issues for hospital CEOs in 2018." *Becker's Hospital CFO Report.* January 28, 2019. Accessed August 9, 2019. https://www.beckershospitalreview.com/finance/no-1-community-hospital-ceo-worry-in-2018-money.html

17. "Top issues confronting hospitals in 2018." American College of Healthcare Executives. January 25, 2019. Accessed August 10, 2019. https://www.ache.org/about-ache/news-and-awards/news-releases/top-issues-confronting-hospitals-in-2018

18. Guide to the GDPR Regulations & Compliance. GPPREU.Org. Accessed September 4, 2020. https://www.gdpreu.org/

19. Una A. Dean and Melis S. Kiziltay Carter. "New guidelines on GDPR's territorial scope confirm it reaches far beyond the EU." *New York Law Journal*. March 1, 2019. Accessed August 12, 2019. https://www.law.com/newyorklawjournal/2019/03/01/new-guidelines-on-gdprs-territorial-scope-confirm-it-reaches-far-beyond-the-eu/?slreturn=20190719160336

20. Adam Satariano. "Google is fined $57 million under Europe's data privacy law." *The New York Times*. January 21, 2019. Accessed August 11, 2019. https://www.nytimes.com/2019/01/21/technology/google-europe-gdpr-fine.html

21. Kate Fazzini. "Europe's huge privacy fines against Marriott and British Airways are a warning for Google and Facebook." *CNBC*. July 10, 2019. Accessed August 11, 2019. https://www.cnbc.com/2019/07/10/gdpr-fines-vs-marriott-british-air-are-a-warning-for-google-facebook.html

22. Kate Fazzini. "Europe's huge privacy fines against Marriott and British Airways are a warning for Google and Facebook." *CNBC*. July 10, 2019. Accessed August 11, 2019. https://www.cnbc.com/2019/07/10/gdpr-fines-vs-marriott-british-air-are-a-warning-for-google-facebook.html; and Mythbusting: General Data Protection Regulations (GDPR) Fact Sheet. European Commission. January 2019. Accessed August 23, 2019. https://ec.europa.eu/info/sites/info/files/100124_gdpr_factsheet_mythbusting.pdf

23. Definitive Healthcare Releases Results of 2019 Annual Healthcare Trends Survey. April 22, 2019. Accessed August 13, 2019. https://blog.definitivehc.com/news/healthcare-trends-survey-2019

24. Keith Anderson, Robert Belfort, Fatema Zanzi. "What marketplace and regulatory drivers are transforming healthcare M&A?" Manatt, Phelps & Phillips, LLP. March 22, 2019. Accessed August 12, 2019. https://www.jdsupra.com/legalnews/webinar-what-marketplace-and-regulatory-23997/

25. Keith Anderson, Robert Belfort, Fatema Zanzi. "Mapping the healthcare M&A landscape." Manatt, Phelps & Phillips, LLP. March 22, 2019. Accessed August 12, 2019. https://www.jdsupra.com/legalnews/mapping-the-healthcare-m-a-landscape-21018/

26. "M&A professionals bullish on healthcare deals for next year, despite political uncertainty concerns." *Merrill Insight*™ Poll. Merrill Corporation. May 22, 2019. Accessed August 16, 2019. https://www.merrillcorp.com/us/en/company/news/press-releases/health-care-it-is-biggest-m-a-investment-opportunity-in--healthca.html

27. "M&A professionals bullish on healthcare deals for next year, despite political uncertainty concerns." *Merrill Insight*™ Poll. Merrill Corporation. May 22, 2019. Accessed August 16, 2019. https://www.merrillcorp.com/us/en/company/news/press-releases/healthcare-it-is-biggest-m-a-investment-opportunity-in--healthca.html

28. Mike Snider. "Verizon shaves $350 million from Yahoo price." *USA Today*. Accessed August 16, 2019. https://www.usatoday.com/story/tech/news/2017/02/21/verizon-shaves-350-million-yahoo-price/98188452/

29. Mike Snider. "Verizon shaves $350 million from Yahoo price." *USA Today*. Accessed August 16, 2019. https://www.usatoday.com/story/tech/news/2017/02/21/verizon-shaves-350-million-yahoo-price/98188452/

30. Avi Salzman. "Electronic health records are becoming a hot investment play—again." *Barron's*. May 17, 2019. Accessed August 16, 2019. https://www.barrons.com/articles/electronic-health-records-investing-51558130302

31. Avi Salzman. "Electronic health records are becoming a hot investment play—again." *Barron's*. May 17, 2019. Accessed August 16, 2019. https://www.barrons.com/articles/electronic-health-records-investing-51558130302

32. "Apple announces effortless solution bringing health records to iPhone." Apple, Inc. January 24, 2018. https://www.apple.com/newsroom/2018/01/apple-announces-effortless-solution-bringing-health-records-to-iPhone/

33. "Apple announces effortless solution bringing health records to iPhone." Apple, Inc. January 24, 2018. https://www.apple.com/newsroom/2018/01/apple-announces-effortless-solution-bringing-health-records-to-iPhone/

34. "A more personal Health app. For a more informed you." Apple.com. September 4, 2020. Accessed September 4, 2020. https://www.apple.com/ios/health/

35. "Institutions that support health records on iPhone and iPod touch (beta)." Apple.com. August 19, 2019. Accessed August 19, 2019. https://support.apple.com/en-us/HT208647

36. "The new health economy in the age of disruption." PwC Health Research Institute. April 2018. Accessed August 16, 2019. https://www.pwc.com/us/en/health-industries/health-research-institute/pdf/pwc-hri-the-new-health-economy-in-the-age-of-disruption.pdf

37. "The new health economy in the age of disruption." PwC Health Research Institute. April 2018. Accessed August 16, 2019. https://www.pwc.com/us/en/health-industries/health-research-institute/pdf/pwc-hri-the-new-health-economy-in-the-age-of-disruption.pdf

38. "The new health economy in the age of disruption." PwC Health Research Institute. April 2018. Accessed August 16, 2019. https://www.pwc.com/us/en/health-industries/health-research-institute/pdf/pwc-hri-the-new-health-economy-in-the-age-of-disruption.pdf

39. Haven. Vision. Accessed August 19, 2019. https://havenhealthcare.com/vision

40. Haven. Vision. Accessed August 19, 2019. https://havenhealthcare. com/vision

41. Sean Day and Megan Zweig. "Beyond wellness for the healthy: Digital health consumer adoption 2018." Rock Health. 2019. Accessed August 18, 2019. https://rockhealth.com/reports/beyond-wellness-for-the-healthy-digital-health-consumer-adoption-2018/

42. Sean Day and Megan Zweig. "Beyond wellness for the healthy: Digital health consumer adoption 2018." Rock Health. 2019. Accessed August 18, 2019. https://rockhealth.com/reports/beyond-wellness-for-the-healthy-digital-health-consumer-adoption-2018/

43. Sean Day and Megan Zweig. "Beyond wellness for the healthy: Digital health consumer adoption 2018." Rock Health. 2019. Accessed August 18, 2019. https://rockhealth.com/reports/beyond-wellness-for-the-healthy-digital-health-consumer-adoption-2018/

44. Samina T Syed, Ben S. Gerber and Lisa K. Sharp. "Traveling towards disease: transportation barriers to health care access." *Journal of Community Health.* Vol. 38, 5 (2013): 976–93. doi:10.1007/s10900–013–9681–1 Accessed August 18, 2019. https://www.ncbi.nlm.nih.gov/pmc/articles/PMC4265215/

45. Ayoub Aouad. "We spoke with the head of Uber Health about how his team built a healthcare organization within a $70 billion tech company". *Business Insider.* August 6, 2019. Accessed August 18, 2019. https://www.businessinsider.com/dan-trigub-uber-health-head-exclusive-interview-2019-8

46. "Built with compliance." UberHealth. Accessed August 18, 2019. https://clearwatercompliance.com/wp-content/uploads/2018/03/Uber_OnePager_safety_SM.pdf

47. Morgan Haefner. "Uber Health chief: With 1,000+ partners, the question is no longer, 'What the heck is Uber doing in healthcare?'" *Becker's Hospital Review.* June 24, 2019. Accessed August 18, 2019. https://www.beckershospitalreview.com/

hospital-management-administration/uber-health-chief-with-1-000-partners-the-question-is-no-longer-what-the-heck-is-uber-doing-in-healthcare.html

48. Farhana Jabeen, Zara Hamid, Adnan Akhunzada, Wadood Abdul and Sanaa Ghouzali. "Trust and reputation management in healthcare systems: Taxonomy, requirements and open issues," in *IEEE Access*, vol. 6, pp. 17246–17263, 2018. doi: 10.1109/ACCESS.2018.2810337 Accessed August 19, 2019. https://ieeexplore.ieee.org/abstract/document/8308716

49. "2019 Healthcare Reputation Report." Reputation.com. 2019. Accessed August 19, 2019. https://d24wdr9t5wf9v7.cloudfront.net/wp-content/uploads/2019/03/2019_Healthcare_Reputation_Report.pdf?x48973

50. "Confidence in institutions." Gallup. 2019. Accessed August 19, 2019. https://news.gallup.com/poll/1597/confidence-institutions.aspx

51. "Confidence in institutions." Gallup. 2019. Accessed August 19, 2019. https://news.gallup.com/poll/1597/confidence-institutions.aspx

52. "Confidence in institutions." Gallup. 2019. Accessed August 19, 2019. https://news.gallup.com/poll/1597/confidence-institutions.aspx

53. "Take a data-centric approach to data protection and privacy." *Forrester Opportunity Snapshot: A Custom Study Commissioned by Virtru*. January 2019. Accessed August 19, 2019. https://inx-mad4bw31barrx17wec71c-wpengine.netdna-ssl.com/wp-content/uploads/2019/01/Virtru-2018-state-of-data-centric-security-and-privacy.pdf

54. 45 CFR §§ 164.400–414

55. James Berman. "The three essential Warren Buffett quotes to live by." *Forbes*. April 20, 2014. Accessed August 19, 2019. https://www.forbes.com/sites/jamesberman/2014/04/20/the-three-essential-warren-buffett-quotes-to-live-by/#6e3c79486543

56. Consumer Intelligence Series: Protect.me. PwC. 2017. Accessed August 19, 2019. https://www.pwc.com/us/en/services/consulting/library/consumer-intelligence-series/cybersecurity-protect-me.html

57. Consumer Intelligence Series: Protect.me. PwC. 2017. Accessed August 19, 2019. https://www.pwc.com/us/en/advisory-services/publications/consumer-intelligence-series/protect-me/cis-protect-me-findings.pdf

Chapter 3: *The Healthcare Cyber Risk Problem*

1. Healthcare Cybersecurity Quotes. GoodReads. (n.d.) Accessed August 31, 2019. https://www.goodreads.com/quotes/tag/healthcare-cybersecurity

2. Health Care Systems and Medical Devices at Risk for Increased Cyber Intrusions for Financial Gain. Private Industry Notification (PIN) #: 140408–009. FBI Cyber Division. April 8, 2014. Accessed August 31, 2019. https://info.publicintelligence.net/FBI-HealthCareCyberIntrusions.pdf

3. Health Care Systems and Medical Devices at Risk for Increased Cyber Intrusions for Financial Gain. Private Industry Notification (PIN) #: 140408–009. FBI Cyber Division. April 8, 2014. Accessed August 31, 2019. https://info.publicintelligence.net/FBI-HealthCareCyberIntrusions.pdf

4. "Hackers attack every 39 seconds." *Security Magazine.* February 10, 2017. Accessed September 1, 2019. https://www.securitymagazine.com/articles/87787-hackers-attack-every-39-seconds

5. "The trust factor: Cybersecurity's role in sustaining business momentum." *2018–2019 Global Application and Network Security Report.* Accessed September 3, 2019. https://www.radware.com/2018-ert-report-lpc-64459

6. "The trust factor: Cybersecurity's role in sustaining business momentum." *2018–2019 Global Application and Network Security*

Report. Accessed September 3, 2019. https://www.radware.com/2018-ert-report-lpc-64459

7. Henry L. Davis. "How ECMC got hacked by cyber extortionists — and how it's recovering." Updated May 22, 2017. Accessed February 18, 2020. https://buffalonews.com/2017/05/20/ecmc-got-hacked-cyber-extortionists/

8. Henry L. Davis. "ECMC spent nearly $10 million recovering from massive cyberattack." Updated July 26, 2017. Accessed February 18, 2020. https://buffalonews.com/2017/07/26/cost-ecmc-ransomware-incident-near-10-million/

9. "$10 Million Cyber Attack Hits New York Hospital". February 13, 2018. Accessed February 18, 2020. https://www.mdsny.com/ten-million-cyber-attack-hits-new-york-hospital/

10. "Collections firm behind LabCorp, Quest breaches files for bankruptcy." *Krebs on Security*. June 19, 2019. Accessed September 1, 2019. https://krebsonsecurity.com/2019/06/collections-firm-behind-labcorp-quest-breaches-files-for-bankruptcy/

11. "Collections firm behind LabCorp, Quest breaches files for bankruptcy." *Krebs on Security*. June 19, 2019. Accessed September 1, 2019. https://krebsonsecurity.com/2019/06/collections-firm-behind-labcorp-quest-breaches-files-for-bankruptcy/

12. Jessica Davis. "The 10 biggest healthcare data breaches of 2019, so far." *Health IT Security*. June 23, 2019. Accessed September 2, 2019. https://healthitsecurity.com/news/the-10-biggest-healthcare-data-breaches-of-2019-so-far

13. Jessica Davis. "The 10 biggest healthcare data breaches of 2019, so far." *Health IT Security*. June 23, 2019. Accessed September 2, 2019. https://healthitsecurity.com/news/the-10-biggest-healthcare-data-breaches-of-2019-so-far

14. Breach Portal. Office for Civil Rights (OCR). U.S. Department of Health and Human Services. Data pulled July 1, 2019. Accessed July 1, 2019. https://ocrportal.hhs.gov/ocr/breach/breach_report.jsf

15. "Non-federal acute care hospital electronic health record adoption." The Office of the National Coordinator for Health Information Technology. *Health IT Dashboard.* 2017. Accessed September 2, 2019. https://dashboard.healthit.gov/quickstats/pages/FIG-Hospital-EHR-Adoption.php

16. Fred Donovan. "Organizations see 878% health data growth rate since 2016." *HIT Infrastructure.* May 8, 2019. Accessed September 2, 2019. https://hitinfrastructure.com/news/organizations-see-878-health-data-growth-rate-since-2016

17. Brady Gavin. "How big are gigabytes, terabytes, and petabytes?" *How-To Geek.* May 25, 2018. Accessed September 1, 2019. https://www.howtogeek.com/353116/how-big-are-gigabytes-terabytes-and-petabytes/

18. Fred Donovan. "Organizations see 878% health data growth rate since 2016." *HIT Infrastructure.* May 8, 2019. Accessed September 2, 2019. https://hitinfrastructure.com/news/organizations-see-878-health-data-growth-rate-since-2016

19. Keith D. Foote. "A brief history of the internet of things." *Dataversity.* August 16, 2016. Accessed September 2, 2019.https://www.dataversity.net/brief-history-internet-things/

20. Jessica Kim Cohen. "How is IoT used in healthcare: 7 statistics." *Becker's Health IT & CIO Report.* March 1, 2017. Accessed September 1, 2019. https://www.beckershospitalreview.com/healthcare-information-technology/how-is-iot-used-in-healthcare-7-statistics.html

21. Bernard Marr. "Why the Internet of Medical Things (IoMT) will start to transform healthcare in 2018." *Forbes.* January 25, 2018. Accessed September 2, 2019. https://www.forbes.com/sites/

bernardmarr/2018/01/25/why-the-internet-of-medical-things-iomt-will-start-to-transform-healthcare-in-2018/#3e9125284a3c

22. Jessica Kim Cohen. "How is IoT used in healthcare: 7 statistics." *Becker's Health IT & CIO Report.* March 1, 2017. Accessed September 1, 2019. https://www.beckershospitalreview.com/healthcare-information-technology/how-is-iot-used-in-healthcare-7-statistics.html

23. Bernardo Bátiz-Lazo. "A brief history of the ATM." *The Atlantic.* March 26, 2015. Accessed September 1, 2019. https://www.theatlantic.com/technology/archive/2015/03/a-brief-history-of-the-atm/388547/

24. Report on Improving Cybersecurity in the Health Care Industry. Health Care Industry Cybersecurity Task Force. June 2017. Accessed August 31, 2019. https://www.phe.gov/Preparedness/planning/CyberTF/Documents/report2017.pdf

25. Report on Improving Cybersecurity in the Health Care Industry. Health Care Industry Cybersecurity Task Force. June 2017. Accessed August 31, 2019. https://www.phe.gov/Preparedness/planning/CyberTF/Documents/report2017.pdf

26. David DeMille. "Will your house be broken into this year?" *A Secure Life.* January 31, 2019. Accessed September 1, 2019. https://www.asecurelife.com/burglary-statistics/

27. David DeMille. "Will your house be broken into this year?" *A Secure Life.* January 31, 2019. Accessed September 1, 2019. https://www.asecurelife.com/burglary-statistics/

28. David DeMille. "Will your house be broken into this year?" *A Secure Life.* January 31, 2019. Accessed September 1, 2019. https://www.asecurelife.com/burglary-statistics/

29. Taylor & Francis. "Risk of crime in gated communities." *ScienceDaily.* March 20, 2013. Accessed September 2, 2019. www.sciencedaily.com/releases/2013/03/130320115113.htm

30. 45 CFR § 164.306(a)(1).

31. "Report on improving cybersecurity in the health care industry." Health Care Industry Cybersecurity Task Force. June 2017. Accessed August 31, 2019. https://www.phe.gov/Preparedness/planning/CyberTF/Documents/report2017.pdf

32. EY Global Information Security Survey (GISS) 2018–19. Accessed September 3, 2019. https://www.ey.com/en_gl/consulting/global-information-security-survey-2018-2019

33. "Burglars using skylights to break into Valley Homes." *ABC15 Arizona*. July 23, 2014. Accessed August 31, 2019. https://www.youtube.com/watch?v=zyD_jLLbf80

34. Marianne Kolbasuk McGee. "HIPAA enforcer reveals audit timeline." *Healthcare Information Security*. December 14, 2012. Accessed September 2, 2019. http://www.healthcareinfosecurity.com/interviews/hipaa-enforcer-reveals-audit-timeline-i-1736

Chapter 4: *The Unique Challenges of Conducting Enterprise Cyber Risk Management*

1. Dennis Chesley, quoted in "Phrases to help us think about cyber attacks." The Cyber Rescue Alliance. Accessed September 15, 2019. https://www.cyberrescue.co.uk/library/quotes

2. HIPAA History. HIPAA Journal. (n.d.) Accessed September 15, 2019. https://www.hipaajournal.com/hipaa-history/

3. HIPAA History. HIPAA Journal. (n.d.) Accessed September 15, 2019. https://www.hipaajournal.com/hipaa-history/

4. Jessica Davis. "7 largest data breaches of 2015." *HealthcareITNews*. December 11, 2015. Accessed September 15, 2019. https://www.healthcareitnews.com/news/7-largest-data-breaches-2015

5. Elinor Mills. "Researcher battles insulin pump maker over security flaw." *CNET*. August 26, 2011. Accessed

September 15, 2019. https://www.cnet.com/news/ researcher-battles-insulin-pump-maker-over-security-flaw/

6. Peter Jaret. "Exposing vulnerabilities: How hackers could target your medical devices." *AAMC News.* November 13, 2018. Accessed September 15, 2019. https://news.aamc.org/patient-care/article/ exposing-vulnerabilities-how-hackers-could-target/

7. Omnibus Final Rule, 78 Fed. Reg. 5566 (Jan. 25, 2013).

8. 45 CFR § 164.514

9. 45 CFR § 160.103

10. USA: Data Protection 2019. International Comparative Legal Guides (ICLG); Global Legal Group (GLG). Accessed September 18, 2019. https://iclg.com/practice-areas/data-protection-laws-and-regulations/ usa

11. Caleb Skeath and Brooke Kahn. State Data Breach Notification Laws: 2018 in Review. Inside Privacy from Covington & Burling, LLP. December 31, 2018. Accessed September 19, 2019. https://www.insideprivacy.com/data-security/data-breaches/ state-data-breach-notification-laws-2018-in-review/

12. "Privacy and data security update: 2018." Federal Trade Commission January 2018—December 2018. FTC. Accessed September 18, 2019. https://www.ftc.gov/system/files/documents/reports/ privacy-data-security-update-2018/2018-privacy-data-security-re-port-508.pdf

13. Facebook, Inc.: Stipulated Order for Civil Penalty, Monetary Judgement, and Injunctive Relief. U.S. District Court for the District of Columbia. Case No. 19-cv-2184. Filed July 24, 2019. Accessed September 18, 2019. https://www.ftc.gov/system/files/ documents/cases/182_3109_facebook_order_filed_7–24–19.pdf

14. "CVS Caremark settles FTC charges: Failed to protect medical and financial privacy of customers and employees; CVS Pharmacy

also pays $2.25 million to settle allegations of HIPAA violations."
FTC. February 18, 2009. Accessed October 15, 2019. https://
www.ftc.gov/news-events/press-releases/2009/02/cvs-caremark-set-
tles-ftc-chargesfailed-protect-medical-financial; and "Rite Aid settles
FTC charges that it failed to protect medical and financial privacy
of customers and employees." FTC. July 27, 2010. Accessed October
15, 2019. https://www.ftc.gov/news-events/press-releases/2010/07/
rite-aid-settles-ftc-charges-it-failed-protect-medical-financial; and
"Accretive Health settles FTC charges that it failed to adequately
protect consumers' personal information." FTC. December 21,
2013. Accessed October 15, 2019. https://www.ftc.gov/news-events/
press-releases/2013/12/accretive-health-settles-ftc-charges-it-failed-
adequately-protect; and "Provider of medical transcript services
settles FTC charges that it failed to adequately protect consumers'
personal information." FTC. January 31, 2014. Accessed October
15, 2019. https://www.ftc.gov/news-events/press-releases/2014/01/
provider-medical-transcript-services-settles-ftc-charges-it

15. "CVS Caremark settles FTC charges: Failed to protect med-
    ical and financial privacy of customers and employees; CVS
    Pharmacy also pays $2.25 million to settle allegations of HIPAA
    violations." FTC. February 18, 2009. Accessed October 15,
    2019. https://www.ftc.gov/news-events/press-releases/2009/02/
    cvs-caremark-settles-ftc-chargesfailed-protect-medical-financial

16. Una A. Dean and Melis S. Kiziltay Carter. "New guidelines on
    GDPR's territorial scope confirm it reaches far beyond the EU."
    New York Law Journal. March 1, 2019. Accessed August 12,
    2019. https://www.law.com/newyorklawjournal/2019/03/01/
    new-guidelines-on-gdprs-territorial-scope-confirm-it-reaches-far-be-
    yond-the-eu/?slreturn=20190719160336

17. "Accretive Health settles FTC charges that it failed to ade-
    quately protect consumers' personal information." FTC Press
    Release. December 31, 2013. Accessed September 20, 2019.

https://www.ftc.gov/news-events/press-releases/2013/12/
accretive-health-settles-ftc-charges-it-failed-adequately-protect

18. Elizabeth Stawicki. "Accretive agrees to $2.5M fine; company
    to withdraw from Minn." *MPR News*. July 31, 2012. Accessed
    September 19, 2019. https://www.mprnews.org/story/2012/07/31/
    accretive-agrees-to-25m-fine-company-to-withdraw-from-minn

19. Elizabeth Stawicki. "Accretive agrees to $2.5M fine; company
    to withdraw from Minn." *MPR News*. July 31, 2012. Accessed
    September 19, 2019. https://www.mprnews.org/story/2012/07/31/
    accretive-agrees-to-25m-fine-company-to-withdraw-from-
    minn; and "Accretive Health settles FTC charges that it failed
    to adequately protect consumers' personal information." FTC
    Press Release. December 31, 2013. Accessed September 20,
    2019. https://www.ftc.gov/news-events/press-releases/2013/12/
    accretive-health-settles-ftc-charges-it-failed-adequately-protect

20. Peter Frost. "Accretive Health delisted from NYSE." *Chicago
    Tribune*. March 17, 2014. Accessed September 19, 2019. https://
    www.chicagotribune.com/business/ct-xpm-2014-03-17-chi-
    accretive-health-delisted-from-nyse-20140317-story.html

21. Dave Barkholz. "Accretive Health changes performance,
    then name, to R1." *Modern Healthcare*. January 5, 2017.
    Accessed September 19, 2019. https://www.modern-
    healthcare.com/article/20170105/NEWS/170109953/
    accretive-health-changes-performance-then-name-to-r1

22. Dave Barkholz. "Accretive Health changes performance,
    then name, to R1." *Modern Healthcare*. January 5, 2017.
    Accessed September 19, 2019. https://www.modern-
    healthcare.com/article/20170105/NEWS/170109953/
    accretive-health-changes-performance-then-name-to-r1

23. Belinda A. Bain and Loarraine Mastersmith. "'Eyes open, nose in, fin-
    gers out': Understanding and managing the potential risks of signing

on as a corporate director." Gowling WLG. *Lexology.com*. September 19, 2017. Accessed September 15, 2019. https://www.lexology.com/library/detail.aspx?g=f670c6ea-23cf-4c96-bd5b-e6d1b75bfde9

24. "Widespread HIPAA vulnerabilities result in $2.7 million settlement with Oregon Health & Science University." OCR Press Office. July 18, 2016. Accessed September 15, 2019. https://wayback.archive-it.org/3926/20170127185938/https:/www.hhs.gov/about/news/2016/07/18/widespread-hipaa-vulnerabilities-result-in-settlement-with-oregon-health-science-university.html

25. "Widespread HIPAA vulnerabilities result in $2.7 million settlement with Oregon Health & Science University." OCR Press Office. July 18, 2016. Accessed September 15, 2019. https://wayback.archive-it.org/3926/20170127185938/https:/www.hhs.gov/about/news/2016/07/18/widespread-hipaa-vulnerabilities-result-in-settlement-with-oregon-health-science-university.html

26. "Widespread HIPAA vulnerabilities result in $2.7 million settlement with Oregon Health & Science University." OCR Press Office. July 18, 2016. Accessed September 15, 2019. https://wayback.archive-it.org/3926/20170127185938/https:/www.hhs.gov/about/news/2016/07/18/widespread-hipaa-vulnerabilities-result-in-settlement-with-oregon-health-science-university.html

27. Cybersecurity Cheat Sheets for the C-suite and Board. *Advisory Board*. May 9, 2018. Accessed October 15, 2019. https://www.advisory.com/research/health-care-it-advisor/resources/2018/cybersecurity-cheat-sheets-for-the-c-suite-and-board

28. 45 CFR 164.308(a)(1)(ii)(A).

29. UMASS Resolution Agreement and Corrective Action Plan. OCR. HHS.gov. November 16, 2016. Accessed September 18, 2019. https://www.hhs.gov/sites/default/files/umass_ra_cap.pdf

30. Martin Mickos. "The cybersecurity skills gap won't be solved in a classroom." *Forbes*. June 19, 2019. Accessed September 18, 2019.

https://www.forbes.com/sites/martenmickos/2019/06/19/the-cyber-security-skills-gap-wont-be-solved-in-a-classroom/#205d98e1c30e

31. "Cybersecurity skills shortage is impacting organizations." *Security.* May 10, 2019. Accessed September 18, 2019. https://www.securitymagazine.com/articles/90218-cybersecurity-skills-shortage-impacting-organizations; and Jon Oltsik. "Is the cybersecurity skills shortage getting worse?" *ESG Blog.* May 10, 2019. Accessed September 18, 2019. https://www.esg-global.com/blog/is-the-cybersecurity-skills-shortage-getting-worse

32. "Cybersecurity skills shortage worsening for third year in a row, sounding the alarm for business leaders." ESG/ISSA. May 9, 2019. Accessed September 18, 2019. https://www.esg-global.com/hubfs/pdf/ISSA-ESG-Press-Release-2018.pdf

33. Bill Siwicki. "Outsourced cybersecurity staff, one way healthcare is getting around the talent shortage." *HealthcareITNews.* June 23, 2017. Accessed September 18, 2019. https://www.healthcareitnews.com/news/outsourced-cybersecurity-staff-one-way-healthcare-getting-around-talent-shortage

34. Prochaska, J. O., & Velicer, W. F. (1997). "The Transtheoretical Model of Health Behavior Change." *American Journal of Health Promotion*, 12(1), 38–48. https://doi.org/10.4278/0890–1171–12.1.38 Accessed September 21, 2019. https://journals.sagepub.com/doi/10.4278/0890–1171–12.1.38#articleCitationDownloadContainer; and Prochaska, J.O. & Prochaska, J.M. (2016). *Changing to Thrive: Overcome the Top Risks to Lasting Health and Happiness.* Center City, MN: Hazelden Publishing. ISBN 13:9781616496296. https://www.hazelden.org/store/item/375144?Changing-to-Thrive

Chapter 5: *Learn ECRM Essentials for the C-suite and Board*

1. "Security and Privacy Controls for Federal Information Systems and Organizations." NIST Special Publication 800–53. Revision

    4. National Institute of Standards and Technology (NIST). April 2013. Accessed October 24, 2019. https://nvlpubs.nist.gov/nist-pubs/SpecialPublications/NIST.SP.800-53r4.pdf

2. Health Care Systems and Medical Devices at Risk for Increased Cyber Intrusions for Financial Gain. FBI Private Industry Notification (PIN) # 140408–009. April 8, 2014. Accessed October 24, 2019. https://info.publicintelligence.net/FBI-HealthCareCyberIntrusions.pdf

3. "Asset." Glossary. Computer Security Resource Center (CSRC). National Institute of Standards and Technology (NIST). Accessed October 24, 2019. https://csrc.nist.gov/glossary/

4. Resolution Agreement between HHS and Triple-S. HHS.gov. November 30, 2015. Accessed November 4, 2019. https://www.hhs.gov/sites/default/files/Triple-S%20-%20OCR%20Resolution%20Agreement%20and%20Corrective%20Action%20Plan%20in%20Final%20%28508%29.pdf

5. Resolution Agreement and Corrective Action Plan between OCR and Advocate. HHS.gov. July 8, 2016. Accessed November 4, 2019. https://www.hhs.gov/sites/default/files/Advocate_racap.pdf

6. UMASS Resolution Agreement and Corrective Action Plan. HHS.gov. November 16, 2016. Accessed November 4, 2019. https://www.hhs.gov/sites/default/files/umass_ra_cap.pdf

7. "Threat." Glossary. Computer Security Resource Center (CSRC). National Institute of Standards and Technology (NIST). Accessed October 24, 2019. https://csrc.nist.gov/glossary/

8. 2019 Internet Security Threat Report (ISTR). Symantec. February 2019. Accessed October 24, 2019. https://symantec.broadcom.com/symc-istr-v24-2019-6819

9. "Threat Event." Glossary. Computer Security Resource Center (CSRC). National Institute of Standards and Technology (NIST). Accessed October 24, 2019. https://csrc.nist.gov/glossary/

10. Barbara Feder Ostrov. "California hospitals and nursing homes brace for wildfire blackouts." *Kaiser Health News.* September 11, 2019. Accessed October 24, 2019. https://khn.org/news/california-hospitals-and-nursing-homes-brace-for-wildfire-blackouts/?utm_source=STAT+Newsletters&utm_campaign=e1b5d35314-MR_COPY_01&utm_medium=email&utm_term=0_8cab1d7961-e1b5d35314-150885145

11. "Vulnerability." Glossary. Computer Security Resource Center (CSRC). National Institute of Standards and Technology (NIST). Accessed October 24, 2019. https://csrc.nist.gov/glossary/

12. "Security Controls." Glossary. Computer Security Resource Center (CSRC). National Institute of Standards and Technology (NIST). Accessed October 24, 2019. https://csrc.nist.gov/glossary/

13. 45 CFR § 164.530(c)(1)

14. "Likelihood." Glossary. Computer Security Resource Center (CSRC). National Institute of Standards and Technology (NIST). Accessed October 24, 2019. https://csrc.nist.gov/glossary/

15. "Likelihood of Occurrence." Glossary. Computer Security Resource Center (CSRC). National Institute of Standards and Technology (NIST). Accessed October 24, 2019. https://csrc.nist.gov/glossary/

16. Paul Mah. "10 things to do before you lose your laptop." *CIO.* September 10, 2015. Accessed October 24, 2019. https://www.cio.com/article/2981970/10-things-to-do-before-you-lose-your-laptop.html

17. "Impact." Glossary. Computer Security Resource Center (CSRC). National Institute of Standards and Technology (NIST). Accessed October 24, 2019. https://csrc.nist.gov/glossary/

18. "Risk Analysis" and "Risk Assessment." Glossary. Computer Security Resource Center (CSRC). National Institute of Standards and Technology (NIST). Accessed October 24, 2019. https://csrc. nist.gov/glossary/

19. "Risk Management." Glossary. Computer Security Resource Center (CSRC). National Institute of Standards and Technology (NIST). Accessed October 24, 2019. https://csrc.nist.gov/glossary/

20. Cybersecurity Framework. NIST. (n.d.). Accessed October 24, 2019. https://www.nist.gov/cyberframework

21. Rob Suárez, Director of Product Security, BD (Becton, Dickinson and Company) quoted in "Choosing an Information Risk Management Framework: The Case for the NIST Cybersecurity Framework in Healthcare Organizations." Clearwater. (n.d.) Accessed October 24, 2019. https://clearwatercompliance.com/wp-content/uploads/2017/10/Choosing-an-IRM-Framework_The-Case-for-the-NIST-CSF-in-Healthcare_Clearwater-White-Paper.pdf"

22. March 2011. Accessed November 4, 2019. Managing Information Security Risk. NIST Special Publication 800-39. National Institute of Standards and Technology (NIST). March 2011. Accessed November 11, 2019. https://nvlpubs.nist.gov/nistpubs/Legacy/SP/nistspecialpublication800-39.pdf

23. Martin Fowler. MaturityModel. August 26, 2014. Accessed October 24, 2019. https://martinfowler.com/bliki/MaturityModel.html#targetText=A%20maturity%20model%20is%20a,order%20to%20improve%20their%20performance.

24. "Plan-Do-Check-Act Cycle," U.S. Department of Health and Human Services, Agency for Healthcare Research and Quality, Health Information Technology. (n.d.). Accessed October 24, 2019. https://healthit.ahrq.gov/health-it-tools-and-resources/evaluation-resources/workflow-assessment-health-it-toolkit/all-workflow-tools/plan-do-check-act-cycle

25. *See* Resolution Agreements and Civil Money Penalties. Health Information Privacy. U.S. Department of Health and Human Services. https://www.hhs.gov/hipaa/for-professionals/compliance-enforcement/agreements/index.html

26. Clearwater analysis of data publicly available at: Resolution Agreements and Civil Money Penalties. Health Information Privacy. U.S. Department of Health and Human Services. (n.d.) Accessed October 24, 2019. https://www.hhs.gov/hipaa/for-professionals/compliance-enforcement/agreements/index.html

27. "Anthem pays OCR $16 million in record HIPAA settlement following largest U.S. health data breach in history." HHS Press Office. October 15, 2018. Accessed October 24th, 2019. https://www.hhs.gov/about/news/2018/10/15/anthem-pays-ocr-16-million-record-hipaa-settlement-following-largest-health-data-breach-history.html

28. "Anthem pays OCR $16 million in record HIPAA settlement following largest U.S. health data breach in history." HHS Press Office. October 15, 2018. Accessed October 24th, 2019. https://www.hhs.gov/about/news/2018/10/15/anthem-pays-ocr-16-million-record-hipaa-settlement-following-largest-health-data-breach-history.html

29. 45 CFR §164.308(a)(1)(ii)(B)

30. Clearwater analysis of data publicly available at: Resolution Agreements and Civil Money Penalties. Health Information Privacy. U.S. Department of Health and Human Services. (n.d.) Accessed April 20, 2020. https://www.hhs.gov/hipaa/for-professionals/compliance-enforcement/agreements/index.html

31. Clearwater analysis of data publicly available at: Resolution Agreements and Civil Money Penalties. Health Information Privacy. U.S. Department of Health and Human Services. (n.d.) Accessed April 20, 2020. https://www.hhs.gov/hipaa/

for-professionals/compliance-enforcement/agreements
/index.html

32. 45 CFR § 164.306 https://www.ecfr.gov/cgi-bin/text-idx?SID=e-
65ba48f13a8d861a04609bc86369384&mc=true&node=se45.2.
164_1306&rgn=div8

Chapter 6: *Set ECRM Objectives*

1. Andrew Cave. "Culture eats strategy for breakfast. So what's for
lunch?" *Forbes.* November 9, 2017. Accessed November 11, 2019.
https://www.forbes.com/sites/andrewcave/2017/11/09/culture-
eats-strategy-for-breakfast-so-whats-for-lunch/#78282ef27e0f

2. Managing Information Security Risk. NIST Special Publication
800–39. National Institute of Standards and Technology (NIST).
March 2011. Accessed November 11, 2019. https://nvlpubs.nist.
gov/nistpubs/Legacy/SP/nistspecialpublication800–39.pdf

3. Bob Chaput. "CEO-to-CEO: Top 5 questions CEOs should ask
themselves & board about risk management." *IT Toolbox Blog.*
(n.d.). Accessed November 11, 2019. https://it.toolbox.com/blogs/
bobchaput/ceo-to-ceo-top-5-questions-ceos-should-ask-themselves-
board-about-risk-management-111914

4. Cyber Risk Oversight Certificate. National Association of Corporate
Directors (NACD). (n.d.). Accessed November 11, 2019. https://
www.nacdonline.org/events/detail.cfm?ItemNumber=37092

5. Cyber Risk Oversight Certificate. National Association of Corporate
Directors (NACD). (n.d.). Accessed November 11, 2019. https://
www.nacdonline.org/events/detail.cfm?ItemNumber=37092

6. Process. BusinessDictionary.com. (n.d.) Accessed November 11,
2019. http://www.businessdictionary.com/definition/process.html

7. "Guidance on risk analysis requirements under the HIPAA Security
Rule." Office for Civil Rights (OCR). July 14, 2010. Accessed

November 11, 2019. https://www.hhs.gov/hipaa/for-professionals/ security/guidance/final-guidance-risk-analysis/index.html ; and Managing Information Security Risk. NIST Special Publication 800–39. National Institute of Standards and Technology (NIST). March 2011. Accessed November 11, 2019. https://nvlpubs. nist.gov/nistpubs/Legacy/SP/nistspecialpublication800–39.pdf; and Guide for Conducting Risk Assessments. NIST Special Publication 800–30, Revision 1. National Institute of Standards and Technology (NIST). September 2012. Accessed November 11, 2019. https://nvlpubs.nist.gov/nistpubs/Legacy/SP/nistspecialpublication800–30r1.pdf

8. Managing Information Security Risk. NIST Special Publication 800–39. National Institute of Standards and Technology (NIST). March 2011. Accessed November 11, 2019. https://nvlpubs. nist.gov/nistpubs/Legacy/SP/nistspecialpublication800–39.pdf; and Guide for Conducting Risk Assessments. NIST Special Publication 800–30, Revision 1. National Institute of Standards and Technology (NIST) September 2012. Accessed November 11, 2019. https://nvlpubs.nist.gov/nistpubs/Legacy/SP/nistspecialpublication800–30r1.pdf

9. André Brodeur, Kevin Buehler, Michael Patsalos-Fox, Martin Pergler. "A board perspective on enterprise risk management." McKinsey & Company. February 2010. Accessed November 12, 2019. https://www.mckinsey.com/~/media/mckinsey/dotcom/ client_service/risk/working%20papers/18_a_board_perspective_on_enterprise_risk_management.ashx

Chapter 7: *Take Six Initial Actions to Establish or Improve Your ECRM Program*

1. "Sorting diamonds from toothbrushes: New guide to protecting personal information." National Institute of Standards and Technology (NIST). January 13, 2009. Accessed December

9, 2019. https://www.nist.gov/news-events/news/2009/01/
sorting-diamonds-toothbrushes-new-guide-protecting
-personal-information

2. "Guidance on risk analysis requirements under the HIPAA
   Security Rule." OCR/HHS. July 14, 2010. Accessed December
   9, 2019. https://www.hhs.gov/sites/default/files/ocr/privacy/hipaa/
   administrative/securityrule/rafinalguidancepdf.pdf

3. 45 CFR § 164.306(a)

4. "Guidance on risk analysis requirements under the HIPAA
   Security Rule." OCR/HHS. July 14, 2010. Accessed December
   9, 2019. https://www.hhs.gov/sites/default/files/ocr/privacy/hipaa/
   administrative/securityrule/rafinalguidancepdf.pdf

5. "Guidance on risk analysis requirements under the HIPAA
   Security Rule." OCR/HHS. July 14, 2010. Accessed December
   9, 2019. https://www.hhs.gov/sites/default/files/ocr/privacy/hipaa/
   administrative/securityrule/rafinalguidancepdf.pdf

6. "Guidance on risk analysis requirements under the HIPAA
   Security Rule." OCR/HHS. July 14, 2010. Accessed December
   9, 2019. https://www.hhs.gov/sites/default/files/ocr/privacy/hipaa/
   administrative/securityrule/rafinalguidancepdf.pdf

7. "Guidance on risk analysis requirements under the HIPAA
   Security Rule." OCR/HHS. July 14, 2010. Accessed December
   11, 2019. https://www.hhs.gov/sites/default/files/ocr/privacy/hipaa/
   administrative/securityrule/rafinalguidancepdf.pdf

8. "Guidance on risk analysis requirements under the HIPAA
   Security Rule." OCR/HHS. July 14, 2010. Accessed December
   11, 2019. https://www.hhs.gov/sites/default/files/ocr/privacy/hipaa/
   administrative/securityrule/rafinalguidancepdf.pdf

9. "Guidance on risk analysis requirements under the HIPAA
   Security Rule." OCR/HHS. July 14, 2010. Accessed December

11, 2019. https://www.hhs.gov/sites/default/files/ocr/privacy/hipaa/administrative/securityrule/rafinalguidancepdf.pdf

10. "Guidance on risk analysis requirements under the HIPAA Security Rule." OCR/HHS. July 14, 2010. Accessed December 12, 2019. https://www.hhs.gov/sites/default/files/ocr/privacy/hipaa/administrative/securityrule/rafinalguidancepdf.pdf

11. "Guidance on risk analysis requirements under the HIPAA Security Rule." OCR/HHS. July 14, 2010. Accessed December 12, 2019. https://www.hhs.gov/sites/default/files/ocr/privacy/hipaa/administrative/securityrule/rafinalguidancepdf.pdf

12. "Guidance on risk analysis requirements under the HIPAA Security Rule." OCR/HHS. July 14, 2010. Accessed December 12, 2019. https://www.hhs.gov/sites/default/files/ocr/privacy/hipaa/administrative/securityrule/rafinalguidancepdf.pdf

13. 45 CFR §§ 164.306(e) and 164.316(b)(2)(iii)

14. "Guidance on risk analysis requirements under the HIPAA Security Rule." OCR/HHS. July 14, 2010. Accessed December 13, 2019. https://www.hhs.gov/sites/default/files/ocr/privacy/hipaa/administrative/securityrule/rafinalguidancepdf.pdf

15. Larry Clinton, Josh Higgins and Friso van der Oord. "Cyber-Risk Oversight 2020: Key Principles and Practical Guidance for Corporate Boards." National Association of Corporate Directors (NACD). Accessed March 4, 2020. https://nacdonline.org/insights/publications.cfm?ItemNumber=67298

16. Framework for Improving Critical Infrastructure Cybersecurity, Version 1.1. National Institute of Standards and Technology (NIST). April 16, 2018. Accessed December 16, 2019. https://nvlpubs.nist.gov/nistpubs/CSWP/NIST.CSWP.04162018.pdf

17. Framework for Improving Critical Infrastructure Cybersecurity, Version 1.1. National Institute of Standards and Technology

(NIST). April 16, 2018. Accessed December 16, 2019. https://nvlpubs.nist.gov/nistpubs/CSWP/NIST.CSWP.04162018.pdf

18. Framework for Improving Critical Infrastructure Cybersecurity, Version 1.1. National Institute of Standards and Technology (NIST). April 16, 2018. Accessed December 16, 2019. https://nvlpubs.nist.gov/nistpubs/CSWP/NIST.CSWP.04162018.pdf

19. Framework for Improving Critical Infrastructure Cybersecurity, Version 1.1. National Institute of Standards and Technology (NIST). April 16, 2018. Accessed December 16, 2019. https://nvlpubs.nist.gov/nistpubs/CSWP/NIST.CSWP.04162018.pdf

20. Framework for Improving Critical Infrastructure Cybersecurity, Version 1.1. National Institute of Standards and Technology (NIST). April 16, 2018. Accessed December 16, 2019. https://nvlpubs.nist.gov/nistpubs/CSWP/NIST.CSWP.04162018.pdf

21. Managing Information Security Risk. NIST Special Publication 800–39. National Institute of Standards and Technology (NIST). March 2011. Accessed December 17, 2019. https://nvlpubs.nist.gov/nistpubs/Legacy/SP/nistspecialpublication800–39.pdf

22. Managing Information Security Risk. NIST Special Publication 800–39. National Institute of Standards and Technology (NIST). March 2011. Accessed December 17, 2019. https://nvlpubs.nist.gov/nistpubs/Legacy/SP/nistspecialpublication800–39.pdf

23. Managing Information Security Risk. NIST Special Publication 800–39. National Institute of Standards and Technology (NIST). March 2011. Accessed December 17, 2019. https://nvlpubs.nist.gov/nistpubs/Legacy/SP/nistspecialpublication800–39.pdf

24. Sasha Romanosky, Lillian Ablon, Andreas Kuehn, and Therese Jones. "Content analysis of cyber insurance policies: how do carriers price cyber risk?" *Journal of Cybersecurity*, Volume 5, Issue 1, 2019, tyz002. Accessed December 18, 2019. https://doi.org/10.1093/cybsec/tyz002

25. Sasha Romanosky, Lillian Ablon, Andreas Kuehn, and Therese Jones. "Content analysis of cyber insurance policies: how do carriers price cyber risk?" *Journal of Cybersecurity*, Volume 5, Issue 1, 2019, tyz002. Accessed December 18, 2019. https://doi.org/10.1093/cybsec/tyz002

26. 2019 HIMSS Cybersecurity Survey. Healthcare Information and Management Systems Society (HIMSS). 2019. Accessed December 18, 2019. https://www.himss.org/sites/hde/files/d7/u132196/2019_HIMSS_Cybersecurity_Survey_Final _Report.pdf

27. GB&A Insurance. "Avoiding the most common cyber insurance claim denials." (n.d.) Accessed December 19, 2019. https://www.gbainsurance.com/avoiding-cyber-claim-denials

28. Judy Greenwald. "Insurer cites cyber policy exclusion to dispute data breach settlement." *Business Insurance*. May 15, 2015. Accessed December 19, 2019. https://www.businessinsurance.com/article/20150515/NEWS06/150519893/Insurer-cites-cyber-policy-exclusion-to-dispute-data-breach-settlement-

29. Margaret A. Reetz., Lauren B. Prunty, Gregory S. Mantych, and David J. Hommel. "Cyber risks: Evolving threats, emerging coverages, and ensuing case law." *Penn State Law Review*. Vol. 122:3, pages 727–762. 2018. Accessed December 19, 2019. http://www.pennstatelawreview.org/print-issues/cyber-risks-evolving-threats-emerging-coverages-and-ensuing-case-law/ and http://www.pennstatelawreview.org/wp-content/uploads/2018/07/Symposium-Reetz-et-al.pdf

30. Adam Satariano and Nicole Perlroth. "Big companies thought insurance covered a cyberattack. They may be wrong." *The New York Times*. April 15, 2019. Accessed December 20, 2019. https://www.nytimes.com/2019/04/15/technology/cyberinsurance-not-petya-attack.html

31. Joshua Gold. "War risk exclusions threaten cyber coverage." *Risk Management.* April 1, 2019. Accessed December 20, 2019. http://www.rmmagazine.com/2019/04/01/war-risk-exclusions-threaten-cyber-coverage/

32. Adam Satariano and Nicole Perlroth. "Big companies thought insurance covered a cyberattack. They may be wrong." *The New York Times.* April 15, 2019. Accessed December 20, 2019. https://www.nytimes.com/2019/04/15/technology/cyberinsurance-not-petya-attack.html

33. "Communicating the value of cybersecurity to boards and leadership: Seven strategies for life sciences and health care organizations. A report by the Deloitte Center for Health Solutions." *Deloitte Insights.* 2019. Accessed December 27, 2019. https://s3-prod.modernhealthcare.com/2019–05/DI_Value-of-cyber-investments.pdf

34. "Communicating the value of cybersecurity to boards and leadership: Seven strategies for life sciences and health care organizations. A report by the Deloitte Center for Health Solutions." *Deloitte Insights.* 2019. Accessed December 27, 2019. https://s3-prod.modernhealthcare.com/2019–05/DI_Value-of-cyber-investments.pdf

35. "Communicating the value of cybersecurity to boards and leadership: Seven strategies for life sciences and health care organizations. A report by the Deloitte Center for Health Solutions." *Deloitte Insights.* 2019. Accessed December 27, 2019. https://s3-prod.modernhealthcare.com/2019–05/DI_Value-of-cyber-investments.pdf

Chapter 8: *Fund Your ECRM Program*

1. Michael Gabriel. "How much cybersecurity funding is enough—is it a bottomless pit?" *CIO.* September 23, 2019. Accessed January

8, 2020. https://www.cio.com/article/3440261/how-much-cyber-security-funding-is-enough-is-it-a-bottomless-pit.html

2. Jamie Dimon. "CEO Letter to Shareholders, 2018." JPMorgan Chase. April 4, 2019. Accessed January 8, 2020. https://www.jpmorganchase.com/corporate/investor-relations/document/ceo-letter-to-shareholders-2018.pdf

3. Jessica Davis. "AMCA files Chapter 11 after data breach impacting Quest, LabCorp." *Health IT Security.* June 18, 2019. Accessed January 10, 2020. https://healthitsecurity.com/news/amca-files-chapter-11-after-data-breach-impacting-quest-labcorp

4. Jessica Davis. "AMCA files Chapter 11 after data breach impacting Quest, LabCorp." *Health IT Security.* June 18, 2019. Accessed January 10, 2020. https://healthitsecurity.com/news/amca-files-chapter-11-after-data-breach-impacting-quest-labcorp

5. "2020 Cost of a Data Breach Report." IBM Security/Ponemon Institute. 2020. Accessed August 1, 2020. https://www.ibm.com/security/digital-assets/cost-data-breach-report/#/

6. "2020 Cost of a Data Breach Report." IBM Security/Ponemon Institute. 2020. Accessed August 1, 2020. https://www.ibm.com/security/digital-assets/cost-data-breach-report/#/

7. "2019 Cost of a Data Breach Report." IBM Security/Ponemon Institute. 2019. Accessed January 24, 2020. https://f.hubspotusercontent40.net/hubfs/2783949/2019_Cost_of_a_Data_Breach_Report_final.pdf

8. "2019 Cost of a Data Breach Report." IBM Security/Ponemon Institute. 2019. Accessed January 24, 2020. https://f.hubspotusercontent40.net/hubfs/2783949/2019_Cost_of_a_Data_Breach_Report_final.pdf

9. "$2.14 million HIPAA settlement underscores importance of managing security risk." HHS Press Office. U.S. Dept. of Health

and Human Services. October 18, 2018. Accessed February 15, 2020. https://wayback.archive-it.org/3926/20170129143439/ https://www.hhs.gov/about/news/2016/10/18/214-million-hi-paa-settlement-underscores-importance-managing-security -risk.html

10. "$2.14 million HIPAA settlement underscores importance of managing security risk." HHS Press Office. U.S. Dept. of Health and Human Services. October 18, 2018. Accessed February 15, 2020. https://wayback.archive-it.org/3926/20170129143439/https:// www.hhs.gov/about/news/2016/10/18/214-million-hipaa-settle-ment-underscores-importance-managing-security-risk.html

11. "$2.14 million HIPAA settlement underscores importance of managing security risk." HHS Press Office. U.S. Dept. of Health and Human Services. October 18, 2018. Accessed February 15, 2020. https://wayback.archive-it.org/3926/20170129143439/https:// www.hhs.gov/about/news/2016/10/18/214-million-hipaa-settle-ment-underscores-importance-managing-security-risk.html

12. Bob Chaput, "Compliance Risk Management and Cyber Risk Management," in *2019 Mid-Year Health Law and Compliance Update*, ed. Harold J. Bressler (Wolters Kluwer). Updated June 17, 2019. Accessed February 15, 2020. https://lrus.wolterskluwer.com/store/ product/health-law-and-compliance-update-2019-mid-year-edition/

13. Bob Chaput, "Compliance Risk Management and Cyber Risk Management," in *2019 Mid-Year Health Law and Compliance Update*, ed. Harold J. Bressler (Wolters Kluwer). Updated June 17, 2019. Accessed February 15, 2020. https://lrus.wolterskluwer.com/store/ product/health-law-and-compliance-update-2019-mid-year-edition/

14. "Anthem pays OCR $16 million in record HIPAA settle-ment following largest U.S. health data breach in history." HHS Press Office. October 15, 2018. Accessed February 15, 2020. https://www.hhs.gov/about/news/2018/10/15/

anthem-pays-ocr-16-million-record-hipaa-settlement-following-largest-health-data-breach-history.html

15. "Anthem pays OCR $16 million in record HIPAA settlement following largest U.S. health data breach in history." HHS Press Office. October 15, 2018. Accessed February 15, 2020. https://www.hhs.gov/about/news/2018/10/15/anthem-pays-ocr-16-million-record-hipaa-settlement-following-largest-health-data-breach-history.html

16. "Anthem pays OCR $16 million in record HIPAA settlement following largest U.S. health data breach in history." HHS Press Office. October 15, 2018. Accessed February 15, 2020. https://www.hhs.gov/about/news/2018/10/15/anthem-pays-ocr-16-million-record-hipaa-settlement-following-largest-health-data-breach-history.html

17. "Anthem pays OCR $16 million in record HIPAA settlement following largest U.S. health data breach in history." HHS Press Office. October 15, 2018. Accessed February 15, 2020. https://www.hhs.gov/about/news/2018/10/15/anthem-pays-ocr-16-million-record-hipaa-settlement-following-largest-health-data-breach-history.html

18. Marianne Kolbasuk McGee. "A new in-depth analysis of Anthem breach." *BankInfoSecurity*. January 10, 2017. Accessed February 15, 2020. https://www.bankinfosecurity.com/new-in-depth-analysis-anthem-breach-a-9627

19. Fred Donovan. "Judge gives final OK to $115M Anthem data breach settlement." *Health IT Security*. August 20, 2018. Accessed February 15, 2020. https://healthitsecurity.com/news/judge-gives-final-ok-to-115m-anthem-data-breach-settlement

20. Fred Donovan. "Judge gives final OK to $115M Anthem data breach settlement." *Health IT Security*. August 20, 2018.

Accessed February 15, 2020. https://healthitsecurity.com/news/judge-gives-final-ok-to-115m-anthem-data-breach-settlement

21. Clearwater analysis, based on publicly available documents and media reports. 2020.

22. EY Global Information Security Survey 2018–19. Accessed January 25, 2020. https://assets.ey.com/content/dam/ey-sites/ey-com/en_ca/topics/advisory/ey-global-information-security-survey-2018–19.pdf

23. EY Global Information Security Survey 2018–19. Accessed January 25, 2020. https://assets.ey.com/content/dam/ey-sites/ey-com/en_ca/topics/advisory/ey-global-information-security-survey-2018–19.pdf

24. Lisa Schencker. "Hospitals spending lags on digital security." *The Courier-Tribune*. March 11, 2019. Accessed January 26, 2020. https://www.courier-tribune.com/news/20190311/hospitals8217-spending-lags-on-digital-security

25. Report on Improving Cybersecurity in the Health Care Industry. Health Care Industry Cybersecurity Task Force. June 2017. Accessed January 26, 2020. https://www.phe.gov/Preparedness/planning/CyberTF/Documents/report2017.pdf

26. CMS Data and Program Reports. Medicare and Medicaid Promoting Interoperability Programs payment and registration data. Page last modified January 27, 2020. Accessed January 31, 2020. https://www.cms.gov/Regulations-and-Guidance/Legislation/EHRIncentivePrograms/DataAndReports; and Joseph Conn. "Federal health IT payments top $28 billion after December surge." *Modern Healthcare*. February 13, 2015. Accessed January 31, 2020. https://www.modernhealthcare.com/article/20150213/NEWS/302139932/federal-health-it-payments-top-28-billion-after-december-surge; and CMS Promoting Interoperability (PI) Program report. October 2018. Accessed February 14, 2020. https://www.cms.gov/Regulations-and-Guidance/

Legislation/EHRIncentivePrograms/Downloads/October2018_ SummaryReport.pdf

27. Medicare & Medicaid EHR Incentive Program. Meaningful Use Stage 1 Requirements Overview. 2010. Accessed February 1, 2020. https://www.cms.gov/Regulations-and-Guidance/Legislation/ EHRIncentivePrograms/downloads/MU_Stage1_ReqOverview.pdf

28. Medicare & Medicaid EHR Incentive Program. Meaningful Use Stage 1 Requirements Overview. 2010. Accessed February 1, 2020. https://www.cms.gov/Regulations-and-Guidance/ Legislation/EHRIncentivePrograms/downloads/MU_Stage1_Req Overview.pdf

29. Stage 1 vs. Stage 2 Comparison Table for Eligible Hospitals and CAHs. CMS. August 2012. Accessed February 1, 2020. https://www.cms.gov/Regulations-and-Guidance/ Legislation/EHRIncentivePrograms/Downloads/ Stage1vsStage2CompTablesforHospitals.pdf

30. Security Risk Analysis Tip Sheet: Protect Patient Health Information. March 2016. Accessed February 1, 2020. https://www.cms.gov/ Regulations-and-Guidance/Legislation/EHRIncentivePrograms/ Downloads/2016_SecurityRiskAnalysis.pdf

31. 2020 Medicare Promoting Interoperability Program Overview Fact Sheet. CMS. 2019. Accessed February 1, 2020. https://www.cms.gov/Regulations-and-Guidance/ Legislation/EHRIncentivePrograms/Downloads/Medicare_ FactSheetFY2020.pdf

32. 2019 Medicare Promoting Interoperability Program Scoring Methodology Fact Sheet. CMS. 2019. Accessed February 8, 2020. https://www.cms.gov/Regulations-and-Guidance/ Legislation/EHRIncentivePrograms/Downloads/ScoringMeth_ FactSheet-.pdf ; and 2020 Medicare Promoting Interoperability Program Overview Fact Sheet. CMS. 2019. Accessed February

1, 2020. https://www.cms.gov/Regulations-and-Guidance/ Legislation/EHRIncentivePrograms/Downloads/Medicare_ FactSheetFY2020.pdf

33. Risk Management Framework for Information Systems and Organizations. NIST Special Publication 800–37, Revision 2. National Institute of Standards and Technology (NIST). December 2018. Accessed February 2, 2020. https://nvl-pubs.nist.gov/nistpubs/SpecialPublications/NIST.SP.800 –37r2.pdf

34. "Moody's names Derek Vadala as Global Head of Cyber Risk for MIS." *Moody's Investor Relations.* October 17, 2018. Accessed February 2, 2020. https://ir.moodys.com/news-and-financials/ press-releases/press-release-details/2018/Moodys-Names-Derek-Vadala-as-Global-Head-of-Cyber-Risk-for-MIS/default.aspx

35. "Moody's names Derek Vadala as Global Head of Cyber Risk for MIS." *Moody's Investor Relations.* October 17, 2018. Accessed February 2, 2020. https://ir.moodys.com/news-and-fi-nancials/press-releases/press-release-details/2018/Moodys-Names-Derek-Vadala-as-Global-Head-of-Cyber-Risk-for-MIS /default.aspx

36. Research Announcement: Moody's—Credit implications of cyberattacks will hinge on long-term business disruptions and rep-utational impacts. February 28, 2019. Accessed February 3, 2020. https://www.moodys.com/research/Moodys-Credit-implications-of-cyberattacks-will-hinge-on-long-term--PBC_1161216

37. Research Announcement: Moody's—Credit implications of cyberattacks will hinge on long-term business disruptions and rep-utational impacts. February 28, 2019. Accessed February 3, 2020. https://www.moodys.com/research/Moodys-Credit-implications-of-cyberattacks-will-hinge-on-long-term--PBC_1161216

38. Research Announcement: Moody's—Credit implications of cyberattacks will hinge on long-term business disruptions and reputational impacts. February 28, 2019. Accessed February 3, 2020. https://www.moodys.com/research/Moodys-Credit-implications-of-cyberattacks-will-hinge-on-long-term--PBC _1161216

39. Cross-Sector — Global: Credit Implications of Cyber Risk Will Hinge on Business Disruptions, Reputational Effects. *Moody's Investors Services*. February 28, 2019. Accessed February 14, 2020. https://www.moodys.com/research/Moodys-Credit-implications-of-cyberattacks-will-hinge-on-long-term--PBC_1161216

40. Cross-Sector — Global: Credit Implications of Cyber Risk Will Hinge on Business Disruptions, Reputational Effects. *Moody's Investors Services*. February 28, 2019. Accessed February 14, 2020. https://www.moodys.com/research/Moodys-Credit-implications-of-cyberattacks-will-hinge-on-long-term--PBC_1161216

41. Nicole Lindsey. "Equifax downgrade shows the lasting financial impact of a massive data breach." *CPO Magazine*. June 3, 2019. Accessed February 3, 2020. https://www.cpomagazine.com/ cyber-security/equifax-downgrade-shows-the-lasting-financial-impact-of-a-massive-data-breach/

42. Rating Action: Moody's affirms Equifax's runs at Baa1, revises outlook to negative from stable. *Moody's Investors Service*. May 17, 2019. Accessed February 4, 2020. https://www.moodys.com/ research/Moodys-affirms-Equifax-sr-uns-at-Baa1-revises-outlook-to--PR_400804

43. Cybersecurity Insurance. Cybersecurity & Infrastructure Security Agency (CISA), U.S. Department of Homeland Security. (n.d.). Accessed February 4, 2020. https://www.cisa. gov/cybersecurity-insurance

44. Cybersecurity Insurance. Cybersecurity & Infrastructure Security Agency (CISA), U.S. Department of Homeland Security. (n.d.). Accessed February 4, 2020. https://www.cisa.gov/cybersecurity-insurance

45. Jeremiah Talamantes. "How to lower your cybersecurity insurance premiums." *RedTeam blog.* (n.d.). Accessed February 5, 2020. https://www.redteamsecure.com/blog/how-to-lower-your-cybersecurity-insurance-premiums/

46. Captives by Industry: Healthcare Industry. The Captive Landscape: Securing Your Future with a Captive. Marsh & McLennan Companies. June 2019. Accessed February 5, 2020. https://www.marsh.com/us/campaigns/captive-report-2019.html

47. Captives by Industry: Healthcare Industry. The Captive Landscape: Securing Your Future with a Captive. Marsh & McLennan Companies. June 2019. Accessed February 5, 2020. https://www.marsh.com/us/campaigns/captive-report-2019.html

48. The Captive Landscape: Securing Your Future with a Captive. Marsh. June 2019. Accessed February 5, 2020. https://www.marsh.com/us/insights/research/captive-report-2019.html

49. Mark E. Reynolds, President & CEO, CRICO. Personal correspondence (email). July 1, 2019.

Chapter 9: *Experience the Ideal ECRM Board Meeting*

1. Larry Clinton, Josh Higgins, and Friso van der Oord. Cyber-Risk Oversight 2020: Key Principles and Practical Guidance for Corporate Boards. National Association of Corporate Directors (NACD). Accessed March 4, 2020. https://nacdonline.org/insights/publications.cfm?ItemNumber=67298

2. Larry Clinton, Josh Higgins, and Friso van der Oord. Cyber-Risk Oversight 2020: Key Principles and Practical Guidance for

Corporate Boards. National Association of Corporate Directors (NACD). Accessed March 4, 2020. https://nacdonline.org/insights/ publications.cfm?ItemNumber=67298

3. 2019 Cost of a Data Breach Report. IBM Security/Ponemon Institute. 2019. Accessed January 24, 2020. https://f.hubspotus- ercontent40.net/hubfs/2783949/2019_Cost_of_a_Data_Breach_ Report_final.pdf

4. Larry Clinton, Josh Higgins, and Friso van der Oord. Cyber- Risk Oversight 2020: Key Principles and Practical Guidance for Corporate Boards. National Association of Corporate Directors (NACD). Accessed March 4, 2020. https://nacdonline.org/insights/ publications.cfm?ItemNumber=67298

5. Larry Clinton, Josh Higgins, and Friso van der Oord. Cyber- Risk Oversight 2020: Key Principles and Practical Guidance for Corporate Boards. National Association of Corporate Directors (NACD). Accessed March 4, 2020. https://nacdonline.org/insights/ publications.cfm?ItemNumber=67298

6. Alex Hern. "WannaCry, Petya, NotPetya: how ransomware hit the big time in 2017." *The Guardian*. December 30, 2017. Accessed February 23, 2020. https://www.theguardian.com/ technology/2017/dec/30/wannacry-petya-notpetya-ransomware

Chapter 10: *Realize the Benefits of a NIST-based ECRM Approach*

1. Bruce Sussman. "13 top cybersecurity quotes you should read." *SecureWorld*. February 11, 2019. https://www.secureworldexpo. com/industry-news/13-top-cybersecurity-quotes

2. Avoiding Personal Liability: A Guide for Directors and Officers. DLA Piper. (MRS000033897). April 2015. Accessed March 11, 2020. https://www.dlapiper.com/~/media/files/insights/ publications/2015/04/mrs000033897-avoiding-personal-liabili- ty-for-do-guide-v2ip.pdf

3. Affirmative defense, definition. Wex legal dictionary and ency-
    clopedia. Legal Information Institute (LII). Cornell Law School.
    Accessed March 11, 2020. https://www.law.cornell.edu/wex/
    affirmative_defense

4. David J. Oberly. Ohio's Data Protection Act. Ohio State Bar
    Association. July 1, 2019. Accessed March 12, 2020. https://
    www.ohiobar.org/member-tools-benefits/practice-resources/
    practice-library-search/practice-library/2019-ohio-lawyer/
    ohios-data-protection-act/

5. David J. Oberly. Ohio's Data Protection Act. Ohio State Bar
    Association. July 1, 2019. Accessed March 12, 2020. https://
    www.ohiobar.org/member-tools-benefits/practice-resources/
    practice-library-search/practice-library/2019-ohio-lawyer/
    ohios-data-protection-act/

6. Ohio Revised Code. Title XIII Commercial Transactions. Ohio
    Uniform Commercial Code. Chapter 1354. Businesses Maintaining
    Recognized Cybersecurity Programs. 1354.03 Reasonable con-
    formance. Added by 132nd General Assembly File No. TBD, SB
    220, §1, eff. 11/2/2018. Accessed March 12, 2020. http://codes.
    ohio.gov/orc/1354.03v1

7. Ohio Revised Code. Title XIII Commercial Transactions. Ohio
    Uniform Commercial Code. Chapter 1354. Businesses Maintaining
    Recognized Cybersecurity Programs. 1354.03 Reasonable con-
    formance. Added by 132nd General Assembly File No. TBD, SB
    220, §1, eff. 11/2/2018. Accessed March 12, 2020. http://codes.
    ohio.gov/orc/1354.03v1

8. History and Creation of the [NIST Cybersecurity] Framework.
    National Institute of Standards and Technology (NIST). Updated
    November 21, 2019. Accessed March 12, 2020. https://www.
    nist.gov/cyberframework/online-learning/history-and-creation
    -framework

9. Framework for Improving Critical Infrastructure Cybersecurity: Where We Are & Where We Are Going. National Institute of Standards and Technology (NIST). October 29, 2015. Accessed March 11, 2020. https://www.nist.gov/system/files/documents/cyberframework/Dell-Webinar-Oct2015.pdf

10. HIPAA Security Rule Crosswalk to NIST Cybersecurity Framework. U.S. Department of Health and Human Services, Office for Civil Rights (OCR). February 22, 2016. Accessed March 9, 2020. https://www.hhs.gov/sites/default/files/nist-csf-to-hipaa-security-rule-crosswalk-02–22–2016-final.pdf

11. HIMSS Cybersecurity Position Statement, Approved by The HIMSS North America (HNA) Board of Directors. September 30, 2016. Accessed March 26, 2020. https://clearwatercompliance.com/wp-content/uploads/2020/03/HIMSS-cybersecurity-position-statement.pdf

12. 2018 HIMSS Cybersecurity Survey. HIMSS. 2018. Accessed March 12, 2020. https://www.himss.org/2019-himss-cybersecurity-survey

13. Khushbu Pratap, Katell Thielemann, Brent Predovich. (2019, December 30). Implement 4 Essentials NIST Cybersecurity Framework. (ID:G00464751). Retrieved from Gartner database.

14. "Are we required to 'certify' our organization's compliance with the standards of the Security Rule?" HIPAA for Professionals, U.S. Department of Health and Human Services, Office for Civil Rights (OCR). July 26, 2013. Accessed March 12, 2020. https://www.hhs.gov/hipaa/for-professionals/faq/2003/are-we-required-to-certify-our-organizations-compliance-with-the-standards/index.html

15. Evolution of the [NIST Cybersecurity] Framework. National Institute of Standards and Technology (NIST). Updated April 2, 2019. Accessed March 11, 2020. https://www.nist.gov/cyberframework/evolution

16. History and Creation of the [NIST Cybersecurity] Framework. National Institute of Standards and Technology (NIST). Updated November 21, 2019. Accessed March 12, 2020. https://www.nist.gov/cyberframework/online-learning/history-and-creation-framework

17. Kara E. MacLeod, David R. Ragland, Thomas R. Prohaska, Matthew Lee Smith, Cheryl Irmiter, and William A. Satariano. (2015). "Missed or delayed medical care appointments by older users of nonemergency medical transportation." *The Gerontologist*, 55(6), 1026–1037. https://doi.org/10.1093/geront/gnu002

18. Morgan Haefner. "Uber Health chief: With 1,000+ partners, the question is no longer, 'What the heck is Uber doing in healthcare?'" *Becker's Hospital Review*. June 24, 2019. Accessed March 9, 2020. https://www.beckershospitalreview.com/hospital-management-administration/uber-health-chief-with-1–000-partners-the-question-is-no-longer-what-the-heck-is-uber-doing-in-healthcare.html; and Rebecca Pifer. "Uber Health plans to double in size this year." *HealthcareDive*. January 21, 2020. Accessed March 9, 2020. https://www.healthcaredive.com/news/uber-health-plans-to-double-in-size-this-year/570771/

Chapter 11: *The Upshot*

1. Mike Myatt. "Boards should be prioritizing cybersecurity and risk." *Corporate Board Member*. (n.d.). Accessed March 23, 2020. https://boardmember.com/boards-prioritizing-cybersecurity-risk/

Index

CPSIA information can be obtained
at www.ICGtesting.com
Printed in the USA
FSHW021736081120

9 781735 122205